BURSTING
THE BIG DATA
BUBBLE

The Case for Intuition-Based
Decision Making

BURSTING THE BIG DATA BUBBLE

The Case for Intuition-Based Decision Making

EDITED BY JAY LIEBOWITZ

CRC Press
Taylor & Francis Group
Boca Raton London New York

CRC Press is an imprint of the
Taylor & Francis Group, an **informa** business

AN AUERBACH BOOK

CRC Press
Taylor & Francis Group
6000 Broken Sound Parkway NW, Suite 300
Boca Raton, FL 33487-2742

First issued in paperback 2019

ISBN-13: 978-1-4822-2885-4 (hbk)
ISBN-13: 978-0-367-37849-3 (pbk)

Library of Congress Cataloging-in-Publication Data

Bursting the big data bubble : the case for intuition-based decision making / edited by Jay Liebowitz.
    pages cm
    Summary: "With the onslaught of the Big Data revolution, data-based decision making and analytics are now the rage. However, many key decision makers often make complementary judgments based on intuition. This intuition is often insight-based due to their experiential learning, ephemeral factors like spirituality, and other related factors. This book focuses on this intuition-based decision making. It presents stories and vignettes from leaders and senior executives in industry, academe, government, and not-for-profits"-- Provided by publisher.
    Includes bibliographical references and index.
    ISBN 978-1-4822-2885-4 (hardback)
    1. Insight. 2. Intuition. 3. Decision making. 4. Experiential learning. 5. Management. I. Liebowitz, Jay, 1957- editor of compilation.

BF315.5.B875 2014
658.4'03--dc23   2014016486

Visit the Taylor & Francis Web site at
http://www.taylorandfrancis.com

and the CRC Press Web site at
http://www.crcpress.com

Contents

Preface

Why a book on intuition-based decision making? Is it because a November 2012 research study at Tel Aviv University found that executives were 90% accurate in their decisions when relying on just their intuition? Is it because, according to Akinci and Sadler-Smith's 2012 historical review of "Intuition in Management Research," intuition research in management has been conducted since the 1930s and there continues to be a need for greater cross-disciplinary collaboration and integration? Or perhaps do we want to challenge the "Big Data" community to show, as evidenced by Woiceshyn's 2009 research on how CEOs use intuition, that intuition should also be applied to complement rational analysis? Daniel Kahneman talked about the two systems (System 1 as intuition and System 2 as deliberative thinking) and their interaction. In Moxley et al.'s 2012 research on these two systems, their finding was that both experts and less-skilled individuals benefit significantly from extra deliberation no matter how easy or difficult the problem.

This book is not meant to discount "rational thought," or data-based decision making, when making decisions, especially those that are important and complex. However, the contributors want to emphasize the importance of applying intuition, gut feel, spirituality, experiential learning, and insight as key factors in an executive's decision-making process.

An interesting question surfaces: When faced with conflicting opinions (i.e., one formed from data and analytics, and the other based on intuition), which one do you trust the most? For example, does a physician rely strictly on the evidence-based research and lab results in diagnosing a patient's problem? Or does intuition have a key role to play? What are the legal implications if the physician decides to rely more on his or her intuition and experience, which may run counter to the medical data and lab results, even after repeating various lab tests? These are fascinating questions, especially as the big data revolution continues to unfold.

In the 2012 movie, *Trouble with the Curve*, Gus, the experienced, older baseball scout (played by Clint Eastwood), who didn't rely strictly on computer statistics but preferred to judge a player from the sound of a fly ball or from the grip on the bat, used his experiential learning and intuition to determine whether to draft a given baseball player. In the same movie, the younger scout, who favored judging a player by computer data analytics versus even watching the player on the field, made a call to draft a player as their number one pick, but Clint Eastwood thought otherwise and intuition won in this case (as the player couldn't hit a curve ball, along with some fast balls). Sometimes, the old-fashioned method may be the way to go.

My intuition tells me that it's time for a book such as this one. As we get caught in the quagmire of big data and analytics, it is important to be able to reflect and apply insights, experience, and intuition as part of the executive and managerial decision-making process. This book serves to focus on this latter part by having two components. First, there is a "research" track where we have chapter contributions from some of the leading researchers worldwide in intuition-based decision making as applied to management. Second, we have a "practice" track where we have leading global executives and senior managers in industry, government, universities, and not-for-profits discuss vignettes of how they used their intuition in making some key decisions. The research part of the book helps to frame the problem and address leading research in intuition-based decision making. The second part of the book then applies these intuition-based concepts and issues in decision-making scenarios.

I would like to thank all the wonderful contributors for sharing their insights and knowledge with us. I also owe a great debt of gratitude to my publishing editors, John Wyzalek and Rich O'Hanley, and their Taylor & Francis production team in having some intuition that this book is timely in terms of our Big Data environment. Certainly, the book would not have been possible without the support of my university. Finally, my family is the key ingredient for success and I hope my intuition doesn't fail them over the years.

Enjoy!

Jay Liebowitz, DSc
Washington, DC

About the Editor

Dr. Jay Liebowitz is the Orkand Endowed Chair of Management and Technology in the Graduate School at the University of Maryland University College (UMUC). He previously served as a professor in the Carey Business School at Johns Hopkins University. He is ranked one of the top 10 knowledge management researchers/practitioners out of 11,000 worldwide, and was ranked number two in knowledge management strategy worldwide according to the January 2010 *Journal of Knowledge Management*. At Johns Hopkins University, he was the founding program director for the Graduate Certificate in Competitive Intelligence and the capstone director of the MS-Information and Telecommunications Systems for Business Program, where he engaged over 30 organizations in industry, government, and not-for-profits in capstone projects.

Prior to joining Hopkins, Dr. Liebowitz was the first knowledge management officer at NASA Goddard Space Flight Center. Before NASA, Dr. Liebowitz was the Robert W. Deutsch Distinguished Professor of Information Systems at the University of Maryland–Baltimore County, professor of management science at George Washington University, and chair of artificial intelligence at the U.S. Army War College.

Dr. Liebowitz is the founding editor-in-chief of *Expert Systems with Applications: An International Journal* (published by Elsevier), which was ranked fifth worldwide for operations research/management science journals (out of 77 journals), according to the 2011 Thomson Impact Factors. The *ESWA Journal* had 1.8 million articles downloaded worldwide in 2011.

Dr. Liebowitz is a Fulbright Scholar, IEEE-USA Federal Communications Commission Executive Fellow, and Computer Educator of the Year (International Association for Computer Information Systems [IACIS]). He has published more than 40 books and many journal articles on knowledge management, intelligent systems, and IT management. His most recent books are *Knowledge Retention: Strategies and Solutions* (Taylor & Francis, 2009), *Knowledge Management in Public Health* (Taylor & Francis, 2010), *Knowledge Management and E-Learning* (Taylor & Francis, 2011), *Beyond Knowledge Management: What Every Leader Should Know* (Taylor & Francis, 2012), *Knowledge Management Handbook: Collaboration and Social Networking, 2nd edition* (Taylor & Francis, 2012), *Big Data and Business Analytics* (Taylor & Francis, 2013), and *Business Analytics: An Introduction* (Taylor & Francis, 2014). As of January 2014, Dr. Liebowitz is the editor-in-chief of *Procedia-CS* (Elsevier).

In October 2011, the International Association for Computer Information Systems established the Jay Liebowitz Outstanding Student Research Award for the best student research paper at the IACIS Annual Conference. He has lectured and consulted worldwide. He can be reached at jay.liebowitz@umuc.edu.

Contributors

Cinla Akinci
Professor
School of Management
University of St Andrews
St Andrews, Scotland, UK

Ramon C. Barquin
CEO
Barquin International
Washington, DC

Lisa A. Burke-Smalley
UC Foundation Professor
University of Tennessee at
    Chattanooga
Chattanooga, Tennessee

Denise Chenger
Consultant and Instructor
Mount Royal University
Calgary, Alberta, Canada

Caroline S. Clauss-Ehlers
Associate Professor
Department of Educational
    Psychology
Rutgers, The State University of
    New Jersey
New Brunswick, New Jersey

Melanie P. Cohen
Information Technology
    Strategist
IT Strategic Planning and
    Communications
US Department of
    Housing and Urban
    Development
Washington, DC

Barry C. Dorn
Lecturer
National Preparedness
   Leadership Initiative
Harvard School of Public
   Health
Brookline, Massachusetts

Dieter H. Früauff
Senior Vice President
Frankfurt Airport
Frankfurt a. Main, Germany

David Harper
IT Project Manager
Applied Physics Laboratory
The Johns Hopkins University
Baltimore, Maryland

James Howard
Professor
Graduate School
University of Maryland
   University College
Adelphi, Maryland

Linda Hummel
President and CKO
Act Knowledge LLC
Bellbrook, Ohio

Andrew Iserson
Adjunct Assistant Professor
University of Maryland
   University College
Rockville, Maryland

John L. Jacobs
Executive Vice President
The NASDAQ OMX Group,
   Inc.
New York, New York

Marion Kahrens
Programme Manager
1&1 Telecommunication AG
Montabaur, Germany

Jay Liebowitz
Orkand Endowed Chair
   in Management and
   Technology
University of Maryland
   University College
Adelphi, Maryland

Simon Y. Liu
Director
National Agricultural Library
US Department of Agriculture
Beltsville, Maryland

Leonard J. Marcus
Senior Lecturer
National Preparedness
   Leadership Initiative
Harvard School of Public Health
Brookline, Massachusetts

Joan Marques
Assistant Dean
School of Business
Woodbury University
Burbank, California

Michelle Mason
Managing Director
American Society for Quality
Milwaukee, Wisconsin

Eric J. McNulty
Director
National Preparedness
    Leadership Initiative
Harvard School of Public
    Health
and
Harvard's Kennedy School
    of Government Center for
    Public Leadership
Brookline, Massachusetts

Ramesh Menon
US CTO
IBM Corporation
Armonk, New York

Susan K. Neely
President and CEO
American Beverage Association
Washington, DC

Donald S. Orkand
Principal
DC Ventures and Associates,
    LLC
McLean, Virginia

Lynn Pasquerella
President
Mount Holyoke College
South Hadley, Massachusetts

David F. Rico
Professor
University of Maryland
    University College
Adelphi, Maryland

Martin Robson
Professor
University of New England
Armidale, New South Wales,
    Australia

Eugene Sadler-Smith
Professor
Surrey Business School
University of Surrey
Guildford, Surrey, UK

Lesley-Ann Shneier
Consultant
World Bank Group
Washington, DC

Marta Sinclair
Senior Lecturer and Author
Griffith Business School
Griffith University
Gold Coast, Queensland,
    Australia

Rick Smith
Deputy Director
Transportation Training Services
    and Public Works
Division of Enterprise
    Development
Austin, Texas

Tara M. Sullivan
Deputy Project Director
K4Health
Center for Communication
    Programs
The Johns Hopkins Bloomberg
    School of Public Health
Baltimore, Maryland

Jaana Woiceshyn
Professor
University of Calgary
Calgary, Alberta, Canada

PART I
RESEARCH TRACK

RESEARCHING INTUITION

A Curious Passion

EUGENE SADLER-SMITH

Surrey Business School
University of Surrey

Contents

1.1 Introduction

"Big Data" is big news; it's heralded by some as the "new oil."[*] So, in a world where computer-based processing applications enable technologists to capture, curate, manage, and process unimaginably large amounts of hard data is there any place for human judgment? The Big Data hype suggests not: Analysis of petabytes of data will allow us to say "correlation is enough" without the need for causal models let alone human judgment and the Big Data future promises simulations of the brain and nervous system and new entities that lie somewhere in between "wetware" and "software."[†] It's undeniable that Big Data opens up new possibilities for building business' analytical capabilities and helping managers to make more informed decisions. But is it all about hard data science? Are we returning to a world governed by assumptions of unbounded rationality albeit in a nonhuman form?

---

[*] http://blogs.hbr.org/2012/11/data-humans-and-the-new-oil/ Accessed 10/29/2013.
[†] http://www.wired.com/science/discoveries/magazine/16-07/pb_theory Accessed 10/29/2013.

Is there room at the decision-making table for that most ineffable attribute of the human mind, intuition? By way of background, I offer some personal insights about what brought me, a die-hard analytic type, to intuition research. I then go on to consider the pros and cons of making intuition-based decisions, and finish up by taking stock of where we are, where intuition research might be headed next, and what value it can add to the art of management decision making as a counter or complement to the hard analytics of the burgeoning Big Data bubble.

1.2 Background

I still remember my first face-to-face encounter with intuition in business: it was when I was working in the training and development department of British Gas in the late 1980s and early 1990s. As are most young managers, I was keen to progress in what had become a dynamic and forward-thinking business following its privatization by the UK government under Margaret Thatcher in 1986. In one of my performance appraisals, my manager and I went through the usual "review against targets," but then at the end of the meeting when it came to looking ahead, my manager said something that at the time perplexed and slightly irritated me. He said, "You know, if you want to get to the top in this business you're going to have to start using your intuition a bit more." As an unseasoned twenty-something I didn't "get" what he meant. My job at the time was the epitome of rational analysis and the demands it made on me resonated with the mindset of someone trained more in the natural and physical sciences than social sciences or humanities. It was data-driven, albeit small data: it involved analyzing employees' training needs in minute, almost microscopic, detail (hierarchical task analysis was my favorite technique); meticulously and systematically planning training projects; trying to ensure, but not always succeeding, that projects came in on target and to budget; and evaluating, as objectively as was possible, the impact our projects had on the business. So why would anyone want to cultivate anything as fuzzy as intuition. Anyway, I "parked" his comment and the idea.

As well as doing my "day job" at British Gas I did my PhD part-time at the University of Birmingham, supervised by Dr. Richard Riding, an educational psychologist and expert on thinking (cognitive) styles. At British Gas we considered ourselves to be very much at the forefront of the early 1990s technology-based training "revolution" and my supervisor gave me the ambitious target of designing and validating a self-adapting computer-based training package—self-adapting, that is, to the cognitive style of the learner. This, on reflection, was a crucial turning point in my professional life: it was cognitive styles that brought me back into contact with intuition post-PhD, opened the door to an academic career, and led to my Damascene conversion from a data-driven, out-and-out rational analytic type to an aspirant—and still aspiring—intuitive.

Cognitive styles research was (and still is, some would say) much like a supermarket. There are almost as many different "brands" and types of style as there are boxes of breakfast cereals on the supermarket shelves. No one could research them all; a choice had to be made. The "Eureka!" moment that ignited what has turned out to be a curious and long-lasting passion for intuition research occurred when I came across a paper by Chris Allinson and John Hayes (both at my alma mater, the University of Leeds) published in the *Journal of Management Studies* and with whom I later had the pleasure to work (Sadler-Smith, Allinson, and Hayes, 2000). Allinson and Hayes' paper was a rigorous, not to say trenchant, critique of Honey and Mumford's much-renowned "Learning Styles Questionnaire" (Honey and Mumford, 1986). Not only had they the temerity to criticize what for many in corporate training was the be all and end all of learning styles, they also suggested an alternative model of cognitive style based on, of all things, an intuition-analysis construct which they claimed reflected a fundamental dichotomy in human thinking. They claimed it was mappable onto gross hemispheric differences in brain function, best captured in their phrase, "intuition, [is] characteristic of the right brain orientation" (p. 122), but now seen not so much as a scientific model but as a convenient metaphor (Hodgkinson et al., 2009).

Now it made sense. Of course, no manager could get by using analysis alone; for example, there might not be time to gather all the necessary facts and figures, there might be too much information, or the data simply might not be available. Only a cursory digging into the archaeology of intuition in management revealed this insight to have been long recognized and well documented and there for all to see. Herbert Simon's foundational article in *The Academy of Management Executive* journal entitled "Making Management Decisions: The Role of Intuition and

Emotion" (Simon, 1987), captured the essence of managerial intuition. Even earlier, Chester Barnard's essay "The Mind in Everyday Affairs," which was the appendix to his magnum opus *The Functions of the Executive* (Barnard, 1938/1968), had laid the groundwork for Simon's contribution. It's worth noting that Barnard was not an academic or a researcher, but a practicing executive, and the acuity of his practical intelligence on this matter is worth sharing in full:

> Mental processes consist of two groups which I shall call "non-logical" and "logical". By non-logical processes I mean those not capable of being expressed in words or as reasoning, which are only made known by judgment, decision or action. This may be because the processes are unconscious, or because they are so complex and so rapid that they could not be analyzed by the person within whose brain they take place. (Barnard, 1938/1968, p. 302)

This insight was what my manager at British Gas back in the early 1990s was surely referring to, but I was not only naïve to the literature on the subject I actually couldn't or wouldn't see its relevance and the practical implications at that time. Like many insights, in retrospect it's obvious: business environments are uncertain, fast-moving, and complex and becoming increasingly so, and it's inevitable that as managers learn explicitly and implicitly how to deal, day to day, with the challenges they face they build up intuitive "muscle power". Eventually, after several years of experience (the rule of thumb is 10 years), their analyses, in the words of Herbert Simon, become "frozen into habit" (Simon, 1987, p. 63) allowing them to know *what* to do under time and informational constraints without necessarily knowing *why* they do it. This isn't to say they can't unpack their reasons under skilled questioning (this very approach is the basis of much of Gary Klein's seminal research on the subject; see Klein, 2003), it's just that they "compress and automate" highly complex tasks, and have to do so in order to be able to perform.

These developments took place in the early 2000s, but focusing my research on what at the time was a marginal and obscure topic might have seemed like a perverse if not risky choice for an aspiring academic. Up until that point there hadn't been much in the way of explanatory intuition research; instead researchers had focused on descriptive studies of intuition in use (e.g., Burke and Miller, 1999). But also at around that time theories of dual processing and "unconscious cognition" were beginning to permeate from psychology into management. At last it seemed that there could be a scientific rationale for "thinking without thinking." This enabled intuition to be rescued from the fringes and absorbed into the mainstream.

A vital first step was defining intuition as more than just knowing without knowing how. Encouragingly, there was convergence of views on this matter. For example, Gigernzer (2007, p. 16) defined an intuition as a judgment that appears quickly in consciousness, whose underlying reasons we are not fully aware of, but nevertheless is potent enough to be able to guide behavior; moreover unlike the conscious process of deliberation, a person cannot explain the reasons for his or her intuitions. Dane and Pratt's (2007) definition encapsulated succinctly the key attributes of intuition, "Intuitions are affectively charged judgments that arise through rapid, non-conscious and holistic associations" (Dane and Pratt, 2007, p. 30). A chronological summary of selected definitions is shown in Table 1.1.

Intuition researchers have been able to pull together numerous strands from various disciplines into a coherent argument that has formed the basis for a sustained and on-going program of research,

Table 1.1 Selected Definitions of Intuition Arranged Chronologically

DEFINITION	SOURCE
"This feeling 'in our marrow' is probably an outcome of previous experience that has not yet emerged into articulate thought."	Barnard, 1938: p. 302
"… simply analyses frozen into habit and into the capacity for rapid response through recognition."	Simon, 1987: p. 63
"Intuition is knowledge gained without rational thought. It comes from some stratum of awareness just below the conscious level and is slippery and elusive. Intuition comes with a feeling of 'almost, but not quite knowing.'"	Rowan, 1989: p. 96
"A feeling of knowing with certitude on the basis of inadequate information and without conscious awareness of rational thinking."	Shirley and Langan-Fox, 1996: p. 564
"Intuition is a capacity for attaining direct knowledge or understanding without the apparent intrusion of rational thought or logical inference."	Sadler-Smith and Shefy, 2004: p. 77
"A non-sequential information processing mode, which encompasses both cognitive and affective elements and results in direct knowing without any use of conscious reasoning."	Sinclair and Ashkanasy, 2005: p. 357
"Affectively charged judgments that arise through rapid, nonconscious and holistic associations."	Dane and Pratt, 2007: p. 33

writing, and teaching on the subject of intuition (Akinci and
Sadler-Smith, 2012; Sinclair, 2011). In the remainder of this chapter,
I summarize some of the key findings by encapsulating what we know
about perils and powers of intuition and examine if and how, in the
age of Big Data, it can hinder or help managers and leaders in taking
decisions and solving problems.

1.3 Downside of Intuition

Historically, 2002 was an auspicious year for intuition research: it was
the year in which Daniel Kahneman was awarded the Nobel Prize in
Economic Sciences for "having integrated insights from psychological
research into economic science, especially concerning human judgment and decision-making under uncertainty." The Nobel Prize was
awarded for work that Kahneman and Amos Tversky (1937–1996)
produced together during their intense collaborations in the 1970s
and 1980s. Their work is truly seminal. The heuristics and biases program of research that flowed from their insights focuses principally
upon the downside of intuition which may be stated simply as follows:
relying on certain types of cognitive shortcuts (heuristics) in particular situations can produce less than optimal decisions.

The underlying theoretical assumption of this and related research
in behavioral decision making is that the full rationality assumed by
economists in the rational choice model was an "unrealistic standard for
human judgment" (Gilovich and Griffin, 2002, p. 2). To be perfectly
rational would entail an indefinite search for complete data and would
impose insatiable demands upon the finite data-processing capacity of
the human brain; clearly this is impossible. The idea of "bounded rationality" was mooted by another intellectual giant of our age, Herbert
Simon (1916–2001). Simon and various colleagues of his argued that
organizations can never be perfectly rational; if we try to explain behavior in terms of the economic model we are destined to be frustrated.
This is because managers' choices are always exercised with respect to a
limited, approximated, and simplified model of reality that is commensurate with the human brain's processing capacity. Simon asserted that
although human behavior may be *intendedly* rational, in the real world
it is only *boundedly* so; hence was born the theory of bounded rationality
and with it psychology was placed on an equal footing with economics

in the study of decision making in organizations. Simon was awarded the Nobel Prize in Economic Sciences in 1978 "for his pioneering research into the decision-making process within economic organizations."

Kahneman and Tversky's own take on bounded rationality was to develop models of various types of heuristics (i.e., mental shortcuts) based on the simple computations that the human mind evolved to make in the ancestral environment (Gigerenzer, 2007; Gilovich and Griffin, 2002) but which are quite different from the environments that human beings live in today (Gore and Sadler-Smith, 2011). For example, when asked to estimate the relative frequency of cocaine use among rock stars the human mind's highly efficient memory retrieval processes is likely to recall examples of drug-abusing rock stars and base its (biased) assessments on this highly available example as indicating the actual frequency of use of cocaine among rock stars in general. The judgment piggybacks on a very crude computation but is in fact a biased cue for the actual frequency of drug abuse among rock stars, which is typical of the types of judgments we all make day in and day out (Gilovich and Griffin, 2002, p. 3). This heuristic is the availability heuristic. In their foundational research Kahneman and Tversky identified a variety of general-purpose heuristics and their attendant biases, for example, "anchoring and adjustment" describes our tendency to rely too heavily or anchor our decision on one piece of information and then adjust from that (e.g., the opening bid from a salesperson); "availability" describes our tendency to base predictions of the frequency of an event, or the proportion of people within a population with a given trait, based on how easily an example can be brought to mind (e.g., drug abuse among rock stars in general); and the conjunction fallacy, in which we assume that specific conditions are more probable than a general condition that contains the specific condition.* If you doubt the potency of mental shortcuts, try this simple example for yourself from Tversky and Kahneman (1983). Which of the following is more likely?

(A) A massive flood somewhere in North America in which more than 1,000 people drown

(B) An earthquake in California causing a flood in which more than 1,000 people drown

---

* http://www.blackswanreport.com/blog/2010/04/daniel-kahneman-a-bat-and-a-ball-cost-1-10/ Accessed 10/29/2013.

(A) A massive flood somewhere in North America in which more than 1,000 people drown is more likely than (B) an earthquake in California causing a flood in which more than 1,000 people drown. (B) is a subset of (A). Although flood alone (A) is necessarily more probable than earthquake and flood (B), the conjunction of an earthquake and a flood in a vivid and plausible scenario is judged as more probable than a flood alone. Fallacious reasoning contributes to "the appeal of scenarios and to the illusory insight that they often provide" (Tversky and Kahneman, 1983, p. 308). Other heuristics have been added to Tversky and Kahneman's original list of "availability," "representativeness," and "anchoring and adjustment," for example, the "affect heuristic" (Slovic et al., 2004).

Heuristics and biases (HB) research suggests that the fast, low-effort intuitive judgments that we deploy, often automatically, can be disadvantageous and even dangerous when processing abstract probabilistic information. Intuitive judgment is inherently fast and has evolved to work efficiently by means of holistic associations rather than logical processing, which can be time-consuming and cognitively resource-hungry. Intuition is a blunt instrument when dealing with statistical and probabilistic judgments because this is not something the human mind evolved to do with the necessary mathematical accuracy, hence systematic errors are likely. HB researchers' motivation in their extensive program of laboratory studies was not to point out the fallibility of human judgment. They're keen to point out that intuitive judgments based on representativeness, availability, or anchoring and adjustment aren't necessarily wrong. Such mental shortcuts can be quite useful sometimes, but they can lead to "severe and systematic errors" (Tversky and Kahneman, 1974, p. 1124) and in certain situations are "less trustworthy than intuitions that are rooted in specific experiences" (Kahneman and Klein, 2009, p. 522). Kahneman has summarized the HB research in a highly accessible style in his 2011 book, *Thinking, Fast and Slow*.

1.4 Upside of Intuition

It is with regard to the trustworthiness or otherwise of intuition and its relationship to expertise that two of the leading intuition researchers, Daniel Kahneman and Gary Klein, famously "failed to disagree" in a jointly authored *American Psychologist* article in 2009 (Kahneman and Klein, 2009). Kahneman's HB tradition of decision research is often viewed as being at odds with the parallel view offered by naturalistic decision-making (NDM) researchers such as Klein. But when the two set out to explore the differences between their two schools of thought they were surprised to find themselves agreeing most of the time.

It's ironic that Klein didn't set out to research intuition. Among his various achievements (such as being one of the leaders of the team who redesigned the White House situation room in the West Wing*), Klein is one of the founders of NDM, a discipline that seeks to understand and improve decision making in field settings by getting to grips with how people handle complex tasks and environments (Salas and Klein, 2001). One such complex task and environment that NDM researchers have studied is how firefighters make fast, high-stakes decisions, for example, if and when to evacuate a burning building in spite of the stress, dynamism, and uncertainty of the setting. This was one of the many response scenarios in the emergency services and military settings that NDM researchers have studied since the inception of the field in the 1990s.

In the 1980s, Klein and colleagues were researching experienced firefighters' decisions. They were intrigued especially by how these people made high-pressure life-or-death decisions in the face of rapidly growing fire or other type of evolving emergency. Contrary to the conventional multiattribute models of decision making in which the pros and cons should be weighed up, it seemed self-evident to Klein and colleagues that this couldn't hold in the emergency situation. Instead they expected that under the time pressure firefighters wouldn't be able to weigh up lots of options, but instead would narrow the choices down to comparing only two options at each decision point. Contrary to their own expectations Klein and colleagues found themselves to be wrong: the firefighters they interviewed insisted that they weren't comparing any options as such, "They just came up with a single course of action and carried it out" (Klein, 2003, p. 15). The puzzle for Klein and colleagues was how it could be that the first decision that was arrived at could be trusted. The answer was experience, what Simon was referring to when he described intuitions as "analyses frozen into habit and the capacity for rapid response through recognition" (Simon, 1987, p. 63). Salas and colleagues

---

* http://macrocognition.com/LOCKED%20PDF/GKlein%20Biosketch%208-17-10.pdf Accessed 10/28/2013.

neatly summarized this key point when they described intuition as "how people rapidly detect coherent patterns in complex environments ... how they generate solutions that work without the luxury of limitless time" (Salas, Rosen, and DiazGranados, 2010, p. 966).

As a result of their experiences in becoming and being fire-ground commanders, the firefighters Klein studied had internalized a large set of complex patterns. This is similar to the way in which the approximately 50,000 patterns Simon estimated chess grandmasters have internalized enable them to play the game to a high level of expertise fluently and intuitively without having to calculate all the potential outcomes. The principle is this: faced with a familiar problem which has been dealt with successfully in the past, there's a good chance that the first solution which pops into the decision-maker's head is likely to be acceptable (Klein, 2003). As Klein noted, it may not be the "best" solution but, under the circumstances, it may be good enough, especially because in a firefighting situation there simply isn't the time to search for the best (Klein, 2003). The second crucial point that Klein's research uncovered was the role that mental simulation played in evaluating the potential course of action of following the intuitive identification of a first response. The firefighters evaluated the proposed courses of action by "consciously imagining what would happen when they carried it out," playing out or fast-forwarding a "DVD in their heads." If the option seems as though it will work, it's carried through; if not, it's jettisoned and another response is considered. This is the basis of Klein's recognition-primed decision model (RPD).

Klein has written at length and engagingly on this research in his 2003 book *Intuition at Work*. The essence of his argument is that intuitive and analytical approaches to decision making are contingent and contextually appropriate. Conditions that favor analysis are conflict resolution, optimization, justification, and computational complexity. Conditions that favor intuition are time pressure, ill-defined goals, dynamic conditions, and, perhaps most important, experienced participants; see Table 1.2.

Kahneman and Klein (2009) in their agreeing on the specification of the conditions that favor the exercising of intuitive expertise single out high-validity environments as a condition for the development of skilled (or informed) intuitions. A high-validity environment is one in which "there are stable relationships between objectively identifiable cue and subsequent events" (Kahneman and Klein, 2009, p. 524) such as medicine

Table 1.2 Attributes of Situations Favoring Intuitive Processing and Analytical Processing

FAVORING ANALYSIS	FAVORING INTUITION
Conflict resolution	Time pressure
Optimization	Ill-defined goals
Justification	Dynamic conditions
Computational complexity	Experienced participants
Low validity environments	High validity environments
Objective criteria	Subjective criteria
Tightly structured problems	Loosely structured problems

Source: Adapted from Dane and Pratt, 2007; Kahneman and Klein, 2009; Klein, 2003.

and firefighting. Low-validity environments in which outcomes are effectively unpredictable are not conducive to the development of intuitive expertise, for example, predicting the future value of individual stocks or long-term forecasting of political events (Kahneman and Klein, 2009).

1.5 The State of Intuition Research

As far as progress in intuition research over the past 10 years is concerned there have been at least three significant developments.

First, rather than having to rely on vague notions of intuition as a "capacity for attaining direct knowledge or understanding without the apparent intrusion of rational thought or logical inference" (Sadler-Smith and Shefy, 2004, p. 77), we're in the fortunate position of being able to define intuition fairly precisely using a number of its key attributes: (1) intuitions are uninvited and instantaneous: they're automatic involuntary responses to complex, hard-to-quantify problems, decisions, and dilemmas; (2) intuitions have an affective (feeling) tone: they're accompanied by "gut feelings" (affect) that may vary in terms of valence (positive/negative) and level of intensity; (3) intuitions are based on holistic associations: they allow the decision maker to "parallel process" information quickly and efficiently and get the bigger picture and match cues in the environment to patterns and scripts for action stored in long-term memory; (4) intuitions are nonconscious: the decision maker is aware only of the outcomes of intuition, the lead-in is backstage and nonconscious; (5) intuitions are judgments that cannot be determined as right or wrong *ex ante*, in this sense they are hypotheses for action (Sadler-Smith, 2010).

Second, conceptually and theoretically we are, all of us, of two minds so to speak. Intuition can be understood in terms of a "two-minds model" or, more correctly, dual-processing theory. In several subfields of psychology there's an emerging consensus that it's possible to delineate two complementary systems of information processing, often referred to as System 1 ("the intuitive mind") and System 2 ("the analytical mind"). In this two-system view, System 1 processing is contextually dependent, associative, heuristic, tacit, intuitive, and implicit/automatic in nature. System 1 is a slow-learning system (i.e., it learns through repeated exposure and experience in environments conducive to effective learning) but is fast in operation and is relatively undemanding in terms of its use of the brain's scarce cognitive resources. System 2 processing on the other hand is contextually independent, rule-based, analytic, and explicit in nature. System 2 is a relatively fast-learning system but is comparatively slow in operation; furthermore, it makes greater demands on cognitive resources than its System 1 counterpart (Epstein, 1994, 2008; Hodgkinson, Langan-Fox, and Sadler-Smith, 2008). It's important to note that this isn't the same as the old idea of the so-called "split brain," with intuition and creativity housed in the right hemisphere and analysis and rationality in the left; modern neuroscience paints a much more complex picture of the neural geography of intuition and analysis. The respective properties of the two systems are summarized in Table 1.3.

The third key point to have been consolidated over the past 10 years is how best to use intuition. Neither the analytical mind nor

Table 1.3 The Two-Minds Model

INTUITIVE MIND	ANALYTICAL MIND
Holistic; Automatic, Effortless; Affective; Associationistic connections; Behavior mediated by "vibes"; Encodes in concrete images, metaphors, narratives; Rapid processing; More resistant to change	Analytic; Intentional; Effortful; Rational; Logical connections; Behavior mediated by conscious appraisal; Encodes in abstract symbols, words, numbers; Slower processing; Less resistant to change
Parallel processing; Faster operating; Slower learning; Nonreflective consciousness; Spontaneous; Sensory; Unaffected by cognitive load; Phylogenetically older	Serial processing; Slower operating; Fast learning; Reflective consciousness; Intentional; Linguistic; Affected by cognitive load; Phylogenetically newer

Source: Adapted from S. Epstein, *American Psychologist*, 49: 709–724, 1994 and M.D. Lieberman, *Annual Review of Psychology*, 58: 259–289, 2007. (With permission.)

the intuitive mind is intrinsically better than the other; it's simply that they're good at different sorts of things. Having two minds gives us the potential to be cognitively ambidextrous, to think, problem-solve, and decide using analysis or intuition depending on the circumstances. But this is a skill that needs to be honed. One problem we face is that management and management education are dominated by an analytical model. The obsession with data, and increasingly so with Big Data, means that analytics (which of themselves are desirable) can obscure and devalue the potential that intuition offers experienced managers who may not have any choice but to take decisions under time pressure and with incomplete data. In talking about the benefits of intuition it's important to be clear that intuition should not be advocated as a panacea. As we have seen, it's wholly inappropriate in many situations, especially those involving quantification; here it's better to rely on the power of the analytical mind (or a computer). The key to using intuition effectively is being able to recognize if, when, and how to use it (Sadler-Smith, 2010).

Intuition is useful for managers

1. in sensing potential problems, for example, when someone's story doesn't stack up or there's an ethical dilemma;
2. when they need to perform well-learned behavior patterns rapidly (this is the essence of "intuitive expertise");
3. if expectations are violated, for example, when we expect a situation to go a certain way but it doesn't—this can set off our intuitive alarm bell;
4. in synthesizing the bigger picture, when faced with multiple isolated bits of data and information, harnessing intuition lets us stand back, avoid analysis paralysis, and sense how the pieces might fit together in a coherent and convincing way;
5. in checking out the results of rational analytics with a sense for whether they stack up, intuition can be deployed when the hard data, or our analysis of it, doesn't feel quite right (prompting us to seek out more or better data, or to take a new or different look at the data we have and the way they've been analyzed).

Development of intuitive expertise is the cornerstone of informed intuition. However, the more subjective aspects of intuition also offer decision makers an option that would be hard to achieve using a data-based approach. As has been noted, one of intuition's distinctive features is its affect tone (in common parlance we talk about gut feel, hunch, or vibe). We know enough about the behavioral and brain sciences to say that feelings and emotions exist in the human organism for a reason. Therefore, recognizing gut feelings as a valid source of "data" means listening attentively to them and correctly interpreting them, but also not mixing them up with basic emotions such as fear, bias, prejudice, or wishful thinking as these can hijack good intuitive judgment.

It would be inappropriate to discuss where we are without also thinking about where we go from here. A key thinker in this field and very much in the vanguard of intuition research in the early 2000s, Robin Hogarth, argued that the greatest challenge facing intuition researchers is in going beyond current conceptualizations, for example, by classifying different types of intuitive phenomena (Hogarth, 2010). In this regard, researchers, including Hogarth, have successfully delineated intuition from related phenomena such as insight (Dane and Pratt, 2007; Hogarth, 2001), and others have gone on to suggest different types of intuition, for example, problem-solving intuition (i.e., intuitive expertise), moral intuition, social intuition, and creative intuition (Dane and Pratt, 2009; Gore and Sadler-Smith, 2011). However, we must be careful to avoid a proliferation of typologies of intuition, and there are still misconceptions to be dispelled (Sinclair, 2010).

One of the paradoxes of intuition in the age of Big Data is that it's an evolved capacity which is not well understood, and therefore not a capability that we can design into our machines (Gigerenzer, 2007). Whether we will ever be able to is an intriguing question. New challenges and opportunities for intuition research are also arising out of the great leaps forward that are taking place in the brain sciences, and perhaps the prospects are raised for a "neuroscience of intuition" (e.g., Lieberman, 2007; Volz, Rübsamen and von Cramon, 2008). From the perspective of management and organization studies as an applied field, we should never let the need for fundamental conceptual and theoretical advances obscure the requirement to explore intuition-in-use. We now know enough about intuition to be able to go out into the field and find out much more about what makes intuition work effectively in practice and how managers' use of intuition might be developed and improved.

1.6 Conclusion

It's more than 10 years since the 2002 meeting of the Academy of Management in Denver, Colorado when I took my first tentative steps at presenting intuition research at a management conference. Now intuition in management is taken for granted as a legitimate research topic, but back then it was still on the fringes of mainstream management research, and there was a quite limited scientific literature on which students of intuition could draw (e.g., Burke and Miller, 1999; Simon, 1987). I'm pleased to say that the situation has changed, and very much for the better: research articles on intuition have appeared in world-leading management journals (e.g., *Academy of Management Review*, *Academy of Management Executive*, *Journal of Management*, etc.); moreover managers themselves never cease to be fascinated by what intuition is and how they can make better use of it, and they're hungry for more of these kinds of insights. That said, intuition research is still very much in its infancy, and I remain convinced that not only do we have a lot more to learn about it, it can actually teach us a lot about ourselves as well.

Our gut feelings are "neither impeccable nor stupid" (Gigerenzer, 2007, p. 228) but in an increasingly data-rich world intuition is a skill that we need, more than ever, to cultivate and on which to place a value. To this extent intuition research has been for me, and remains, a curious passion and a privilege to be part of the decade-long endeavor that it has been. Back in 2002 Big Data in business was merely a twinkle in the technologists' eye, but as Steve Lohr writing in *The New York Times* in 2012* noted, listening to the messages that can be gleaned from Big Data is important but so too is listening to intuition. Intuition can make us not only smarter but wiser. Intuition at its best is data filtered through and processed by the most complex system in the known universe, the human brain.

References

Akinci, C. and Sadler-Smith, E. (2012). Intuition in management research: A historical review. *International Journal of Management Reviews*, 14(1): 104–122.

Barnard, C. (1938/1968). *The Functions of the Executive*. Cambridge, MA: Harvard University Press.

---

* http://www.nytimes.com/2012/12/30/technology/big-data-is-great-but-dont-forget-intuition.html?_r=0 Accessed 3/16/2014.

Burke, L.A. and Miller, M.K. (1999). Taking the mystery out of intuitive decision making. *Academy of Management Executive,* 13(4): 91–99.

Burke, L. and Sadler-Smith, E. (2006). Instructor intuition in the educational context. *Academy of Management Learning and Education*, 5(2): 169–181.

Dane, E. and Pratt, M.G. (2007). Exploring intuition and its role in managerial decision making. *Academy of Management Review*, 32(1): 33–54.

Dane, E. and Pratt, M.G. (2009). Conceptualizing and measuring intuition: A review of recent trends. In G.P. Hodgkinson and J.K. Ford (Eds.), *International Review of Industrial and Organizational Psychology*, 24: 1–40.

Epstein, S. (1994). Integration of the cognitive and the psychodynamic unconscious. *American Psychologist*, 49: 709–724.

Epstein, S. (2008). Intuition from the perspective of cognitive-experiential self-theory. In H. Plessner, C. Betsch, and T. Betsch (Eds.), *Intuition in Judgment and Decision Making*. New York: Taylor and Francis, pp. 23–37.

Gigerenzer, G. (2007). *Gut Feelings. The Intelligence of the Unconscious*. New York: Viking Press.

Gilovich, T. and Griffin, D. (2002). Introduction – Heuristics and biases: Then and now. In T. Gilovich, D. Griffin, and D. Kahneman (Eds.), *Heuristics and Biases: The Psychology of Intuitive Judgment*. New York: Cambridge University Press, pp. 1–18.

Gore, J. and Sadler-Smith, E. (2011). Unpacking intuition: A process and outcome framework. *Review of General Psychology*, 15(4): 304–316.

Hodgkinson, G.P., Langan-Fox, J., and Sadler-Smith, E. (2008). Intuition: A fundamental bridging construct in the behavioural sciences. *British Journal of Psychology*, 99(1): 1–27.

Hodgkinson, G.P., Sadler-Smith, E., Burke, L., Claxton, G., and Sparrow, P. (2009) Intuition in organizations: Some implications for strategic management. *Long Range Planning*, 42: 277–297.

Hogarth, R.M. (2001). *Educating Intuition*. Chicago: University of Chicago Press.

Hogarth, R.M. (2010). Intuition: A challenge for psychological research on decision making. *Psychological Inquiry*, 21(4): 338–353.

Honey, P. and Mumford, A. (1986). *The Learning Styles Questionnaire*. Maidenhead, UK: Peter Honey.

Kahneman, D. (2011). *Thinking, Fast and Slow*. New York: Farrar, Straus & Giroux.

Kahneman, D. and Klein, G. (2009). Conditions for intuitive expertise: A failure to disagree. *American Psychologist*, 64(6): 515–526.

Klein, G. (2003). *Intuition at Work*. New York: Doubleday.

Lieberman, M.D. (2007). Social cognitive neuroscience: A review of core processes. *Annual Review of Psychology*, 58: 259–289.

Rowan, R. (1989). What it is. In H.A. Weston (Ed.), *Intuition in Organizations: Leading and Managing Productively*. Newbury Park, CA: Sage, pp. 78–88.

Sadler-Smith, E. (2010). *The Intuitive Mind: Profiting from the Power of Your Sixth Sense*. Chichester, UK: John Wiley and Sons.

Sadler-Smith, E. and Shefy, E. (2004). The intuitive executive: Understanding and applying "gut feel" in decision making. *Academy of Management Executive*, 18(4): 76–91.

Sadler-Smith, E., Allinson, C.W., and Hayes, J. (2000). Cognitive style and learning preferences: Some implications for CPD. *Management Learning*, 31: 239–256.

Salas, E. and Klein, G. (2001). Expertise and naturalistic decision making: An overview. In E. Salas and G. Klein (Eds.), *Linking Expertise and Naturalisitic Decision Making*. Mawah, NJ: Lawrence Erlbaum, pp. 3–8.

Salas, E., Rosen, M.A., and DiazGranados, D. (2010). Expertise-based intuition and decision making in organizations. *Journal of Management*, 36: 941–973.

Shirley, D.A. and Langan-Fox, J. (1996). Intuition: A review of the literature. *Psychological Reports*, 79(2): 563–584.

Simon, H.A. (1987). Making management decisions: The role of intuition and emotion. *Academy of Management Executive*, 1: 157–164.

Sinclair, M. (2010). Misconceptions about intuition. *Psychological Inquiry*, 21(4): 378–386.

Sinclair, M. (Ed.) (2005). *Handbook of Intuition Research*. Cheltenham, UK: Edward Elgar.

Sinclair, M. and Ashkanasy, N.M. (2005). Intuition: Myth or a decision-making tool? *Management Learning*, 36(3): 353–370.

Slovic, P., Finucane, M.L., Peters, E., and MacGregor, D.G. (2004). Risk as analysis and risk as feelings: Some thoughts about affect, reason, risk, and rationality. *Risk Analysis*, 24(2): 311–322.

Tversky, A. and Kahneman, D. (1974). Judgment under uncertainty: Heuristics and biases. *Science*, 185: 1124–1131.

Tversky, A. and Kahneman, D. (1983). Extensional versus intuitive reasoning: The conjunction fallacy in probability judgment. *Psychological Review*, 90(4): 293.

Volz, K.G., Rübsamen, R., and von Cramon, D.Y. (2008). Cortical regions activated by the subjective sense of perceptual coherence of environmental sounds: A proposal for a neuroscience of intuition. *Cognitive, Affective, and Behavioral Neuroscience*, 8(3): 318–328.

2

FEELING OUR WAY WITH INTUITION

MARTIN ROBSON

The University of New England, New South Wales, Australia

Contents

2.1 Introduction

Intuition became the focus of my attention in fulfillment of an undergraduate "leadership" assignment set by Professor Peter Miller, a prominent leadership expert in Australia. We had been tasked to interview a leader we admired, find out what we could about his or her leadership, and then compare the findings to theory. I had recently completed a "Men in Separation" workshop (for men recently divorced or separated) led by John. In his 60s, gray, but still well muscled from daily surfing, John impressed me with his confidence, compassion, and wisdom. I remember the moment well when the word "intuition" popped up. I asked him "You have a diverse bunch of men—different ages, backgrounds, experiences, personalities, and so on; how do you know what technique or strategy to employ"? He said, "Intuition." As have most people, I had heard the word used before, but not given it much thought; the focus was usually on what the intuition was about, rather than the concept itself. When I later came to look for the topic in leadership and management theory, I could not find it. There seemed to be an assumption that leaders exclusively used analysis for their decision making. I had to seek out books and articles specifically focusing on intuition to gain an understanding. Thus, intuition immediately came to mind as a topic for postgraduate research.

This chapter summarizes my postgraduate investigations into intuition conducted between 2002 and 2011. Some of what I have learned is from the literature (theory), as well as from interviewing 38 "elite" Australian leaders: chairs, directors, CEOs, and senior executives of public and private companies, as well as a barrister, two politicians, and a former chief of defense. Most of these leaders had been selected by their peers as "True Leaders" (see, e.g., Macken, 2002).* My research, based in "grounded theory", was one of discovery, and one that took me far beyond where I expected to go. It changed me as a person and it gave me a new perspective on my own culture. This chapter is structured in two sections discussing the research questions I sought to answer. Section 2.2 addresses what intuition is and how participants used it. I also focus on an issue that arose from my Honors research (and the research of others), which had never been investigated: why do leaders say they use and value intuition, but for the most part, don't talk about it? This was important to investigate because knowledge about intuition use in organizations is less potent unless the social context in which it is used is also understood.

Section 2.3 reveals that the answer was surprising and complex and a good example of the value of the research methodology I used, "grounded theory" (further explained in Robson and Cooksey's chapter in Sinclair, in press) the principal advantage of which is "discovery" in describing and explaining social processes. My research was essentially a study of humans and human interaction. It did not seek to test hypotheses, rather, it sought to understand intuition use and disclosure from the perspective of participants and to develop an explanatory theory. My approach to intuition research complements and contextualizes the findings of the deductive, positivist psychological approaches that have dominated extant theory. Viewed together, they present a more complete picture, not unlike the complementary way the elite participants themselves said they used intuition and analysis.

---

* True Leaders lists are published by *Boss Magazine*, a supplement of the Australian Financial Review.

2.2 What Is Intuition?

2.2.1 Definition

Participants experienced intuition as an internal, received, holistic, subconscious sense or feeling of knowing. Intuition as a feeling/knowing flags the rightness or wrongness of a person, group, choice, strategy, or proposal, the timeliness of a decision, or the need for action or caution, and particularly further investigation.

Participants were remarkably consistent in their descriptions of intuition: a feeling of knowing that "appeals to you as being correct, something you should go with ... an internal force" (Robson, 2011, p. 136), that often stands in contrast to other information, opinions, and data. Intuition is experienced as internal because it comes from an ancient, preconscious cognitive system. Intuition draws on tacit knowledge: we know more than we know we know (Polanyi, 1966). Intuition is nonrational (as opposed to irrational) because it is a feeling of knowing, without knowing why. Knowing why would require reasoning, which, by definition, would be conscious: "[I]t's not a conscious process, it's just the sort of gut feel that something else is going on here;" "[I]t's telling me that I should go left and I'm told I should go right;" "[I]t just doesn't feel right ... something is nagging at me" (Robson, 2011, p. 137). Intuition is literally "*in*-tuition", being taught or guided from the inside. At the broadest level, it could be said that every sort of feeling can guide decisions: emotions (fear or desire), hunger, or addictive cravings. However, intuition can be distinguished from these other feelings. Section 2.3 shows that an ability to discriminate between feelings was key for some participants.

Although ubiquitously described as a feeling, participants were very keen to point out that intuition is not emotion but rather an innate human capacity that was "honed" by years of experience. Many participants talked about intuition and pattern recognition: "[P]atterns you have seen before and therefore are very familiar to you" (Robson, 2011, p. 140). Therefore, intuition is dependent on both natural capacity and experience, the way that intelligence is both a natural capacity and developed through education. If experience informs intuition, it is therefore no surprise that participants argued that "The very reason you are chosen as a non-executive director is the sum of your experience and ideally the breadth of that experience ... which you are expected to

Table 2.1   Experiential and analytical cognitive systems

EXPERIENTIAL	ANALYTICAL SYSTEMS
Thinks quickly; primed for immediate action	Thinks slowly, deliberately
Closely connected with emotions	Oriented toward planning and consideration
Experiences passively and automatically	Analytic, thinks in terms of cause and effects
Experiences events as self-evidently valid	Separates logic from emotions
Intuitive, holistic	Sees the world in abstract symbols
Interprets experience and guides conscious thoughts and behavior	Experiences actively and consciously
	Requires justification by logic and evidence

draw on for decision-making and counseling at that level; so it [intuition] is a fundamental prerequisite for the job" (Robson, 2011, p. 140).

From an evolutionary perspective, intuition is primal intelligence (Epstein, 1994). As early mammals, our ancestors' survival literally depended on pattern recognition and associated feeling. Some patterns, for example, cheetah spots and scent, invoked fright and flight, whereas fruity colors and smells invoked hunger and attraction. Human intuition operates in the same basic way; however, humans have an added layer of brain (the prefrontal cortex) that facilitates conscious, rational cognitive processing. Thus, dual process theorists (see, e.g., Epstein, 1998) posit that we have two oppositional but complementary cognitive systems that explain conflicts between the head and heart, or intuition and analysis. Table 2.1 depicts the characteristics associated with each "mind".

2.2.2 Role of Intuition for Leaders

Analysis is infallible only when all variables are known, accurately quantified, and the calculation is performed flawlessly. As one participant pointed out, if all information were perfectly known, there would not really be a decision to make. In real life, this is seldom the case. Universities do not prepare people for such a complex and uncertain world: "When I went to the university, all the problems were presented in a very neat and tidy way – this is the problem, and this is how you solve it. My experience was my life was always messy, and the problems presented to me and my work were always messy" (Robson, 2011, p. 150). Participants repeatedly pointed out that making judgments on incomplete, complex, uncertain, and sometimes contradictory information was the essence of their job as leaders: "As a leader, you can't not make decisions;" "[I]t's what I'm paid to do;" "[N]o matter how good the business case, if you go with the business case without making any further judgment ... it's not your judgment. You're saying well, these guys know what they're doing, so we will follow them" (Robson, p. 156). Leadership, at its most basic level, is about making decisions. Participants said they were not always comfortable making decisions based on gut-feeling, however, "[Y]ou've got to call it one way or another" (Robson, p. 148).

It is clear from my research and the research of others that intuition is very important for leaders in organizations because it can deal with more uncertainty than our conscious rational minds (see, e.g., Brockman and Simmons, 1997; Sadler-Smith, 2008). Most commonly, participants cited their use of intuition in relation to a "feeling of knowing" about whether someone or something would work: "You listen to alternatives and to the scenarios and you get a certain feeling about what you think is right" (Robson, 2011, p. 155). Intuition was associated with judgments about people and qualitative factors in organizations. However, participants did have intuitions about analyses: "We had the numbers and we went through a very rational process of doing a forecast every quarter ... but just from kicking the tires and wandering around, my sense was we were going to do better" (Robson, p. 156). Moreover, "objective" information always has a context. Some participants pointed out that the information they relied on for their decisions could never be entirely separated from the individuals who provided the information: "It may be that the person presenting the evidence is too risk averse ... so you weigh that up and put on a different weighting than that person did" (Robson). Participants said they developed a "feel" over time for where there were missing data, incorrect data, and detecting the "spin" others might place on data, piercing the intentions and motivation of the messenger.

> As a leader, you do get filtered information and it's unintentional, it's just human nature. Everyone has their own perspectives and I think one of the key things in making a decision is assessing what are the key drivers, intentions and desires of the people that are providing you that information, so you can recalibrate it accordingly before you make the decision. I think that is a key step. (Robson, 2011, p. 156)

Intuition was therefore acknowledged as an indispensible tool at the intersection of the subjective and objective (people and data).

Intuition is particularly useful for making judgments about people, because people are often complex, uncertain, and thus unpredictable, even deceptive and Machiavellian. Participants placed a high priority on these judgments because they perceived that people were intertwined and critical to the success of all aspects of organizational strategy: "[V]irtually everything we do is people". Intuition tells us: "[I]f this person is going to be detailed, make decisions, going to be an irritant or going to be a 'mood Hoover'"[mood destroyer] (Robson, 2011, p. 156). Intuition is the only tool for the intangible and qualitative factors in decision making:

> [T]here are themes and factors that aren't measureable that you take into account when making decisions ... how will this decision play out, how will employees feel about this, how will management feel about this, how will I feel about this, will the directors feel challenged by this? So thinking about the different perspectives of the stakeholders involves intuition. (Robson, 2011, p. 159)

Many participants said they used intuition in recruiting and appointing. Curriculum vitae and other evidence are considered in making these judgments, however, not solely relied on because: "[S]ometimes the picture painted on a piece of paper is rosier than the reality, so you've got to see through that" (Robson, 2011, p. 158). Only one participant from the sample regarded intuition with some skepticism. He argued that the word intuition is sometimes used as "an excuse for inadequate analysis". Despite his mistrust of others' intuition, he did admit, "I suppose if I was to use intuition, and I certainly consciously don't do it, it would be in the area of judging people" (Robson, p. 158). Interestingly, the next thing he said was, "I've spent more time picking people to carry out tasks than almost anything else" (Robson, p. 158). He later agreed that: "[Y]es, one gets a feel for people" (Robson, p. 169). Ironically, this participant clearly relied on intuition and obviously trusted in his own intuition, yet, at the same time, regarded it as "muck and mystery" (Robson, p. 168).

For some, intuition was the only defense against the "articulate incompetent" or a dysfunctional, deceitful, corrupt individual or "organizational psychopath". Two women gave significant examples of intuitions from CEO appointment interviews:

> ... and then I met him and I said to my fellow directors and to the managing director, I have a terrible sense about this man. I said, he can't relate to me ... he gives me the sense of being slippery, shonky, whatever. And I don't know why I felt that ... I said, look, I can't give you chapter and verse, but this man gives me the creeps. This man has trouble written all over him. And subsequently we had no end of trouble. (Robson, p. 158)

Participants also described how intuition was useful for interpreting the dynamics of interpersonal relations, particularly within an organization: "I come from a finance background, so let's look at the composites of the assets [people]. I mean you actually do want your assets working for you so that you've got an optimum outcome and output. You do not want those assets working as a liability" (Robson, 2011, p. 159). Intuition gives insights into hidden agendas including moods, attitudes, desires, needs, motivations, and tensions between individuals (sexual or otherwise), all of which may contradict written or spoken information. Commonly referred to as reading subtext, participants discussed intuition as useful in sensing subtle signals, typically body language, intonation, gestures, or just picking up on a "vibe" in an individual or organization: "What are the vibes in this organization about how people are feeling? I mean, people will use words like, '[W]hat's the temperature in the organization,' you know, 'you need to listen to what's not said'" (Robson, p. 159). These qualitative judgments were shown to be important for leaders: "It might be the different cultures of the organization. It might be the strength of character of the leadership of the other organization or it can be a whole variety of things. At the end of the day they may impinge on the business, and you make that judgment about those qualitative factors and you try and quantify it if you can, but you know, they can be showstoppers" (Robson, p. 151). Aspects such as culture were seen as critical to the value of an organization by many participants: "[I]f you get the people right and the culture right, you're there, you don't have to manage the business, they manage it for you" (Robson, p. 214).

Consistent with psychological theory about intuition, leaders said that their intuition was fallible but reliable, especially where they had significant experience. Thus, where they had less experience, participants said they tended to listen to somebody who has more experience. Some said their faith in their own intuition had grown through their use of it, and subsequent reflection: seeing the results. Thus, participants indicated a reflexive use of intuition that had contributed to their development as leaders over the years: "For me, hearing the voice, but having the experience to validate it, so there's a reason to trust it … my experience as a leader has actually, has deepened – has evolved" (Robson, p. 149). A consistent theme in the data was intuition as a signal or warning that something was not right. Participants said intuition told them if something was wrong, suspicious, did not add up, or that the situation was not as it appeared. This would cause them to seek further information in order to confirm or deny their feeling: "I get a sense that something is not right or I get a sense, for example, that we need to go and dig and ferret a bit more for some information because I have got the sense that it might end up on a political agenda or it might hit the media, or something like that" (Robson, p. 157). Thus, intuition would often cause participants to be cautious or develop alternative strategies. For example, "If my intuition was telling me that something was not going to work out the way that people were presenting it to me based on evidence I would not totally ignore my intuition. I would not fully launch into a plan of action that denied my intuition. I would probably make some allowances for it and I would take it in smaller steps" (Robson). Thus, rather than using intuition as a substitute for analysis, participants would use intuition hand in hand with analysis.

2.2.3 Complementary Use of Intuition and Analysis

Given the discussed fallibility of both intuition and analysis, it was not surprising that a repeated theme in the research was the complementary and conditional use of both. Decision making in organizations occurs in a rich, complex, dynamic interplay of decision conditions. In response to this perceived inherent uncertainty of decision making, many participants strongly emphasized that they would do as much as possible, particularly for important decisions, to verify their intuition through research and analysis: "I would never say that I would just go with intuition. … I would always endeavor to try and understand cognitively or intellectually using the evidence that is available, and I would try and link that up to what my intuition is telling me" (Robson, 2011, p. 150).

Consequently, nearly all decision making was perceived as various blends of analysis and intuition. The relative mixture or blend of intuition and analysis was found to depend on the nature of the problem (qualitative or quantitative) and its context. Figure 2.1 represents a conditional matrix derived from the study that depicts the conditions feeding into decision-making scenarios that influence the cognitive mode.

Figure 2.1 suggests that although decision making might be dominated by one mode or another, intuition and analysis are almost never mutually exclusive processes. Qualitative decisions are most likely to invoke intuition in cases where there is high precedent, and therefore a high level of experience, low "hard" information, high urgency, high complexity and ambiguity, and low perceived gravity, whereas the reverse would normally be true for analysis. Participants had intuitions about their analyses; conversely, they also analyzed their intuitions. Participants sought to align their intuitions and analyses. Thus, most decision making was perceived to be a mixture of intuition and analyses to the extent that the difference between them became indistinct: a "quasirationality" (Hammond, 1996); "I think now after all these years, there's no defined edge. To me it's a blurred process" (ibid, p. 150). Thus, the "take-home" message from Section 2.2 is that

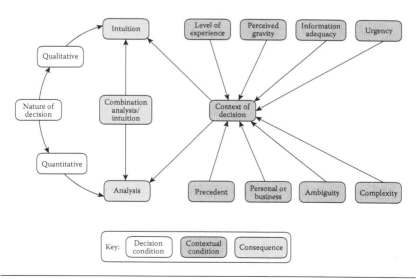

Figure 2.1 Conditional matrix of intuitive/analytical decision making. (Reprinted from M. J. Robson, *The Use and Disclosure of Intuition(s) by Leaders in Australian Organisations: A Grounded Theory*, 2011, p. 154. With permission.)

intuition and analysis are both considered vital to decision making and leadership. Despite this, Section 2.3 shows that intuition is most often not acknowledged in organizations.

2.3 Intuition as a Secret Practice

Intuition was seen as something that is seldom discussed, especially in the public domain, and especially with stakeholders and the media. Intuition use was described as a silent or private practice confided only to close associates. I found that intuition's long association with the mystical and magical was a contributing factor for keeping the use of intuition a secret: "There has been a lot of pressure on making management seem very scientific and it [intuition] seems to be tantamount to crystals;" "[I]t's not scientific, it's not necessarily based on fact, it's not able to be backed up by research;" "[I]t sounds fluffy, non-business-like" (Robson, 2011, p. 170). In addition, some participants (mostly female) argued that intuition was generally perceived as a feminine characteristic associated with emotion, and therefore inferior and weak, in the predominantly male-dominated, often sexist world of organizations: "Generally, it [intuition] has a prefix – women's intuition ... and it's pooh poohed. ... People think that if women make decisions based on intuition then it has no factual basis, it's unsupportable, it's just, you know, girl talk" (Robson, p. 171). As a consequence: "[N]o female in the boardroom would ever want to have her decisions referred to as based on women's intuition. You would die a thousand deaths if you thought anybody thought that's what you were doing" (Robson, p. 173). Therefore, the negative connotations of intuition as being "voodoo ... weird ... a girl thing" (Robson, p. 171) might alone explain the silent nature of intuition use, because people might be frightened of being ridiculed. However, I found an additional, more subtle, explanation for the lack of intuition disclosure upon examining perceptions about gender and intuition, as well as the starkly different ways men and women in the study talked about their subjective experience of intuition and how intuition feels[*].

Many participants believed that women have better intuition or were more in touch with their intuition than men and would be more likely

---

[*] As a consequence of discovering this gender difference early in the study, I modified my sampling strategy to include as many women as possible in the study (nearly 50%).

to use intuition. Indeed, some male participants suggested they would sometimes invite the intuitive judgments of women they knew and trusted. Significantly, women were perceived by both men and women in the study to be more likely to use the word "intuition", or words that can be seen to imply intuition, particularly "feeling" words: "The women want to talk about what they're feeling and experiencing and the blokes want to talk about [laughs], you know, they get very irritated by this process because they don't want to talk about this stuff" (Robson, 2011, p. 177). Women, in general, were perceived to be more in touch with their feelings and, as a consequence, their intuitions: "I just think that women have a deeper sense of how we feel about things. We're more in touch with feeling okay, feeling not okay, and we express those views. We use different words 'that doesn't feel right to me,' that sort of thing. So I think it is a bit of self-awareness. It's a very different language" (Robson, p. 200). Thus, awareness and orientation to feelings and intuitions, and the willingness and ability to express them, became an important theme in the research because it could also explain the lack of disclosure of intuitions in organizations. Moreover, this perception of women being more in touch with their feelings and more able to express them was supported by the difference in responses to questions about participants' internal subjective experience of intuition.

The women in the study, without hesitation, gave lengthy replies and seemed very comfortable with the question. For example: "[The feeling is] not physical, you don't feel like it's a blow or a bit of a wrench or anything. It's just an unsettling in the guts, a level of discomfort in the guts" (Robson, 2011, p. 181). On the other hand, nearly all men either struggled with the question or avoided answering it by changing the subject. I often had the feeling that they thought the question to be strange, inappropriate, and not serious. I remember very well how awkward I felt asking the chairman of one of Australia's largest companies about his subjective experience of intuition. The tension was palpable; the noise from his fingers tapping on the arm of his chair was audible on the interview recording. After pausing for some time, he finally replied, "I don't see that it's an experience. I wouldn't say that it's a huge sensation" (Robson, p. 181), which was a typical response for the men. Intuition can be like a column of smoke: it disappears when we reach out to grab it. The subconscious nature of intuition is the reason why intuition is experienced as internal and is so hard to grasp and talk about.

However, in contrast to the men, the women interpreted the question with a more highly developed subjective self-awareness* coupled with a willingness and ability to articulate this awareness.

I saw this distinction as a dimension of personality and labeled it "interiority". I proposed the properties of this new dimension of personality to be a high ability to be aware of and acknowledge feelings (including intuitions) and distinguish between these feelings (e.g., between emotions and intuition). In addition, the women in the study actively sought to "surface" intuitions. Surfacing intuitions involves taking time out from often hectic and charged critical decision-making processes to foster receptivity to one's internal feeling realm: "You still yourself and you kind of wait for the inner turmoil to kind of settle. And if you just sit with it, you can be clear about what it is that you are experiencing", and "Stepping aside, being on your own – taking time out just to try and get the whole thing in perspective and to get all of that kind of deep knowledge to come to the surface and to be part of the active decision making" (Robson, p. 189). Thus, I theorized that part of the reason intuitions were not acknowledged and disclosed as such was that some people—those with lower interiority, particularly men—were not as aware of the role that intuition played in their own internal decision-making process.[†]

Based on the analysis of data gathered, I also theorized that interactions between people and within organizations can have interiority or not. Do we talk about our feelings and intuitions, or do we talk about external things: money, cars, sports, or data? At the organizational level, the women participants talked about organizations characterized by the need to appear scientific, rational, and objective where strong hierarchies and leadership style determine social organization, power, and the right to speak. I labeled these "assertive cultures". Assertive cultures, often led by men, value strong and active decision making, evidence, and economics, and tough, assertive, interpersonal relations where mistakes are punished. Thus, feelings in these assertive cultures go largely unacknowledged. Assertive cultures can therefore be described as having low interiority.

---

[*] Objective self-awareness, on the other hand, is awareness of how others perceive you.
[†] This finding was recently supported by Sinclair, Ashkanasy and Chatopadyay (2010). They reported that the women in their study were guided more by their intuition because "they can access it more easily through their heightened awareness of emotions" (p. 393).

As depicted in Figure 2.2, individuals in assertive cultures may silence their intuitions. In the following example, the participant talks about deliberations on a multimillion-dollar rescue package for a failed company: "If I would have to have gone to XXX and said, look, all of it looks good on paper and the objective facts are that we've got to support this position – but having looked at all of that and on the basis of my experience and my intuition about these people, I don't think it's the right thing for us. They would have said go and have some 'expletive' counseling will you" (Robson and Cooksey, 2008, p. 79). Individuals with intuitions in assertive cultures may also find or even fabricate a rationale rather than admit they used intuition. Alternatively, expressions that are culturally congruent and that mask the role of intuition, such as "my experience" and "judgment", are used. Participants acknowledged that there were

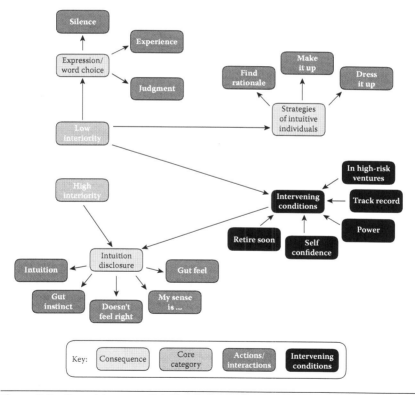

Figure 2.2 The social process of intuition disclosure. (Reprinted from M. J. Robson, *The Use and Disclosure of Intuition(s) by Leaders in Australian Organisations: A Grounded Theory*, 2011, p. 211. With permission.)

circumstances (intervening conditions) in which individuals might go against cultural norms of expression: where there was no precedent and therefore no data (entrepreneurship), where they have power, status, and especially where an individual has established a track record. Intuitions may also be disclosed where the individual is about to retire, or where the leader has high self-confidence. In the words of one participant, "I don't think your intuition will change, but the context in which you are presenting it will change how you present it" (Robson, 2011, p. 211).

On the other hand, participants also described organizations, often led by women, with characteristics very different—even oppositional—from those of assertive cultures. These organizations were found to have integrating values and a focus on developing supportive, inclusive, democratic cultures that are tolerant of mistakes and characterized by open language, where feelings, including intuitions, are consequently acknowledged (Robson, 2011, p. 199):

INTERVIEWER

Could you imagine being in a boardroom full of women and the culture being different?

PARTICIPANT

Absolutely, been there … and the culture is totally different. The conversation is more open … the way in which things are talked about is more around feelings.

INTERVIEWER

It sounds as though there's a pretty stark difference between men and women in these situations. Is it really that stark? Is it really that different?

PARTICIPANT

I think it is absolutely. Yes, that's my personal experience.

2.3.1 *Interiority and Its Implications*

The advantages of a high degree of interiority and thus the acknowledgment and disclosure of feelings and intuitions at the individual level are numerous. For example, the ability to distinguish between intuition and other feelings allows individuals to recognize when their motivation is fear, greed, or desire, rather than intuitions based on experience. Participants perceived that if they were able to acknowledge the emotional context of a decision, it would be less likely to drive or undermine both individual and collective decision-making processes. The lack of an awareness of the internal drivers of decision making could lead to erroneous/self-serving and resource-wasting activities: "I think that, particularly if you are in a senior position, if you are not aware of what is going on internally and how you are reacting to things, you can lead people on a wild goose chase. You have got to think about where this is coming from, why am I feeling in this way about a piece of work that comes to you" (Robson, 2011, p. 191). Acknowledging feelings and emotions that often accompany critical decisions allows them to be dealt with transparently. Interiority enhances complementarity: "I think the more you are self-aware, the better you are able to weight it [intuition] appropriately amongst other considerations in the decision-making process" (Robson, p. 184).

The complementarity of intuition and analysis in decision making is just as important at the collective level as it is at the level of the individual. High organizational interiority has positive consequences for decision making and behavior because intuitions become available for expression, articulation, comparison, discussion, exploration, and scrutiny. Clearly, intuition is used and valued by leaders. However, if intuitions are dressed up as analysis, or if decisions based on intuitions are simply announced, decision making becomes less transparent and thus more vulnerable to error. Moreover, if feelings are given legitimacy and valued, there would be a greater likelihood of ethical decision making, because for most people, unethical decision making "doesn't feel right", even though it may be justifiable through reasoning and rationality.

2.4 The Way Forward

People are individuals and have preferences for cognitive style. Moreover, the nature and context of decisions have impacts on how decisions are approached. However, the findings clearly show that what worked for these elite leaders was a combination of intuition and analysis in nearly all decision-making scenarios. This happens naturally at the intrapersonal/interiority level, however, at the organizational level, complementary use of intuition/analysis is constrained by assertive cultures that regard disclosure of intuitions as deviant, foolish, or unmanly behavior. Clearly, in order to make the most of intuition, attitudes need to change and this can only happen when intuition, as a concept and a process, is better understood. Intuition, its strengths and limitations, when to trust it, how to develop and nurture it, and how to surface it, is almost entirely absent from mainstream education and in particular, management and leadership education (see The University of New England, 2013, as an exception). This is significant because it means that as individuals, as organizations, and as a society, we do not really know or acknowledge the importance of the nonrational in our daily decision making and behavior.

With a better understanding of intuition as an integral cognitive function, irrespective of gender, men might be more likely to be persuaded to develop their interiority. It could be argued that men have a lot of catching up to do. Women have always been perceived as more in touch with their feelings, and in school girls are now outperforming boys in "masculine" subjects (Paton, 2012). From my research, and that of others (Barrett et al., 2000; Sinclair, Ashkanasy, and Chatopadyay, 2010), it seems that men in general are not as in touch with their feelings and do not feel comfortable talking about them. However, there were perceptions that this may be changing, perhaps as a consequence of more modern nonsexist parenting and social conditioning. Moreover, studies concerning brain plasticity show that men are better able to express their feelings given the right motivation. Research shows that due to nontraditional, culturally driven opportunities and pressures, individual brain "gender" varies widely. Moreover, "masculinization" and "feminization" of brain regions may vary within one brain. Thus, an individual may "throw like a boy" but "talk like a girl" (Schulz, 2005, p. 23). Brain plasticity clearly offers the possibility of change for men, but only if they are motivated to do so (Ciarrochi, Hynes, and Crittenden, 2005).

Changing attitudes about intuition and the development of interiority in men may go some way to increasing interiority in organizations. However, culture is notoriously resistant to change. This is because culture is the subconscious of an organization and mostly below awareness. It is for this reason that feminist writers suggest that asking men to acknowledge "masculinities" would be like asking fish to acknowledge "the water in which they swim" (Stivers, 1996 cited in Sinclair, 2005, p. 27). As a consequence, we often do not recognize how culture affects behavior. It is often only through contrast, when we experience a different culture, that we really begin to understand our own. Thus, it is no surprise that it was the women in the study who had the most insight into culture, because in general, women do indeed seem to generate different organizational cultures when they dominate. However, only 2% of Australian organizations are led by women (EOWA, 2008) and only 4% in the United States (Howard, 2012). Therefore, the challenge of bringing intuition into the boardroom, which is still very much a "boys' club", should not be underestimated.

References

Barrett, L.F., Lane, R.D., Sechrest, L., and Schwartz, G.E. (2000). Sex differences in emotional awareness. *Personality and Social Psychological Bulletin*, 26(9): 1027–1035.

Brockman, E. and Simmons, P. (1997). Strategic decision making: The influence of CEO experience and use of tacit knowledge. *Journal of Managerial Issues*, 9(4): 454–467.

Ciarrochi, J., Hynes, K., and Crittenden, N. (2005). Can men do better if they try harder?: Sex and motivational effects on emotional awareness. *Cognition and Emotion*, 19(1): 133–141.

EOWA (2008). Eowa 2008 Australian Census of Women in Leadership. Retrieved from: <http://www.eowa.gov.au/Australian_Women_In_Leadership_Census/2008_Australian_Women_In_Leadership_Census/Media_Kit/EOWA_Census_2008_Publication.pdf >, 10/14/2009.

Epstein, S. (1994). Integration of the cognitive and the psychodynamic unconscious. *The American Psychologist*, 49(8): 709–724.

Epstein, S. (1998). *Constructive Thinking: The Key to Emotional Intelligence*. Westport, CT: Praeger.

Hammond, K. (1996). *Human Judgment and Social Policy: Irreducible Uncertainty, Inevitable Error and Unavoidable Injustice*, New York: Oxford University Press.

Howard, C. (2012). The new class of female CEOs. *Forbes*. Retrieved from: <http://www.forbes.com/sites/carolinehoward/2012/08/22/introducing-the-new-class-of-female-ceos>, 10/22/2013.

Macken, J. (2002). True leaders 2002. *Financial Review*, AFR Boss, pp. 5–6.

Paton, G. (2012). Girls outperforming boys in "masculine" subjects. *The Telegraph*. Retrieved from: <http://www.telegraph.co.uk/education/educationnews/9376466/Girls-outperforming-boys-in-masculine-subjects.html>, 10/22/2013.

Polanyi, M. (1966). *The Tacit Dimension*. Chicago: University of Chicago Press.

Robson, M. and Cooksey, R. (2008). Towards the integration and contextualisation of perspectives on managerial intuition. *Australasian Journal of Business and Social Inquiry*, 6(3): 62–84.

Robson, M. and Cooksey, R. (in press). Theorising intuition in practice: Developing grounded theory with elite business leaders. In M. Sinclair (Ed.), *A Handbook of Intuition Research Methods*. Cheltenham, UK: Edward Elgar.

Robson, M.J. (2011). "The Use and Disclosure of Intuition(s) by Leaders in Australian Organisations: A Grounded Theory." PhD thesis, New England School of Business, University of New England, Armidale, Retrieved from: <https://e-publications.une.edu.au/vital/access/services/Download/une:12114/SOURCE02?view = true>, 13/2/2013.

Sadler-Smith, E. (2008). *Inside Intuition*. London: Routledge.

Schulz, M.L. (2005). *The New Feminine Brain: How Women Can Develop Their Inner Strengths, Genius, and Intuition*. New York: Free Press.

Sinclair, A. (2005), *Doing Leadership Differently: Gender, Power and Sexuality in a Changing Business Culture*, rev. edn. Carlton South, Aus: Melbourne University Press.

Sinclair, C.D., Ashkanasy, N.M., and Chatopadyay, P. (2010). The affective determinants of intuitive decision making. *Journal of Management and Organisation*, 16(3): 382–398.

The University of New England (2013). GSB740 Managerial Thinking and Decision Making, Retrieved from: https://my.une.edu.au/courses/2012/units/GSB740

3

STORIES OF INTUITION-BASED DECISIONS

Evidence for Dual Systems of Thinking

CINLA AKINCI

School of Management
University of St Andrews

Contents

3.1 Introduction

Intuition research started with a practitioner (Barnard, 1938) initiating intuition scholarship in management and organization studies. Over time, the significance of intuition in relation to the cognitive limitations of decision makers became apparent and moved to the fore (Simon, 1987, 1997), but the view of intuition as an attribute of humans as "cognitive misers" gave way to a naturalistic view of intuition (Klein, 1998) as an affective nonconscious mechanism that was both fast and frugal, as well as potentially powerful and perilous (Gigerenzer and Todd, 1999; Kahneman, Slovic, and Tversky, 1982). With the acknowledgment of the role of affect in cognition, intuition's place as a bridging construct was recognized (Slovic et al., 2002). It has come to occupy an important role in the broader dual-process architecture of cognition (Epstein, 1994) as the latter moved center stage in the psychological sciences in the 1990s and beyond. Part way through the story, management researchers were seduced by the lateralization of brain function and wandered down the blind alley of hemispheric dominance with the so-called "split-brain" hypothesis (Mintzberg, 1976). There have been recent overtures in the direction of cognitive neuroscience (Lieberman, 2007) and these developments are not only conceptually and theoretically coherent and compelling, but also they are commensurate with many of the central tenets of dual-process theory. However, as Akinci and Sadler-Smith (2012) note, there is still no fully integrated and holistic theoretical picture of how the fundamental processes of intuiting interact within and between the physiological and psychological processes of analysis.

Drawing from the conceptual foundation of dual-process theories, this chapter presents stories of intuition-based decisions from a police force in the United Kingdom, illustrating an "intuitive hit" and an "intuitive miss" in a managerial and an operational context, respectively. On the basis of the analysis of these stories, a discussion is provided on the theoretical and practical implications of the emerging findings, and the conclusion offers a set of recommendations for the use of intuition and analysis for effective decision making.

3.2 Dual Systems of Reasoning

Although dual-process theories come in a number of forms, what they have in common is the idea offered by Stanovich and West (2000) that there are two different modes of processing. In order to emphasize the prototypical view adopted, the two systems have simply been generically labeled System 1 and System 2. System 1 is characterized as contextually dependent, automatic, largely unconscious, associative, intuitive, and implicit in nature. Thus, it is relatively undemanding in terms of its use of scarce cognitive resources. This system has as its goal the ability to model other minds in order to read intention and to make rapid interactional moves based on those modeled intentions. In contrast, System 2 processing is contextually independent, analytic, rule-based, and explicit in nature. Hence, it is relatively slow and makes greater demands on cognitive resources than its System 1 counterpart. In the last two decades, different forms of dual-process theories have been established by many cognitive and social psychologists (see Table 3.1).

For example, Sloman (1996) asserts that human reasoning is a function of two systems that are designed to achieve different computational goals. One is "associative" and operates reflexively. It draws inferences from a kind of statistical description of its environment by making use of the similarity between problem elements interpreted using such aspects of general knowledge as images, stereotypes, and prototypes. The other system described by Sloman (1996) is "rule-based" which tries to describe the world by capturing different kinds of structure that is logical, hierarchical, and causal–mechanical.

According to Lakoff and Johnson (1999), metaphorical, frame-based, and prototype reasoning are cognitive mechanisms that have developed in the course of human evolution to allow us to function as well as possible in everyday life. Therefore, it would be irrational not to use the cognitive mechanisms that in general allow us to function well overall. The authors claim that if we did not reason automatically and unconsciously using prototypes and conceptual frames, we would probably not survive. Similarly, Epstein (1994) asserts that the experiential (intuitive) system is assumed to have a much longer evolutionary history and to operate in animals as well as in humans, though due to their more highly developed brains, the experiential system processes information in far more complex

Table 3.1   *Dual-Process Theories*

	SYSTEM 1	SYSTEM 2
Reber (1993)	Implicit cognition	Explicit learning
Epstein (1994)	Experiential system	Rational system
Sloman (1996)	Associative system	Rule-based system
Klein (1998)	Recognition-primed decisions	Rational choice strategy

Source: Adapted from K. Stanovich and R. West, *Behavioural and Brain Sciences* 23: 643–726, 2000. With permission.

ways in humans. The experiential system operates in an automatic, holistic, associationistic manner, and is primarily nonverbal. Although it encodes experience in the form of nonverbal concrete representations (e.g., images, feelings, physical sensations), it is able to generalize and to construct relatively complex models for organizing experience and directing behavior by the use of prototypes, metaphors, scripts, and narratives (Denes-Raj and Epstein, 1994).

At the time, this was a new concept, sometimes referred to as the "cognitive unconscious" (Epstein, 1994, p. 710), which holds that most information processing occurs automatically and effortlessly outside of awareness, a mode that is far more efficient than conscious deliberative thinking.

> Conscious thought is the tip of an enormous iceberg. It is the rule of thumb among cognitive scientists that unconscious thought is 95 percent of all thought – and that may be a serious underestimate. Moreover, the 95 percent below the surface of conscious awareness shapes and structures all conscious thought. If the cognitive unconscious were not there doing this shaping, there could be no conscious thought. (Lakoff and Johnson, 1999: 13)

Cognitive-experiential self-theory (Epstein et al., 1996) suggests that neither the experiential (intuitive) nor the rational (analytical) system is superior to the other. Each has its strengths and limitations. The rational system is capable of solving abstract problems, planning, applying principles broadly across situations, and taking long-term considerations into account. The experiential system on the other hand is able effortlessly to direct behavior in everyday life. It is a source of motivation and passion. Without it, the ability of people to engage in motivated behavior would be seriously compromised (see Damasio, 1994). The experiential system can solve problems that are beyond the capacity of the rational system because they require a holistic rather than analytic orientation, because they depend on lessons from lived experiences, or because they require creativity via associative connections. Epstein (2008) argues that without an experiential system, people would be like robots with computers in their heads: they would be incapable of feeling.

To sum up, the message conveyed by the dual-process theories is that behavior and conscious thought are guided by the joint operations of the two systems (intuition and analysis), with their relative influence being determined by various parameters, including the nature of the situation (i.e., does the situation require a holistic or analytic approach?), individual differences in style of thinking (i.e., cognitive styles), and the degree of emotional involvement. As Simon (1987) asserts it concisely, intuition is not a process that operates independently of analysis; rather the two processes are essential complementary components of information processing (Epstein et al., 1996) and effective decision making (Damasio, 1994).

3.3 Intuitive Decision-Making Processes: Stories from a Police Force

This section presents two recent stories from a police force in the United Kingdom (gathered in focus group interviews with the senior management team and the operational team) to illustrate the intuition-based decision processes in the contexts of organizational change by senior police officers (intuitive hit) and police law enforcement by operational officers (intuitive miss). The name of the police force shall remain anonymous for confidentiality purposes.

3.3.1 Intuitive Hit: Organizational Restructure

The police force was under considerable pressure both externally and internally to restructure the organization in order to "re-engineer" the way they did business. Externally, there was a drive from the government to deliver an "effective and efficient" police service. On the other hand, internally, staff workloads were extremely high mainly due to unclear lines of accountability, which led to high anxiety and sickness levels within the organization. This in turn resulted in poor performance around detection and reduction of crime, thus causing poor satisfaction and confidence within the local community. The crime performance figures were in the red, and the senior officers were under scrutiny from the chief officers' group.

The senior officers started looking at some of the best practices in other parts of the country by visiting various police forces similarly positioned to them, to see what models they had, and how they were structured and operated. It became apparent that they needed to reduce the number of the neighborhood policing teams and divide the resources between the three major divisions of policing within the organization: the neighborhood policing team including response functions, the investigation of serious and organized crime, and the crime management and custody division. However, this presented uncertainty and complexity because there was no straightforward formula they could apply to the allocation of resources. Furthermore, at the time, the government changed their view on how the police would be assessed, and the single top-down indicator was going to be based on public confidence. The senior officers had to find the right balance of resources among the three areas in order to deliver what the government was demanding from them.

> I think it's fair to say there is no magic formula in this. There is no logarithm you can apply to policing that says, you need to put X percent into uniform policing, X percent into neighborhood policing, X percent into CID, X percent into back office support and through applying that distribution of resources success is guaranteed. That formula does not exist. So you then really do have to rely upon intuition and professional judgment. (Participant A)

In the beginning of the change process, an external consulting firm was brought in to analyze the demand of policing across the organization and to provide a "formula" based on that demand establishing how many people were needed in each division, which could then be applied to the business in terms of redistribution of the resources. Following a few months' work, the consultants were not able to deliver a resourcing formula and they had not managed to take the process forward.

> We had an outside firm come in and say, okay, we're being tasked to look at the Force, and find the resource formula, and find the magic button that's going to tell everybody how the whole Force should look, and that just collapsed and faded. (Participant D)

In the discussions with the consultants, the senior officers were asked: "So what are your business rules in terms of how you redistribute staff, and what is your rationale in terms of deploying X and Y, and how have you decided that you can take from there and add to here for instance?" Through these discussions, it became obvious that there was no magic formula to apply to the redistribution of resources, and hence the external consultants, who had no personal experience of policing had not been successful in delivering one. The big realization for the senior officers was that it was not only the analysis of demand and supply of policing that was needed to take into account in making the resourcing decisions, but also there was something about knowing the business. These senior officers had many years of policing experience, therefore they were best placed to make the resourcing decisions themselves. What they had to do was to rely on their professional judgment. Indeed, the senior officers were referring to their intuitive judgment:

I think it is intuitive, there's a lot about knowing your business. (Participant E)

I think a lot of it was down to that, to the gut feeling at the end of the day, but it was also backed up in terms of professional judgment around supply and demand, etcetera, levels of staff and other things … when you put them all together, there's not a magic formula, it is about knowing that's what I think, a lot of it was about that. (Participant D)

There is no magic equation, there is no magic formula and it's relying upon experience and the understanding … perhaps more professional judgment of what's needed to deliver policing in […]. (Participant C)

The senior officers explained that their intuitive judgments were influenced by the accumulation of their learning and experiences through the years in the police service suggesting that their past experience was the underlying foundation of their intuitions.

I think there was intuition for the whole, it comes from something in the back of your mind, your experiences, and we've all got a certain amount of experience to stand up here. (Participant E)

Inevitably we are a product of our learning and our experiences through the police service, the routes we have taken to the position we're in now, and the positions, the other various roles we've had will affect those opinions and things. (Participant F)

The Detective Chief Inspector for Crime Management attempted to explain his personal experience of intuiting, which he described as having a "gut feeling". He stated that all the information gets processed in his mind nonconsciously and the solution appears suddenly as a feeling, the basis of which is based in his knowledge and experience of the business.

Another senior officer stated that their intuitive judgments around the distribution of resources were based on what each of them "felt" was the right balance to have in their respective divisions, again emphasizing the fact that the model they had come up with was not an outcome of analysis of hard data alone, but of their judgment and gut feeling of what was needed to operate effectively.

> The division up of where those officers went was based around I think, the needs in various areas. … The decisions we were making were an awful lot based on our intuition of what we feel is the right thing to do. (Participant F)

After long-lasting and tense discussions, eventually the senior officers arrived at a place where they could all agree on the level of staff that was required in different divisions to operate effectively. From the perspective of these officers, the whole process in effect brought them together and made them stronger as a management team. The senior officers described this decision as an intuitive hit as they developed the resource allocation model based on their extensive experience and knowledge of policing, and knowing the business well helped them build a model that would work. The new structure based on these officers' intuitive decisions was a success leading to the perception of increased effectiveness and efficiency in the organization.

3.3.2 Intuitive Miss: Failed Search Operation

The operational officers were preparing to execute multiple search warrants as part of a "week of action" against drug dealers that the intelligence unit provided them to target. Strong intelligence was coming through continuously from various sources detailing that a number of well-known drug dealers who were selling drugs in and around the town center were linked to this one particular address.

Prior to the week of action, the Sergeant sent officers to the address several times to walk around the house in civilian clothes in order to check if there was any activity in and around the address. The Police Constable (PC) who was leading this drug search operation also went to the address a couple of days before the execution of the search. Looking at and around the house, the PC's gut feeling was that there was certainly drug activity going on at this address. Especially based on his previous experience of places used by drug dealers, it matched the prototype he had in his mind. He explained that the curtains were always closed, the garden was a mess, and from its appearance, the state of the address corroborated the intelligence they were receiving.

> Yeah, you know, it's not a nice address with the curtains drawn and flowers on the window sill, and, yeah, it looks like a drugs address, I'll be happy with that. (Participant K)
>
> … we go into enough addresses that are used by drug addicts, and more often than not drug addicts will keep their curtains closed, and more often than not, drug addicts maybe don't do their washing up, and they've got rubbish strewn all over the kitchen, and from what these guys saw when they did the little recce's on the address, that's what it looked like. (Participant J)

As with any intelligence the police force receives, this information also had to be analyzed and corroborated to get evidence from at least two reliable sources. Therefore, in addition to the PC and his colleagues checking around the house, the intelligence unit had done some regular checks on the address and also gathered source information from people previously tried and tested by the police.

The PC and his team were highly experienced officers in executing drug search warrants and had high success rates in similar jobs. As far as they were concerned, it was just another job that they were going to attend. The PC's comment suggests that they did not put a lot of conscious effort into this operation as they were fairly confident in what they were doing. "We do a lot of these warrants, it's bread and butter for us, and it's not an issue potentially, we weren't as cautious and as worried about it, because it's our bread and butter…" (Participant K).

On the operation day, the execution of the warrant was perfect: the entry into the address was quick, the address was secured quickly, two people in the address were detained and handcuffed as they would do in every drug warrant arrest. But there was only one problem: these were not the subjects of the warrant the police were looking for. As soon as the Sergeant entered the house, her immediate gut feeling was that this was not the right address. She saw the young couple and a baby so she knew they were not the people for whom they were looking. She immediately ordered to un-handcuff the young couple and cleared the officers out of the premises.

> It's a gut feeling, the second, the second we got into the house, my gut feeling was that, I saw the bloke that was there, my gut feeling the second we got into the house is "Oh my God, it's either the wrong address or the people aren't here anymore," the second we got in! (Participant J)
>
> When I got inside, it's pretty instant, wrong address. (Participant K)

After the failed operation it became obvious that the subjects of the warrant had moved out of the address some time ago, but when they were stopped by the police they kept giving this address as their current residence, and still had their cars registered to that address. Hence, in the intelligence unit's database this information appeared to be current but in fact it was inaccurate. Additionally, contrary to what was assumed by the operations team, the intelligence unit had not done a comprehensive investigation to confirm that the subjects were current residents at the targeted address. The Sergeant explained that normally more search would be done before going on an operation, however because there were many addresses to target that week, the officers could not carry out a thorough investigation on the subjects of this particular warrant.

> At the right address, where everything was right, it was still a mistake, because there were a few checks that went undone, and potentially we could have avoided going through that door on the morning that we did. (Participant J)

Because it was a week of action, the police invited the local press to go along with them as they were expecting that there would be successful drug arrests to provide positive coverage. In fact, this led to a damaging story on the front page of the local newspaper the next day, creating a PR nightmare for the senior team and great embarrassment for the operations team. This incident was a hard-learned lesson for the officers involved. As a result of this experience, they now recognize that in the future they have to make sure that all the checks are carried out fully.

This case is an example of an intuitive miss whereby relying on inaccurate information provided by the intelligence unit (as a result of lack of investigation) led to an unsuccessful drug search. Although the PC was certain about his gut feeling that the address looked like a drug dealer's house, his comments about drug searching being their bread and butter indicates that they were not being very cautious. Also, it could be argued that their previous experience and success in similar situations might have nonconsciously biased his judgment, not giving any consideration to the thought that it might not have been a drug dealer's address. As a result his gut feeling had failed him.

3.4 Characterization of Intuition-Based Decisions

A number of theoretical themes emerged from these stories that highlight certain characteristics of intuition (see Table 3.2). Conceptual foundations of these themes are discussed here in relation to their implications on the decision-making process and by drawing evidence from the stories illustrated above.

3.4.1 Intuitive Expertise and Affect

A common attribute of the participants of the above stories refers to intuition as coming from their past experiences and appearing as a gut feeling in the form of judgment that felt right or wrong. Furthermore, some officers used the term "professional judgment" to refer to intuitive judgment (see Prietula and Simon, 1989; Hayashi, 2001; Patton, 2003). The terms intuition and gut feeling were used by these officers interchangeably without the distinction of the expertise and feeling characteristics that are the most commonly noted in the literature on intuition.

Table 3.2   Characterization of Intuition-Based Decisions

CHARACTERISTICS	DESCRIPTION	SOURCE
Expertise	Based on prior learning, knowledge and experience	Simon, 1987
Affective	Feelings-based signals	Damasio, 1994
Certitude	Having confidence in one's intuitions	Shirley and Langan-Fox, 1996
Speed of intuiting	Gut feelings arising rapidly	Burke and Miller, 1999
Subjective	Based on accumulated personal experiences	Dane and Pratt, 2007
Nonconscious	Knowing without knowing how one knows	Epstein, 1994
Collective	Drawing advice and experience from others	Jett and Brown, 2002
Scanning	Searching for information	Prietula and Simon, 1989
Analyzing	Conscious and deliberate processing of information	Simon, 1987

Sadler-Smith and Shefy (2004) suggested that intuition relies on both expertise (through explicit and implicit learning processes, manifested as subconscious decision heuristics) and feelings (manifested as affect associated with a particular stimulus). The authors called these two notions "intuition-as-expertise" and "intuition-as-feeling", respectively. The former is consistent with Simon's (1987, p. 63) assertion of intuition as "analyses frozen into habit", whereas the latter is consistent with Epstein's (1998) notion of experiential processing that involves affect.

Simon (1987) also acknowledged this distinction by asserting that the intuition of the emotion-driven* manager is very different from the intuition of the expert: the latter's behavior is the product of learning and experience, and is largely adaptive, whereas the former's behavior is a response to more primitive urges and is more often than not inappropriate. On the contrary, Damasio (1994) claimed that somatic markers play a crucial role in helping the decision maker filter various possibilities quickly, even though the conscious mind might not be aware of it.

In these stories, there is evidence of intuition as expertise and intuition as feeling. For example, in intuitive hit, the senior officers' intuitions were based on their expertise that the officers attributed to their prior learning and professional seniority. On the other hand in intuitive miss, the officers' intuitions appeared in the form of a strong affectively charged gut feeling that appeared quickly and nonconsciously. In the latter case the gut feeling acted as a warning sign requiring the decision maker to respond to the situation. This finding supports research in neuroscience that the intuitive processes, manifesting themselves as automatic somatic alarm bells, provide feelings-based signals to the decision maker for or against a course of action (Le Doux, 1996; Damasio, 1994).

3.4.2 Confidence in Intuitions

Although the police officers were not able to explain fully what happens during the process of intuiting, they referred to several

---

* It is not uncommon to find in the literature that the terms "emotion" and "affect" are used interchangeably (Sinclair and Ashkanasy, 2005); however, it is important to note that intuitions are affectively charged judgments (Dane and Pratt, 2007), and this is different from emotions.

characteristics of intuition. For example, the officers indicated the feeling of certitude in their intuitions (Shirley and Langan-Fox, 1996) commonly expressed by statements such as, "It felt right" or, "It was the right thing to do", constituting belief that their intuitions were correct (Shapiro and Spence, 1997) despite the inadequate information around the decision. Dane and Pratt (2007, p. 39) stated that the feeling of certitude which accompanies intuition may be due to its "affective and associative properties".

Having high levels of confidence in their intuitions meant that sometimes the senior officers were taking a risk by following their gut feeling (Slovic et al., 2002). For example, in intuitive miss whereby the officers felt certain of their intuitions about the house looking like a drug dealer's place, they were misguided by their gut feelings.

3.4.3 Speed of Intuiting

The officers also made reference to the speed of intuitive processing, the aspect of intuition that drew the most attention in the field of managerial decision making (Agor, 1986; Eisenhardt, 1989, 1990; Burke and Miller, 1999; Khatri and Ng, 2000; Klein, 2003). This was particularly evident in intuitive miss when, upon entering the house, the officers had an affectively charged gut feeling about the situation that arose rapidly. Evidence suggests that nonconscious recognition occurs almost immediately upon engagement with relevant stimuli (Hensman and Sadler-Smith, 2011).

3.4.4 Intuiting as a Subjective Phenomenon

Additionally, the senior officers emphasized the subjective nature of intuition by stating that the intuitive judgments they made were subjective on the basis of their accumulated personal experiences and how they felt about the situation. Because intuitions are derived from tacit and explicit ways of learning (Dane and Pratt, 2007; Hogarth, 2001), giving rise to differences in subjective perceptions of people, the senior officers in intuitive hit acknowledged that the quality and effectiveness of the decisions depended on the experiences of the decision makers involved in the decision-making process.

3.4.5 Nonconscious Processing

Miller and Ireland (2005) stated that intuitive decision makers cannot explain why they feel the way they do, or why they make the choices they make. This resonates with Epstein's (2008, p. 29) claim that intuition involves "knowing without knowing how one knows". Accordingly, although there is evidence of attributes of intuition (such as its speed and subjectivity, and being based in experience and attended by affect), the officers were not able to tell exactly what happens while they are intuiting. This supports the previous conceptualization of intuition that it is a nonconscious process (Epstein, 1994; Hogarth, 2001). In intuitive hit, one of the senior officers attempted to describe his personal experience of intuiting:

> I tend to go on gut feelings quite a lot … there's a lot of numbers and stuff going through my head, it's like you can't work it all out, and you wake up in the middle of the night, and there it is, because your brain's processed it all. So yeah, there is a lot of gut feeling … (Participant E)

His explanation suggests that the process of intuiting occurs beyond conscious awareness; he is only aware of the outcome (i.e., intuitive judgment) as a result of intuiting (Dane and Pratt, 2007).

3.4.6 Collective Intuition

Intuiting is an individual level process (i.e., the phenomenon is a personal and highly subjective experience), however, it has emerged from the stories that the officers also engaged in a collective intuiting process, for example, in intuitive hit when trying to come up with a model of structure that would fit the organization's needs. Several authors stated that collective intuitions shared among senior managers are of great value to decision making and may contribute to faster and more accurate reactions (Eisenhardt, 1989, 1990; Eisenhardt and Martin, 2000) and facilitate collective learning processes (Sadler-Smith, 2008). Jett and Brown (2002) found that the development of collective intuition involves drawing advice and experience from other people rather than from sources of explicit information, and making the tacit knowledge of individuals more explicit to the group.

This helps the decision makers develop shared domain-related experiences that lead to collective intuition, problem solving, and organizational learning.

3.4.7 Scanning and Analyzing

Decision makers may engage in scanning to search for knowledge from external or internal sources in order to monitor the environment and gather information that would be useful in the decision process (Huber, 1991; Weick, 2001; Almeida, Phene, and Grant, 2005). In these stories, the officers actively used external and explicit sources of knowledge to analyze information (e.g., in intuitive hit, by bringing in external consultants and looking at resource allocation models of other police forces; in intuitive miss, by corroborating intelligence with a number of different sources). To distinguish between the notions of scanning and analyzing, it should be noted that scanning refers to the search for information, whereas analyzing refers to the conscious and deliberate processing of information (Simon, 1987). The resultant information from scanning may become a source for analyzing or intuiting processes. Prietula and Simon (1989) suggested that by scanning the environment, experts absorb and evaluate large quantities of information quickly, grasping the meaning of certain patterns of operations or activity. This explanation fits well with what happened in intuitive miss. The police officer went to the address in question several times to check whether there was any activity that would corroborate the intelligence; his intuitive judgment was that it looked like a drug dealer's house. This suggests that the officer's intuition relied on the recognition of patterns on the basis of his previous experience of what a drug dealer's house looked like (Klein, 1998).

These stories also suggest that there was a process of analyzing, in varying degrees, in different decision-making circumstances. In an intuitive hit, analyzing occurred prior to intuiting whereby the failure of attempts to develop a resourcing formula solely based on analysis led to the use of intuition by the senior officers. On the other hand, it appears that there was a lack of analyzing in intuitive miss. Although some analyzing took place, admittedly it was less than what they would normally do, therefore leading to the failure of the operation.

The evidence gathered from these stories points to the necessity to use conscious and rational information processing (analyzing) in conjunction with nonconscious and experiential information processing (intuiting) for effective decision making (i.e., intuitive hit), a view consistent with dual-process theories.

3.5 Conclusions and Recommendations

This chapter explored intuition-based decision-making processes with examples of an intuitive hit and an intuitive miss from a police force. The emerging findings are commensurate with the tenets of dual-process theories. In essence, the evidence suggests that for effective decision making, intuitions should be complemented by use of analysis.

Previous research on managerial decision making has mainly focused on the success stories of managers showing only the upside of the role of intuition in decision making. The stories illustrated in this chapter explored both an effective and an ineffective decision process based on intuitive judgments of the decision makers. The investigation of both hits and misses arguably paints a more realistic picture of the perceived effectiveness of intuition in the context of police (operational) and managerial (organizational) decision making, and contributes to our understanding of when it is likely to hit and when it is likely to miss (see Akinci, 2014). The stories presented here solely focused on the police community, therefore the results may not be generalizable. However, the intention was not to generalize the pattern of intuitive decision making found at this police force, but to provide an understanding of what contributes to effective intuition-based decision-making processes more widely.

As demonstrated in these stories, intuition is an important aspect of decision making in police work, both in lower and senior levels of the hierarchy. In this respect, it is promising that police officers in all levels of the organization recognize the significance of, and employ their intuitive judgments in, decision making. Clearly, there are many benefits of using intuitive judgments for police officers, and managers alike in public and private organizations, such that it can enhance the decision making by identifying similar patterns, which aids in the acceleration of the decision-making process. Organizations might usefully include intuition in their policies and procedures and in training programs. As the findings suggest, intuition and analysis should be treated as complementary modes of information processing for effective decision making. The extent to which each is relevant or should be used depends on the circumstances as well as the decision-maker's level of experience and knowledge in the specific domain and context.

It is recommended that managers recognize intuiting as a valid way of information processing in decision making and problem solving, and not just see it as a mysterious phenomenon. Managers can develop habits to become aware of automatically appearing intuitive judgments; it is by paying conscious attention that they will be able to capture their intuitions. However, they should be as aware of the perils of intuition as well as of its power.

At the present juncture, intuition researchers have a rich and diverse set of conceptual, theoretical, and methodological resources from which to draw. History shows that meaningful and long-lasting development in the study of the role of this vital aspect of human cognition in management and organization context cannot come from within the field of management and organization studies alone; instead scientific progress is likely to be maintained and enhanced from seeking a deeper and wider perspective that acknowledges the potential contributions of psychology (e.g., individual differences in information perception), philosophy (e.g., moral intuitions in decision making) and neuroscience (e.g., biological mechanisms underlying cognitive processes).

References

Agor, W. (1986). The logic of intuition: How top executives make important decisions. *Organizational Dynamics*, 14(3): 5–18.

Akinci, C. (2014). Capturing intuition in decision making: A case for critical incident technique. In Sinclair, M. (Ed.) *Handbook of Research Methods on Intuition*. Cheltenham, UK and Northampton, MA: Edward Elgar.

Akinci, C. and Sadler-Smith, E. (2012). Intuition in management research: A historical review. *International Journal of Management Reviews*, 14(1): 104–122.

Almeida, P., Phene, A., and Grant, R. (2005). Innovation and knowledge management: Scanning, sourcing, and integration. In *The Blackwell Handbook of Organizational Learning and Knowledge Management*. Hoboken, NJ: Blackwell.

Barnard, C. (1938). *The Functions of the Executive*. Cambridge, MA: Harvard University Press.

Burke, L. and Miller, M. (1999). Taking the mystery out of intuitive decision making. *Academy of Management Executive*, 13(4): 91–99.

Damasio, A. (1994). *Descartes' Error: Emotion, Reason, and the Human Brain*. New York: Putnam.

Dane, E. and Pratt, M. (2007). Exploring intuition and its role in managerial decision making. *Academy of Management Review*, 32(1): 33–54.

Denes-Raj, V. and Epstein, S. (1994). Conflict between intuitive and rational processing: When people behave against their better judgment. *Journal of Personality and Social Psychology*, 66(5): 819–829.

Eisenhardt, K. (1989). Making fast strategic decisions in high-velocity environments. *Academy of Management Journal*, 32(3): 543–576.

Eisenhardt, K. (1990). Speed and strategic choice: How managers accelerate decision making. *California Management Review*, 32(3): 39–54.

Eisenhardt, K. and Martin, J. (2000). Dynamic capabilities: What are they? *Strategic Management Journal*, 21: 1105–1121.

Epstein, S. (1994). Integration of the cognitive and the psychodynamic unconscious. *American Psychologist*, 49(8): 709–724.

Epstein, S. (1998). Cognitive-experiential self-theory. In *Advanced Personality*. New York: Plenum.

Epstein, S. (2008). Intuition from the perspective of cognitive-experiential self-theory. In *Intuition in Judgment and Decision Making*. Boca Raton, FL: Taylor & Francis.

Epstein, S., Pacini, R., Denes-Raj, V., and Heier, H. (1996). Individual differences in intuitive-experiential and analytical-rational thinking styles. *Journal of Personality and Social Psychology*, 71(2): 390–405.

Gigerenzer, G. and Todd, P. (1999). Fast and frugal heuristics: The adaptive toolbox. In *Simple Heuristics That Make Us Smart*. New York: Oxford University Press.

Hayashi, A. (2001). When to trust your gut? *Harvard Business Review*, 79(2): 59–65.

Hensman, A. and Sadler-Smith, E. (2011). Intuitive decision making in banking and finance. *European Management Journal*, 29: 51–66.

Hogarth, R. (2001). *Educating Intuition*. Chicago: The University of Chicago Press.

Huber, G. (1991). Organizational learning: The contributing processes and the literatures. *Organization Science*, 2: 88–115.

Jett, Q. and Brown, A. (2002). Collective intuition: The formation of shared experience for rapid problem solving in innovation teams. Houston, TX: Working Paper.

Kahneman, D., Slovic, P., and Tversky, A. (Eds.) (1982). *Judgment Under Uncertainty: Heuristics and Biases*. New York: Cambridge University Press.

Khatri, N. and Ng, A. (2000). The role of intuition in strategic decision making. *Human Relations*, 53(1): 57–86.

Klein, G. (1998). *Sources of Power: How People Make Decisions*. Cambridge, MA: MIT Press.

Klein, G. (2003). *Intuition at Work.* New York: Doubleday.

Lakoff, G. and Johnson, M. (1999). *Philosophy in the Flesh: The Embodied Mind and Its Challenge to Western Thought.* New York: Basic.

Le Doux, J. (1996). *The Emotional Brain.* New York: Simon and Schuster.

Lieberman, M. (2007). Social cognitive neuroscience: A review of core processes. *Annual Review of Psychology,* 58: 259–289.

Miller, C. and Ireland, D. (2005). Intuition in strategic decision making: Friend or foe in the fast-paced 21st century? *Academy of Management Executive,* 19(1): 19–30.

Mintzberg, H. (1976). Planning on the left side and managing on the right. *Harvard Business Review,* 54(4): 49–58.

Patton, J. (2003). Intuition in decisions. *Management Decision,* 41(10): 989–996.

Prietula, M. and Simon, H. (1989). The experts in your midst. *Harvard Business Review,* 67(1): 120–124.

Sadler-Smith, E. (2008). The role of intuition in collective learning and the development of shared meaning. *Advances in Developing Human Resources,* 10(4): 494–508.

Sadler-Smith, E. and Shefy, E. (2004). The intuitive executive: Understanding and applying 'gut feel' in decision-making. *Academy of Management Executive,* 18(4): 76–91.

Shapiro, S. and Spence, M. (1997). Managerial intuition: A conceptual and operational framework. *Business Horizons,* 40(1): 63–68.

Shirley, D. and Langan-Fox, J. (1996). Intuition: A review of the literature. *Psychological Reports,* 79: 563–584.

Simon, H. (1987). Making management decisions: The role of intuition and emotion. *Academy of Management Executive,* 1(1): 57–64.

Simon, H. (1997). *Administrative Behaviour,* 4th edn. New York: Free Press.

Sinclair, M. and Ashkanasy, N. (2005). Intuition: Myth or a decision-making tool? *Management Learning,* 36(3): 353–370.

Sloman, S. (1996). The empirical case for two systems of reasoning. *Psychological Bulletin,* 119(1): 3–22.

Slovic, P., Finucane, M., Peters, E., and MacGregor, D. (2002). The affect heuristic. In *Heuristics and Biases: The Psychology of Intuitive Judgment.* New York: Cambridge University Press.

Stanovich, K. and West, R. (2000). Individual differences in reasoning: Implications for the rationality debate? *Behavioural and Brain Sciences,* 23: 643–726.

Weick, K. (2001). *Making Sense of the Organization.* Hoboken, NJ: Blackwell.

4

HEURISTIC, INTUITION, OR IMPULSE

How to Tell the Difference and Why It Is Important to Decision Makers

JAMES HOWARD

Graduate School
University of Maryland University College

Contents

4.1 Introduction

The purpose of this chapter is to summarize and integrate what we know about intuition, heuristics, and impulses and help clarify their role in decision making. This has an important relationship with forward-looking research, because these drivers of decisions have both a conscious and unconscious source. Decision making as a field of study has been popular since the mid-1940s; however, opportunities exist to integrate these efforts into a more holistic framework. For example, Howard (2012) performed a meta-analysis associated with the accumulation of financial decision-making knowledge using a five-paradigm model, as shown in Figure 4.1.

Of the five paradigms included in the model, the first four listed are relatively mature in what they can tell us about financial decision making. The emerging paradigm for the future is exploring the unconscious (that brain activity outside conscious awareness) and its

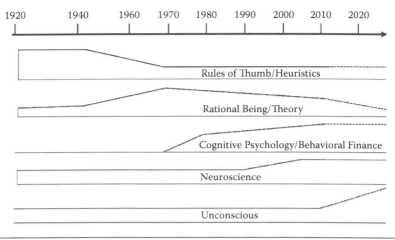

Figure 4.1   Knowledge accumulation/evolution, financial decision making.

role in our decision making, inasmuch as neuroscientists now estimate that up to 90% of our behavior emerges beyond our awareness in the unconscious (Eagleman, 2011). Each of the above paradigms, except the rational being theory, recognizes the importance of intuition, heuristics, and impulses to decision-making outcomes. Because the nature of the unconscious is still not well understood, little progress has been achieved exploring the relationships among intuition, heuristics, and impulses at this level. We know that humans seek control of their environment and have a tendency to assume it is more predictable than it is (Lolinow, 2008). Thus, intuition, heuristics, and impulses may simply be efficient evolutionary adaptations of the brain to allow humans to deal with uncertainty and function effectively in the real world. Alternatively, their nature, relationships, and impacts may be considerably more complex.

Although the brain evolves over time to adapt to new environments, the speed of such adaption is very slow. To a significant degree, we are still carrying ancient baggage in our brains that is inefficient in modern society. If this is the case, then improperly interpreted or controlled emotions in the modern world can have important negative effects on decision making. For example, this can take the form of prematurely acting upon intuition, heuristics, and impulses when a better result is available if the individual has a broader perspective and assesses the situation more accurately before acting.

4.2 Intuition

Merriam-Webster's *Online Dictionary* defines intuition as "immediate apprehension or cognition." An interesting debate has been ongoing between Daniel Kahneman and Gary Klein regarding the nature of intuition, its sources, and its effects on the quality of decisions. Kahneman (2011) analyzes intuition in the context of a System 1 and System 2 framework. System 1 is where intuition resides and is largely characterized as fast, even automatic, in arriving at a decision. System 2 is characterized by deliberation and is slow and conscious. Systems 1 and 2 work together to determine whether the decision facing an individual is one that requires conscious deliberation, analysis, and choice, or whether the "lazy" System 2 defers to the fast-thinking System 1. In Kahneman's framework, there are two types of intuitions emanating from System 1: accurate intuitions explained by practice and inaccurate intuitions based on "gut feel." Here, accurate intuitions have a basis in experience and have been internalized. The more practice, the more automatic and accurate the intuition and decision can be. In explaining what he considers as inaccurate intuitions, this derives from the nature of System 1 and System 2. System 2 takes effort and an individual is reluctant to expend energy when he or she judges a "good enough" decision can be made by System 1. Good decision making requires recognizing when System 1 or System 2 is the best resource in a specific instance.

Klein (2004) focuses on the ability of intuition to improve decision making in the workplace. Like Kahneman, he recognizes intuition as particularly effective when based on internalized experience. He cites the reactions of experienced firemen when facing a dangerous situation in a burning structure, that their reactions become almost automatic. In studies where decisions must be made quickly, there are no lists of alternatives generated for evaluation; the fireman takes the first choice based on intuition and this choice overwhelmingly turns out to be the best one. However, Klein (2004) doesn't discount gut feel coming from a deeper level. Oftentimes, such intuitions resemble impulses and are accompanied by emotions without a strong base of internalized experience. Although one should not react unthinkingly to these impulses/intuitions, according to Klein, they have information content and shouldn't be suppressed or ignored. Another feature of Klein's intuition structure is a discounting of extensive data gathering and evaluating activities as a basis for most decisions in the workplace. He points to the work of Simon (1957) and the concept of bounded rationality, where decision-making quality can be adversely affected by more information and elaborate analytical and alternative ranking procedures. This depends upon situational variables, such as the quality of information, time constraints, and inherent uncertainty in the environment.

The somewhat differing views on when one can trust one's intuition were formally debated by Kahneman and Klein (2010) in the *McKinsey Quarterly*. An area of difference is in the degree of trust in the quality of evaluations by experts based on their experience. Klein considers this a generally trusted source, whereas Kahneman would not necessarily trust the intuition of an expert encountering a situation not directly related to his or her base of experience. Another area of disagreement is how much trust to place in a gut feeling. Kahneman recommends delaying acting on intuition in this case as long as possible in an effort to use cognitive resources to improve decision quality. Klein puts more faith in gut feeling and recommends giving it more credence in decision making. In another driver of the quality of intuition in financial decisions, they agree that overconfidence is an important obstacle. Financial decisions involve risk and uncertainty. An expert with a string of fortunate decisions will tend to overweight her personal intuitive or gut feeling contribution and underweight the role of luck.

Price and Norman (2008) argue that hard distinctions between System 1 (fast thinking, intuitive) and System 2 (slow thinking, cognitive) are misleading. They propose that the mind/brain may be more accurately described along a continuum from focused cognitive effort to a vague gut feel originating in the unconscious. In this scheme, much of what is considered as intuition based on experience would lie somewhere around the midpoint on that continuum as fringe consciousness, as shown in Figure 4.2.

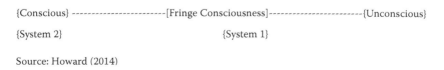

{Conscious} ----------------------[Fringe Consciousness]----------------------{Unconscious}

{System 2}   {System 1}

Source: Howard (2014)

Figure 4.2   The continuum of consciousness.

Fringe consciousness is a state where experienced memories can be triggered and brought to conscious awareness by events, situations, or other stimuli in the environment. As fringe consciousness, the validity of such intuitions varies depending on their strength and the particular configuration of the triggering stimuli. From neuroscience research, we know that experiences cause neurons in the brain to connect in establishing memories. Experiences become intuitions through experience accompanied by emotions. This process is consistent with Kahneman's explanation of how such experienced memories can be automatically called upon by the fast-thinking System 1.

If we accept the concept of fringe consciousness as described by Price and Norman (2008), how can we explain the feeling of knowing what emanates from a level deeper than fringe consciousness? Shull (2011) explores this in her experiences with the coaching of traders. She has adopted a successful strategy of encouraging traders to allow themselves to feel and interpret their emotions instead of repressing them, but not necessarily acting upon them until the source of the emotions and experiences is fully understood. Her approach resembles that of Freudian practitioners by having her clients recall past traumatic experiences during the formative ages through the teenage years. She and her clients have found that many times such repressed past experiences in the unconscious can account for the unconscious triggering of biases and impulses in situations characterized by poor decision making. By taking ownership of these memories and putting them in context, she claims that the trader has better control of his behavior, especially when the emotional content is high and decisions must be made quickly.

Cheng (2010) introduces what he terms a transcendental model, where he proposes that conscious thought is affected by a capacity constraint, whereas the unconscious has no such constraint. With no capacity constraint, improved judgment and decision making are possible through better organization of information in unconscious memory, implying that creativity and acting on legitimate gut feel are largely a product of the unconscious due to its greater capacity and the many unconscious programs at work. For example, when very creative people are asked how they rationally achieved a great discovery, a typical response is that it just came to them without conscious thought. It is as if there were unconscious programs running to support unconscious decision making. Cheng concludes his analysis by proposing a transcendent model for financial decision making, where the total cognitive capacity of an individual consists of a conscious and an unconscious component. It is an interactive model where each component has its own coefficient signifying the relative importance of the conscious and unconscious in this interactive relationship. Given the differences between individual cognitive capacities, each person would have her own unique values to solve the model. Finding ways to test this model is one of the challenges for future researchers. The transcendental model bears a close resemblance to Kahneman's System 1 and System 2 model, where System 1 includes the unconscious component with no capacity constraint. Exploring the mechanics of how intuition, heuristics, and impulses form and are acted upon in this framework may be subject to traditional transcendental techniques.

The unconscious does not necessarily contain only repressed experiences as a source of knowing or intuition. It has been speculated by Mercier and Sperber (2011) that humans are born with an innate confirmation bias, which developed hundreds of thousands of years ago as an efficient survival mechanism. This confirmation bias allowed humans to communicate effectively within their social groups. With a confirmation bias as an anchor, humans developed the ability to justify their positions and argue effectively to secure resources necessary for survival. This would largely explain why a confirmation bias to create sophisticated arguments from a preset perspective to support positions is prevalent across the human spectrum, from the general populace to academic researchers. An innate confirmation bias can be classified as an intuition or make one more likely to act on a misinterpreted gut feel, because it would create a feeling of knowing without necessarily an awareness of its evolutionary source. Although not an intuition that one should act upon without thinking, it is so subtle and ingrained that reactions are automatic in developing justification to support arguments.

4.3 Heuristics

Gigerenzer and Wolfgang (2011) provide a formal definition of heuristics: "A heuristic is a strategy that ignores part of the information, with the goal of making decisions more quickly, frugally, and/or accurately than more complex methods" (p. 454). Heuristics do not attempt to find the optimal solution but one that is best given the context and constraints faced by the decision maker. Using heuristics is not the best approach in every case, but when applied appropriately, may represent the best a decision maker can do in specific situations given the tradeoff between time available to make a decision, uncertainty, and the cost of getting better information. In a situation where there is little uncertainty, adequate information, and sufficient time to process data, structured organization of data and information is likely to be the best approach. However, as uncertainty increases, the time to make a decision becomes constrained, and the quality of the information that supports analysis declines, a heuristic may perform better than a more complex, data-driven approach. The nature of this set of tradeoffs was formalized by Simon (1957) with the term *bounded rationality*. Bounded rationality refers to the fact that the ability of a decision maker to take as much time as needed to make an optimal decision is constrained by the quantity and quality of information provided and the time available to make the decision. The overall constraint is the human mind's cognitive limitations in the pursuit of an optimal rather than satisficing (best decision, given the circumstances) decision.

An issue being dealt with in this chapter is to help clarify the relationship of heuristics to intuition and conscious awareness (System 1 versus System 2). Kahneman (2011) attempts to differentiate "accurate" intuitions better explained by the effects of practice from heuristics (p. 11). This distinction is somewhat artificial, at least for a subset of heuristics that also have their source in experience or practice. For example, if we consider some popular heuristics from economics and finance (Table 4.1), it is clear that they exhibit a solid experiential base.

Table 4.1   Examples of Economics/Financial Heuristics

HEURISTIC	DESCRIPTION
1/N	If there are three investments, then the investor allocates one-third of available funding to each. This heuristic is employed frequently when individuals allocate their 401K retirement funds among various investment options.
Payback criterion of capital investments	Criterion is to invest only when the investment can be recovered in the specified number of years.
DuPont model for ratio analysis	Collapse financial company financial analysis into a series of turnover, profit margin, and leverage ratios.
Pareto principle	Focus on the "vital few rather than the trivial many" (20/80 rule)

Source: J. Howard, *Modern Accounting and Auditing* (2013). With permission.

These examples represent a class of heuristics that share a basis in experience with the "good intuitions" that Kahneman describes. However, these examples tend to be employed at the level of conscious awareness and differ in this respect from intuition that operates below conscious awareness or on the fringes of consciousness.

4.4 Impulses

From Merriam-Webster's *Online Dictionary*, an impulse is "something that arouses action or activity." One type of impulse is the feeling of knowing, which arises from accumulated internalized experience, and is expressed as intuition as a basis for good decision making. Alternatively, the feeling of knowing can also originate from an innate confirmation bias (Mercier and Sperber, 2011), which is expressed as an impulse to take a specific action. Discriminating between these two sources of impulses (valid or invalid signal of internalized experience) and the resulting feeling of knowing/intuition is vital to interpreting validity for the decision maker. From the discussion in the previous sections, impulses have a close association with emotion in moving an individual to take an action or make a decision. The greater the emotion, the more a sense of urgency is attached to acting on the impulse/intuition.

Impulses triggered by emotions are strongly affected by brain chemicals. Certain hormones and neurotransmitters (oxytocin, dopamine, and serotonin) importantly affect decision-making behavior at both the conscious and unconscious levels. In their work with oxytocin, Vercoe and Zak (2010) have established a causal relationship between the levels of oxytocin and feelings of trust/trustworthiness in research subjects. They identified what they call a HOME (human oxytocin mediated empathy) circuit in the brain that is activated by the release of oxytocin. In response to the external environment, the HOME circuit increases feelings of trust/empathy and mediates the release of dopamine in the midbrain and serotonin in the serotonergic neurons to down-regulate distress. In addition, they found that low to moderate amounts of distress increase the release of oxytocin and the feeling of empathy, with the likelihood of pro-social response (e.g., soldiers in combat feel a closer bonding with their fellow soldiers). In one of their experiments, viewing a 100-second video of a father interacting with his son with brain cancer triggered a 150% increase in oxytocin (empathy) and release of the stress hormone cortisol. On the other hand, elevated distress extinguishes the desire to help and motivates desire to escape. The release of these drugs into the bloodstream is automatic and the sources of emotions discussed earlier; they are especially relevant to acting on impulse.

The neurotransmitter dopamine plays a key role in stimulating the nucleus accumbens (NAcc) in the brain's gain/approach circuit by generating an intense feeling of excitement or anticipation, thereby turning motivations into decisions and decisions into action. In a study by Knutson et al. (2001) they found that NAcc activation represents gain prediction, whereas anterior amygdala/insula activation represents loss prediction (Paulus et al., 2003). Functional magnetic resonance imaging (fMRI) experiments have shown how the NAcc reacts to dopamine in differing situations involving anticipated gains:

- Unanticipated gain: Strong reaction and feeling of pleasure in the gain circuit transmitted to the prefrontal cortex
- Gain equal to anticipated gain: Small or no reaction in the gain circuit
- Gain less than anticipated: Activity in the loss circuit of the limbic system, particularly the anterior insula

The action of dopamine can stimulate emotion-related decision actions such as impulses and heuristics, and intuition to a lesser degree. The release of dopamine may be closely related to acting on impulses during the forming of financial bubbles (Lehrer, 2010). Being cognizant of the presence of these brain chemicals, especially in emotion-laden situations, and properly interpreting their role in generating motivations to act are important factors in being an effective decision maker.

There is another type of impulse that originates in the unconscious that the individual is largely unaware of until after action has been taken. Based on recent research in neuroscience (Gazzaniga, 2011), we know how the brain reacts to emergency situations. In a general situation, sensory inputs from the visual and auditory systems provide input to the thalamus, which is responsible for deciding how to react to these stimuli. Impulses are generated and transmitted to the cortex and then to the frontal lobes for interpretation. This is considered the stage where an individual becomes consciously aware of the information and the need for evaluation and action/decision. As explained by Kahneman (2011), cognitive processes are slow (System 2). However, if an emergency arises, the thalamus can direct a nonconscious shortcut through the amygdala. When a memory (or perhaps innate trigger) associated with the danger is sensed by the amygdala, an impulse is sent along a direct connection to the brain stem. This activates the familiar fight-or-flight response and rings the alarm and moves the body to respond through impulse. This can happen so fast that the individual has no conscious recollection of acting until after the fact.

4.5 Conclusion

Intuition, heuristics, and impulses have important roles in decision making. In some instances, the roles are both effective and efficient. The human brain has developed specialized adaptations to deal with different types of decision situations. When there is no emergency, decisions will depend upon on a number of factors: strength of ingrained confirmation bias, emotional content, ability to interpret and control emotions to have a positive outcome, and the degree to which the decision-making situation is familiar through experience or practice. Emotions trigger the release of chemicals, stimulating the gain/approach or loss/avoidance circuits and the strength of impulses. Unmanaged, these emotions take the form of impulses that raise the probability of bypassing the cognitive system (System 2). In emergencies, this may be the best course of action. For example, where speed of action is important, the amygdala may send a message to System 1 causing an automatic reaction to facilitate survival or avoidance of a threat. The individual may be completely unaware of this reaction until after the fact. In other instances, the impulse may result in poor decisions because of youth, where the cognitive area of the brain has not matured, or in old age, as cognitive ability and the value of experience decline.

If emotions can be interpreted and acted upon as claimed by Shull (2011) in her Freudian approach to coaching traders, this can remove much of the regret from systematic flaws in how one makes decisions. An understanding of how the brain coordinates the fast thinking of System 1 with the slow thinking of System 2 raises the awareness of how to process the feelings of knowing (intuition). Connections between neurons and formed memories in the brain can be strengthened by thoughtful learning and practice so that when System 1 takes the lead in decision making, the probability of good decision making is enhanced.

Eagleman (2011) claims that the next generation of neuroscience tools will provide a much clearer picture of how the unconscious works. Integrating the promising new research by Cheng (2010) and Shull (2011), and evolving neuroscience tools, have the potential to give us a much better understanding of how intuition, heuristics, and impulses originate in the unconscious or fringe conscious. With this understanding and increased awareness of our human potential, better models and educational programs directed at improving financial decision making are possible.

Sorting out the differences and relationships among heuristics, intuition, and impulses/emotion will be facilitated by new knowledge about the unconscious. As documented in this chapter, there appears to be a substantial amount of overlap among these human responses, as well as a unique component of each as shown in Figure 4.3.

However, the current state of research has been unable to identify and describe clearly the overlaps and unique features associated with heuristics, intuition, and impulses because a significant source of each resides in the unconscious. Impulses, by definition, are heavily laden with emotion, based on recalling experience, the release of

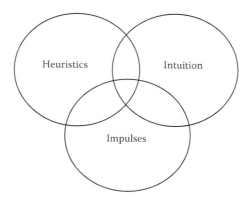

Figure 4.3 Heuristics, intuition, and impulses. (Reprinted from J. Howard, *Modern Accounting and Auditing*, 2013. With permission.)

neurochemicals in the brain, or from inherited mechanisms in the brain from the distant human past. Behavior based on impulses can either be optimal or suboptimal, based upon the context of the situation and the role that cognitive functions are able to play. When there is a life-threatening emergency, the amygdala may initiate danger avoidance actions at the unconscious level where the individual is completely unaware, at least until after the fact. In other contexts, the impulse may arise from the unconscious but be interpreted by the cognitive system along with other information in driving decision-making behavior. A less-developed "emotional intelligence" may move the individual to make a poor financial decision (e.g., retirement planning, investment, merger and acquisition transaction) based solely on the feelings being experienced in the body.

Heuristics may be affected by impulses in some instances by the individual taking needed action based on properly assessing the uncertainty of the environment and urgency needed to act in a timely manner. In other situations, impulses may let System 2 off the hook and open the individual to poor decisions based on biases, poor heuristics, and framing effects. Achieving greater clarity of how heuristics, intuition, and impulses interact should be a major goal of future research into the unconscious and how this knowledge can help decision makers.

References

Cheng, Y. (2010). Improving financial decision making with unconscious thought: A transcendental model. *The Journal of Behavioral Finance*, 11(2), 92–102.

Eagleman, D. (2011). *Incognito: The Secret Lives of the Brain*. New York: Pantheon.

Gazzaniga, M. (2011). *Who's in Charge? Free Will and the Science of the Brain*. New York: HarperCollins.

Gigerenzer, G. and Wolfgang, G. (2011). Heuristic decision making. *The Annual Review of Psychology*, 62: 451–82.

Howard, J. (2012). Behavioral finance: The contributions of cognitive psychology and neuroscience to decision making. *Journal of Organizational Psychology*, 12(2): 52–70.

Howard, J. (2013). Financial decision making: The role of intuition, heuristics, and impulses. *Journal of Modern Accounting and Auditing*, 9(12): 1596–1610.

Kahneman, D. (2011). *Thinking Fast and Slow*. New York: Farrar, Straus and Giroux.

Kahneman, D. and Klein, G. (2010). Strategic decisions: When can you trust your gut? *The McKinsey Quarterly*, 2: 58–67.

Klein, G. (2004). *The Power of Intuition: How to Use Your Gut Feelings to Make Better Decisions at Work*. New York: Currency.

Knutson, B., Adams, C., Fong, G., and Hommer, D. (2001). Anticipation of monetary reward selectively recruits nucleus accumbens. *Journal of Neuroscience*, 21(16;RC159): 1–5.

Lehrer, J. (2010, October 29). Microscopic microeconomics. *The New York Times*. Retrieved from http://www.nytimes.com/2010/10/31/magazine/31FOB-idealab-t.html.

Lolinow, L. (2008). *The Drunkard's Walk: How Randomness Rules Our Lives*. New York: Random House.

Mercier, H. and Sperber, D. (2011). Why do humans reason? Arguments for an argumentative theory. *Behavioral and Brain Sciences*, 34(2): 57–111.

Paulus, M., Rogalsky, C., Simmons, A., Feinstein, J., and Stein, M. (2003). Increased activation in the right insula during risk-taking decision making is related to harm avoidance and neuroticism. *Neuroimage*, 19(4): 1439–1448.

Price, M. and Norman, E. (2008). Intuitive decisions on the fringe of consciousness: Are they conscious and does it matter? *Judgment and Decision Making*, 3(1): 26–41.

Shull, D. (2011). *Market Mind Games*. New York: McGraw-Hill.

Simon, H. (1957). A behavioral model of rational choice. In *Models of Man, Social and Rational: Mathematical Essays on Rational Human Behavior in a Social Setting*. New York: John Wiley & Sons.

Vercoe, M. and Zak, P. (2010). Inductive modeling using causal studies in neuroeconomics: Brains on drugs. *Journal of Economic Methodology*, 17(2): 133–146.

5

MAKING EFFECTIVE DECISIONS BY INTEGRATING

Interaction of Reason and Intuition

JAANA WOICESHYN

Haskayne School of Business
University of Calgary

Contents

5.1 Introduction

Imagine a CEO of a public company contemplating a complex decision, such as whether to move some of his company's operations to a low labor cost country, whether to develop a new product for a new market, or whether to establish an overseas sales office in an emerging market for his company. The particular CEO we observe here heads a mid-sized oil company that operates primarily in the Western Canadian Sedimentary Basin where production rates are declining rapidly.[*] To continue providing shareholders a satisfactory rate of return, the company must discover oil or natural gas elsewhere or boost production in its home base. The CEO is aware of some promising gas discoveries in the Arctic and has been approached by a larger competitor for a potential joint venture in the North. He must decide whether to pursue Arctic exploration.

---

[*] The CEO described here represents a composite of 16 oil company CEOs who participated in my study of executive decision making (Woiceshyn, 2009).

The decision is complex and urgent, as production is declining fast and must be increased. The company's staff has no experience in the Arctic, and the potential joint venture partner does not seem much better in that regard. The CEO also knows that cost-effective transportation of gas from the Arctic requires a new pipeline, subject to a presidential veto in the United States and contested by environmental groups and First Nations in the area, all of which elevates the political risk of the venture. In addition, natural gas prices have been depressed for a long time. The introduction of the hydraulic fracturing technology for cost-effective exploitation of shale gas in the United States is likely to keep gas prices low, making the economics of investing in Arctic exploration highly uncertain.

How does the CEO make a decision about exploring for natural gas in the Arctic, given that he has limited time and less than perfect knowledge about the potential outcomes? He has a few choices: he can order a massive data collection effort about everything in the Arctic and analyze the data to death until he is "paralyzed by analysis" but still without a decision; he can base his decision on a "gut feeling"; or he can decide based on the relevant information available as well as on his own accumulated knowledge about oil and gas exploration in general and about operating a profitable oil company.

The CEO's first alternative is the classical rational analysis approach somewhat caricaturized, the second is what is understood as the intuitive approach, and the third one combines both reason (rational analysis) and intuition but avoids the downsides of the first two methods. It is also the approach used by the oil company CEOs with "good minds" in my study on executive decision making (Woiceshyn, 2009). In the study, the CEOs read a realistic decision scenario with three alternative courses of action and thought out loud what they would do in that situation. The CEOs known as effective thinkers asked a lot of questions about the scenario as a way to gain relevant knowledge and to justify the assumptions they were making. They then drew upon their existing knowledge and applied it to the scenario as follows.

> It's *too risky* for a public company of this size to go exploring in the Arctic. It *does not have the resources* to make a sufficient investment to get *a return large enough to justify the risk*. The *payback* in the Arctic is *too long*; you would not see any production and revenue for 7 to 10 years.

The *production declines* are about 20 percent annually in the Western Canadian Sedimentary Basin; the company cannot wait that long but needs to add production sooner. *The market expects faster returns.* And *the company does not have any expertise in the Arctic*—making the risk even higher. (Woiceshyn, 2009, p. 304)

The CEOs may have had a "gut reaction" against the option of exploring in the Arctic but they did not stop there. They articulated clearly how their previous knowledge about what was essential to success in new ventures—which they had integrated into a few succinct principles, highlighted in the above quotation—applied to the present situation and were therefore able to reach a sound, well-reasoned decision quickly. They were using both rational analysis and intuition to make the decision given in the scenario, by spiraling between the facts they were learning and the integrated knowledge about new ventures stored in their subconscious in the form of principles. This is illustrated in Figure 5.1.

This chapter explains the interaction between the conscious (reason) and the subconscious mind (intuition) depicted in Figure 5.1. But first, let's contrast the effective decision-making process with that of the CEOs who participated in the same study and were not so effective in their thinking processes.

The less-effective CEOs were much less focused in their handling of the decision scenario about oil exploration in the Arctic. They asked fewer questions and instead of focusing on the scenario, they reverted to discussing their own companies. Unlike the more effective CEOs, they did not have an integrated view of the essential success factors of new ventures (such as acceptable level of risk, sufficient resources, appropriate risk–return ratio, adequate payback period, etc.), and therefore they could not apply them to the scenario. Instead, they either decided on emotion, such as a personal dream to expand operations beyond Western Canada, or postponed the decision, waiting to poll others and wanting to adopt the majority view.

In my study, the effective and not-so-effective CEOs alike demonstrated the use of both reason and intuition. This was not surprising, as both are used by everyone, although the quality of these processes varies. I argue that even the well-known examples of "intuitive" business decisions, such as Edwin Land's discovery of instant photography

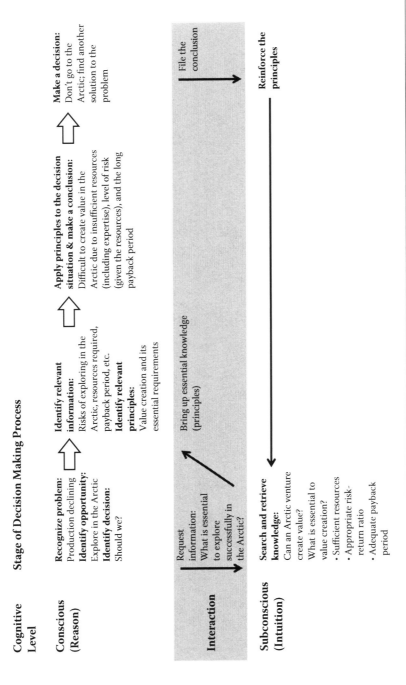

Figure 5.1 Decision-making process: interaction of reason and intuition (with the Arctic exploration example).

which led to the development of Polaroid cameras (Langley et al., 1995), development of the Dodge Viper at Chrysler (Hayashi, 2001), and Ray Kroc's purchase of McDonald's brand from the McDonald brothers (Miller and Ireland, 2005) were not based on intuition alone but depended on its interaction with rational analysis. Next, I elaborate how such interaction works and how cognitive integration makes it effective. I conclude with implications for handling complex decisions and voluminous dynamic information: "Big Data."

5.2 Both Rational Analysis and Intuition Are Needed for Effective Decisions

What is rational analysis and what is intuition, and how do they relate to each other? Much of the research on strategic decision making (Dane and Pratt, 2007; Khatri and Ng, 2000) and cognitive science (Pretz, 2008; Reynolds, 2006) has concluded that rational analysis alone is insufficient for effective decisions and needs to be supplemented by what is called intuition. Rational analysis is understood as systematic sequential processing of factual information that generates decision alternatives which are weighed based on evidence, leading to the choice of the one that is best supported by evidence and most consistent with the chosen goal. Research suggests that this mode of thinking is best suited for structured stable situations with low levels of uncertainty (Miller and Ireland, 2005). Intuition, or the process of intuiting, is described as the inexplicable emergence of a sudden understanding—a "hunch" or a "gut feeling"—seemingly out of nowhere but involving the subconscious and one's previous experience (Dane and Pratt, 2007), often described as recognition of familiar patterns from previous experiences (Klein, 2003). Most studies conclude that intuition is needed in complex situations that require fast decisions (Khatri and Ng, 2000; Klein, 2003).

Based on my own research (Woiceshyn, 2009), that of others (Dane and Pratt, 2007; Khatri and Ng, 2000), and introspective evidence (Rand, 1990), I argue that both rational analysis and subconscious processing (a more descriptive term that I prefer to intuition) are constant interactive elements of all thinking and decision making. Rational analysis depends on subconscious processing, and vice versa. However, the quality of our thinking and decisions depends largely on the interaction between rational analysis and subconscious processing, the effectiveness of which depends primarily on the quality of the rational analysis (Binswanger, 2014).

Let me explain. Our primary means of knowledge is reason: We perceive our surroundings and our own thought processes and use logic to integrate these perceptions, first into concepts based on direct perception and later into higher-level, more abstract concepts and principles. We do this to save mental space; holding multiple perceptions in conscious awareness would soon clog our processing capacity. For example, a child meets for the first time a hairy creature with four legs that barks and wags its tail. Her mother points at the creature and says: "That's a dog." That happens a few times upon meeting hairy, four-legged creatures of different sizes and looks but essentially similar and that often bark, and the child grasps the concept "dog." All information the child learns about dogs she files in one conceptual "folder" labeled "dog." Later, the child integrates her knowledge about dogs and other animals such as cats into broader, more abstract concepts such as "animal" (and eventually differentiates other concepts from it, such as "mammal," "domesticated animal," and "pet"). The child also forms simple generalizations, such as "dogs bark" and "dogs can bite," which she also places in the file folder "dog." Later, she forms more abstract generalizations, such as "dogs are mortal."* These abstract generalizations are principles. They are the broadest integrations: general or fundamental truths upon which other truths depend (Peikoff, 1991, p. 218).

Even with the space-saving power of integrating knowledge into concepts and principles, we cannot hold all of our knowledge in conscious awareness at the same time. Therefore, we store most of our knowledge in subconscious memory "files" and recall it as and when needed, such as when a child meets a new dog and needs to know how to act or to write a homework essay on dogs. This process of storing and recalling knowledge into and from the subconscious is often called intuition (Khatri and Ng, 2000; Reynolds, 2006).

Although subconscious processing is critical to our cognitive functioning, the conscious reasoning process plays a dominant role. The relationship between the conscious and the subconscious mind

---

* For a more in-depth explanation of the concept formation process, see Rand (1990: pp. 10–28, 45–54).

can be described through an analogy. Reason, the conscious mind, can be likened to a CEO who gives orders to subordinates, the subconscious mind (Binswanger, 2014). The CEO, the conscious mind, acquires information through sense perception and integrates perceptions into concepts and principles. If the CEO files the acquired information logically into appropriate conceptual "file folders," she is able to recall and the subordinates (the subconscious mind) are able to retrieve knowledge and bring it back to conscious awareness when needed. For example, if the conscious mind integrates knowledge into concepts and principles arbitrarily, integrating disparate pieces of information, such knowledge will be useless. For example, if a child files knowledge about dogs with knowledge about, say, cars and weather, his subconscious will be sending a miscellany of facts about dogs, cars, and weather when he requests knowledge about dogs. The filing system analogy is apt: if we create a big file folder and label it "miscellaneous important" and put in it various items we consider important at the moment of filing, our filing system will not function very effectively.

The principle governing the relationship between the conscious mind and the subconscious, the CEO and the subordinates, is the same as in computer programming: "garbage in, garbage out." In other words, the more logically the CEO acts, the better her subordinates are able to follow her orders in filing away and retrieving information. Logical conscious processing is based on integration by essentials. Effective thinkers (such as the CEOs in my study) have mastered it, but so can everyone else (Van Damme, 2006).

5.3 Effective Decisions Are Based on Integration by Essentials

Human knowledge must be integrated into concepts and principles; we could not function without integration (Rand, 1990: p. 68). But for concepts and principles to function as helpful tools of cognition, they must be integrated based on essentials. To integrate by essentials, one must identify the essence of whatever one is observing. The essence is the most fundamental characteristic of a thing, event, or issue that gives rise to and makes possible most of its other characteristics (Rand, 1990, p. 52) and differentiates it from other similar things. For example, the faculty of reason is the most fundamental attribute of human beings and gives rise to most of our other characteristics and differentiates us from other animals. Thanks to reason, we are able to project the future and plan for the long term— we buy insurance and save for retirement, for example—and we are able to adjust our environment to ourselves by inventing and producing new materials, products, and services, such as plastics, 3-D printers, and voice-over-Internet communication. The ability to use reason, to think rationally, is what makes us human as opposed to, say, the possession of opposable thumbs (Rand, 1990, p. 65). Other primates also have opposable thumbs and can therefore make primitive tools, but they cannot achieve the human invention and production that only rational thinking makes possible.

The CEO contemplating natural gas exploration in the Arctic has identified the essence of business firms: value creation, or long-term profitability, which is their purpose. A business firm can achieve long-term profitability only by creating value for its customers and making them willing to pay a price for its products or services that exceeds the cost of their production and the firm's cost of capital. And only by creating value for its customers, can the firm create value for its shareholders. But a CEO who thinks effectively will not stop at the identification of value creation as the essence of a business firm. He also identifies other, more specific principles such as acceptable level of risk, sufficient resources, appropriate risk–return ratio, adequate payback period, and so on, that are required for value creation in his industry. Such essentials of value creation are generalizations an effective CEO has integrated from his experience and observations, by focusing on what is indispensable and omitting the rest, into a limited number of principles.

CEOs less effective in their thinking would also have identified value creation as the essence of a business firm. But in contrast to the effective CEO, typically they would not have integrated their experience and observations into clearly identified essential requirements of value creation. For example, the less-effective CEOs in my study (Woiceshyn, 2009) claimed to be "following their gut" without identifying (even when probed) what that actually meant, beyond acting on an emotional reaction such as responding to a personal dream to expand operations internationally, to the particular situation.

Integration by identifying essentials such as value creation in business, or requirements of success in any field gives us indispensable tools of effective decision making: guiding principles (Oliver and Roos, 2005; Peikoff, 1991; Woiceshyn, 2009). Principles are those generalizations in any field that we induce from our observations and condense in a short statement such as "eat a balanced diet from all food groups" (in nutrition), "differentiate your products from those of your competitors" (in competitive strategy), and "do not fake reality to gain a value" (in ethics). Principles such as these condense a wealth of information from various concrete instances and allow us to make quick decisions based on relevant proven knowledge without succumbing to "analysis paralysis" (Langley, 1995). Instead of having to start from scratch and collect reams of information and analyze it every time when we need to make a decision such as what to buy for supper at the grocery store, what new product to launch, or whether to resort to dishonesty, principles allow us to determine quickly what to do by highlighting the essential requirements of success without the need to analyze minute nonessential details. Forming and applying principles is based on the interaction of reason and subconscious processing. If we have used reason to form valid principles based on essentials, they would have been properly filed by the subconscious and brought back again into conscious awareness upon recall when we face a decision where any particular principle applies, helping us make a quick effective decision even in complex situations such as deciding whether to explore in the Arctic.

5.4 How Do Integration by Essentials and Principles Help Us Deal with Complexity and "Big Data"?

Herbert Simon (1957) argued that humans are "boundedly rational." According to him, we have a limited ability to deal with a big volume of data or complex information and therefore we "satisfice": instead of seeking perfect information we settle with good enough information to make decisions. Although this is a valid observation, Simon did not recognize the ability of the human mind to identify essentials and the power of concepts and principles. Therefore, he concluded that satisficing is needed as a coping mechanism to deal with the limitations of our bounded reason.

Cognitive scientists and behavioral economists have built on Simon's view and emphasize biases and limitations of human cognitive ability

(Ariely, 2008; Tversky and Kahneman, 1974). However, humans would not have made the progress that we enjoy without the cognitive ability that differentiates us from all other species. We are fallible (volition is an essential part of human nature) but conceptualization and inducing and applying valid principles have allowed us to solve complex problems. For example, forming concepts and identifying principles has helped to prevent debilitating diseases such as polio through vaccination, to eradicate hunger in many parts of the world through innovations in agriculture, and to generate more wealth (and reduce poverty) through innovative new products, technologies, and business models. Integrative thinking has taken us far: Human life today is more productive, prosperous, healthy, and comfortable than ever, and people at the "bottom of the pyramid" are making tremendous progress as well (Prahalad, 2005) thanks to the advances in communications and other technologies, which are based on integration of knowledge.

In line with Simon's argument, some observers have warned about the challenge of dealing with Big Data (Floridi, 2012; Lycett, 2013). However, accumulating, analyzing, and exploiting Big Data is not a problem when we have tools such as integration by essentials and principles in our toolkit. The need for business analytics and powerful computer technology cannot be ignored, but the critical capabilities (on which business analytics and computer technology depend) is integration of data into meaningful chunks (Floridi, 2012), identification of which information is essential (and which is not), and how to apply principles in decision making.

Whether we are contemplating exploring for oil and gas in a remote but potentially lucrative area, developing a new product, undertaking a major construction project, or any other complex decision, the prospect of complexity does not need to paralyze us. Complexity is not a new phenomenon; today's problems are no more complex than those our ancestors faced. They faced complex decisions and a multitude of options and had to learn to conceptualize and to form principles through integration by essentials, keeping only a limited amount of essential knowledge in the conscious awareness at any given time. The key to solving problems and making effective decisions then was the same as it is now: identifying what is essential to the problem or decision at hand, getting the relevant information, and making the decision.

The fact that there is "Big Data" available today does not mean that we need to sift through and analyze it all before we can make a decision and act. We only need the knowledge essential to our decision, acquisition of which depends on our ability to integrate by essentials. The facts that are relevant to our actions do not change whether we have a little or a lot of data about them. The key to effective decision making is to focus on the essential data and put the rest aside (Aziza, 2013), which is possible when our existing knowledge is properly integrated into concepts and principles. Having too little data, indicated by the inability to answer questions required to solve the problem at hand, warrants more data collection and analysis, but only enough to be able to answer the essential questions.

Consider the CEO in the opening scenario. Having lots of detailed data available about oil and gas exploration in the Arctic (e.g., of geological formations in a great level of detail, exploration success rates of other companies for the last 50 years or more, detailed meteorological data, etc.) does not make his decision any more complex or challenging than if he has less data available. With the help of principles, such as value creation and its essential requirements, he is able to identify which data are essential and base the decision on the essential information only.

The extent to which people, including CEOs, integrate their knowledge by essentials and use principles varies. However, everybody can learn to use these tools of effective thinking and decision making. Ideally, this happens at school. Unfortunately, today's educational philosophy does not emphasize integration, particularly integration by essentials (Van Damme, 2006). But if these important skills were not learned at school, they can be acquired later. Surprisingly, little literature and other resources are available, given what powerful tools of thinking and decision making they are. Some sources for learning more are Moroney (2013), Binswanger (2014), and Oliver and Roos (2005).[*]

There is no mystery as to how intuition helps us make effective decisions. It is a matter of organizing our knowledge into concepts and principles based on integration by essentials, storing the concepts and principles in our subconscious memory files, retrieving them, and

---

[*] For more details on how some oil company CEOs use integration by essentials and principles, see Woiceshyn (2009). For how they can be used in the context of long-term value creation in business, see Woiceshyn (2011) and (2012).

applying them to any decision we face. If we do the first task well—if our concepts and principles are based on proper integrations and our "filing system" therefore logically organized—our subconscious will serve us well and provide essential information when we ask for it, facilitating and speeding up our decisions.

References

Ariely, D. (2008). *Predictably Irrational: The Hidden Forces That Shape Our Decisions*. New York: Harper Collins.

Aziza, B. (2013). The big deal about a big data culture (and innovation). *Sloan Management Review*, 54(2): 1–5.

Binswanger, H. (2014). *How We Know: Epistemology on an Objectivist Foundation*. New York: TOF.

Dane, E. and Pratt, M.G. (2007). Exploring intuition and its role in managerial decision making. *Academy of Management Review*, 32(1): 33–54.

Floridi, L. (2012). Big data and their epistemological challenge. *Philosophy and Technology*, 25: 435–437.

Hayashi, A.M. (2001). When to trust your gut. *Harvard Business Review*, 72(2): 59–65.

Khatri, N. and Ng, H.A. (2000). The role of intuition in strategic decision making. *Human Relations*, 53(1): 57–86.

Klein, G. (2003). *The Power of Intuition*. New York: Doubleday.

Langley, A. (1995). Between "paralysis by analysis" and "extinction by instinct." *Sloan Management Review*, 36(3): 63–76.

Langley, A., Mintzberg, H., Pitcher, P., Posada, E., and Saint-Macary J. (1995). Opening up decision making: The view from the black stool. *Organization Science*, 6(3): 260–279.

Lycett, M. (2013). Datafication: Making sense of (big) data in a complex world. *European Journal of Information Systems*, 22: 381–386.

Miller, C.C. and Ireland, R.D. (2005). Intuition in strategic decision making: Friend or foe in the fast-paced 21st century. *Academy of Management Executive*, 19(1):19–30.

Moroney, J. (2013). *Thinking Directions*. Accessed at www.thinkingdirections. com, October 18, 2013.

Oliver, D. and Roos, J. (2005). Decision-making in high-velocity environments: The importance of guiding principles. *Organization Studies*, 26(6): 889–913.

Peikoff, L. (1991). *Objectivism: The Philosophy of Ayn Rand*. New York: Penguin.

Prahalad, C.K. (2005). *Fortune at the Bottom of the Pyramid: Eradicating Poverty Through Profits*. Upper Saddle River, NJ: Pearson Education.

Pretz, J.E. (2008). Intuition versus analysis: Strategy and experience in complex everyday problem solving. *Memory & Cognition*, 36(3): 554–566.

Rand, A. (1990). *Introduction to Objectivist Epistemology*, expanded 2nd edn. New York: Penguin.

Reynolds, S.J. (2006). A neurocognitive model of the ethical decision-making process: Implications for study and practice. *Journal of Applied Psychology*, 91(4): 737–748.

Simon, H.A. (1957). *Models of Man: Social and Rational*. New York: Wiley.

Tversky, A. and Kahneman, D. (1974). Judgment under uncertainty: Heuristics and biases. *Science*, 185: 1124–1131.

Van Damme, L. (2006). The hierarchy of knowledge: The most neglected issue in education. *The Objective Standard*, 1(1): 55–81.

Woiceshyn, J. (2009). Lessons from "Good Minds": How CEOs use intuition, analysis and guiding principles to make strategic decisions. *Long Range Planning*, 42: 298–319.

Woiceshyn, J. (2011). A model for ethical decision making in business: Reasoning, intuition, and rational moral principles. *Journal of Business Ethics*, 104(3): 311–323.

Woiceshyn, J. (2012). *How to Be Profitable and Moral: A Rational Egoist Approach to Business*. Lanham, MD: Hamilton.

6

INTUITION

A Decision Aid in Academe

LISA A. BURKE-SMALLEY

College of Business
University of Tennessee at Chattanooga

Contents

6.1 Introduction

This chapter is about several cases in which I have invoked intuition in decisions within the academic context as a college-level instructor and unit department head. The case examples span across the research-based categories of when intuition is more appropriately used (Burke and Miller, 1999), including: (a) explicit cues are lacking; (b) precedents for action are absent; (c) time is of the essence; and (d) rational analyses need to be checked.

In the intuition literature, one point of agreement is that the cognitive element of intuitive decision making stems largely from distilled experience (Agor, 1989; Burke and Miller, 1999; Hogarth, 2001; Klein, 2003). Whereas rational decision approaches can be rigid, narrow, and inflexible, the nonrational decision approach of intuition can allow for quick yet informed maneuvering when needed, a balanced check of quantitative solutions, and culturally compatible prescribed courses of action (Burke and Miller, 1999). As such, in addition to quantitative approaches, intuition is used in decision making across various industries, organizations, professions, and job types.

One underexplored venue where intuition is utilized is academe, in the traditional tasks associated with faculty roles such as teaching, as well as in the administration of university operations. In this chapter, I write about several personal cases in which I have invoked intuition in professional decisions in the academic context based upon many years as a college professor at several universities and several years as a department head. The case examples are organized across four research-generated categories of when intuition is more commonly used by managers (see Burke and Miller, 1999), including: (a) explicit cues are lacking, (b) precedents for action are absent, (c) time is of the essence, and (d) rational analyses need to be checked. By reviewing such personal cases and stories in these specific categories, it is hoped that readers will have a more vivid understanding of how, when, and why intuition can be a useful decision aid.

6.2 Situations Where Explicit Guidelines/Rules Are Absent

When specific written guidelines, rules, and policies are lacking to steer worker behavior, which is possible even in stereotypically bureaucratic university settings, intuition can be a useful decision aid. As stated by Burke and Sadler-Smith (2006, p. 170), intuition is "likely to be born out of previous analyses, experiences, and trial-and-error learning that are holistically 'frozen' into a repertoire of routines related to dealing with a specific set of [instructional] circumstances." In recalling almost three years as a department chair at another university, there were multiple times I was confronted with challenging situations in dealing with tenured, tenure-track, and part-time faculty members, where no formal procedures existed to outline my next step.

One such situation occurred as a newly appointed department chair trying to process mounds of paperwork, just as supervisors do in the corporate venue. Given that my predecessor had his own ways of implementing and executing certain administrative tasks, I often had to establish my own approaches for making decisions. One such seemingly mundane task was considering "late add" requests of students to the multiple classes in my area of responsibility. While naïvely plugging away at my desk one morning, a senior professor entered my office without notice, face flushed red, and stood over my desk waving a piece of paper in front of my face. He went on to insist loudly that my handling of a late add to one of his classes was processed (by me) without his approval. I proceeded to inform this professor that my understanding was that I could make these decisions as the head, especially when they appeared to be routine scenarios. However, he continued to escalate in his anger and insist that I had overstepped my bounds. It seemed to me that this professor wanted to impress upon me, early in my stint as chair, how little decision discretion (he believed or perceived) I had and to ensure I realized he desired an active voice in any matter (routine or not) dealing with his classes. I could sense the situation was heating up such that my ability to have a rational conversation with him appeared futile. So, with a desire to squelch what I perceived to be ultimately an over-reactive power move, I stood up—to be on a comparable physical eye contact playing field with him—and he then not only at least took a step back, but lowered his voice, albeit a tad. This move certainly did not fully deter him though, so I then sensed that it might be useful to starting walking toward my door, sending him the signal that he needed to leave my office. While doing so, I also verbally informed him that I would be happy to investigate any formal procedures on making late add decisions should they exist (which they didn't) and that I would talk to him when things "cooled down" to an appropriate level so that we could have a more effective exchange. Looking back, I realize that I not only invoked my intuition in making the particular late add decision, and in other administrative decisions, as there were no explicit or formal guidelines for doing so, but I also counted on my intuition for dealing with this highly agitated colleague. Written policies for responding certainly did not exist in either case, but I needed to try to deal with each adequately.

6.3 Situations Where Precedents for Action Are Absent

Other times in university life I have found myself navigating personally uncharted territory, absent precedents. One such area of "firsts" for most instructors is dealing with students' wide array of physical, mental, emotional, and learning disabilities and their associated accommodation requests. Certainly, this is an area that is vitally important not only legally for a university but also for a student's personal learning situation.

Most of the time, instructors merely carry out written instructions from the relevant university center, provided by the student to the instructor at the beginning of the semester for accommodating a particular student's disability. Although I am used to being in such a response role, I was not prepared to identify and deal with a student who over the course of the semester exhibited in my opinion a potential mental or learning disability about which I was never informed. In this case, invoking intuition enabled me to tune into the cues in my midst and call upon a large well of knowledge and understanding (Burke and Sadler-Smith, 2006) in order to make sense of the situation and develop a reasonable response.

Specifically, this student had become more and more disruptive in class during the course of the semester, blurting out responses and interrupting me during the lecture component of class. He was bright and his comments/questions were typically relevant and sometimes really useful; however, his timing for interjections seemed to lack any social awareness of others' reactions around him and any deference to the "speaker on the floor." After weeks of observing this behavior, I started to notice the disruption his behavior caused for the rest of the class and decided to take some action. I checked with other instructors in my subfield who had likely had him in class previously, and although they acknowledged his disrupting behaviors they never considered it was potentially indicative of what I became increasingly convinced was Asperger's syndrome. Because I had never accommodated this condition, it was new to me, but I had heard our resource center director talk about the condition. So I called up the center and talked to them about the behavioral indicators I was witnessing; they had no record of this student in their center but they gave me a few pointers for dealing with him during the rest of the semester. Then, I decided to call the student into my office and delicately broach the topic. I relayed that I wanted to help him learn the material but that certain behaviors of his, which I detailed, were disruptive to the class. He was surprisingly receptive to my specific, impersonal feedback (although unaware of how his behavior was being received by others). We mutually agreed upon feasible alternatives for dealing with his questions and comments during lecture, and I was just thankful

I acted upon my hunch in a thoughtful manner. It is hoped that all parties involved will benefit long-term from my discernment and our resolution.

6.4 Situations Where Time Is of the Essence

Often, college professors, just like their executive counterparts in industry, must determine a course of action without the luxury of abundant time. Situations can arise in the classroom, for example, that are unexpected and novel, but the instructor needs to identify an appropriate response to preserve the integrity of the learning setting. Relevant examples include a class discussion that quickly and unexpectedly gets students heated about personal opinions that are contrary to others, natural and man-made disasters that require instructors to take lead roles in managing a safe response, or swift changes to planned lecture schedules that must be modified in a timely manner to meet student expectations.

Another more common yet seemingly random occurrence for instructors is when classroom technology goes awry during (a critical point in) a lecture and the instructor must respond quickly yet appropriately in order to salvage the learning environment. In such situations, as Burke and Sadler-Smith (2006) point out, intuition allows instructors to utilize their prior experiences in melding and shaping the classroom context exactly "where the learning is situated." Recently, I experienced such a technology glitch in an MBA class of 23 executives at a most inopportune time, but quickly realized that I could either spiral down with the glitch or swiftly "go with it" in a seemingly unaffected manner so that students did not become distracted. As with most, at my university instructors rotate among many classrooms, each having their own technological idiosyncrasies and ultimately most experience varying emergent problems that expert technology staff must address.

In my experience, showing short Internet videos to demonstrate course concepts can be quite useful but they can also pose multiple challenges, including volume and loading issues and other potential glitches. However, after years as an instructor, I realize the importance of not becoming visibly frustrated in front of students, as it can make the entire learning situation suffer. In this specific situation, after an enthusiastic introduction to an Internet video I was getting ready to show that was instrumental in illustrating a point on innovation,

I clicked play and the video started just fine. Great so far, right? Well, the Internet connection must have slowed or encountered a hitch of some sort, and the video abruptly stopped midstream. Compared to my earlier days as a professor when such an event would trigger panic and verbal frustration, I proceeded to laugh and make light of the oddity and then seamlessly went on to explain the final major points of the video, using the whiteboard. And then, as serendipity would have it, the video started back up on its own and ultimately finished my impromptu mini-lecture. In this case, relying upon and trusting my intuition to quickly remedy a classroom mishap paid off.

6.5 Situations Where Rational Analyses Need to Be Checked

Lastly, intuition can help instructors (and other professionals) to perform a meaningful check and balance of quantitative data. For college professors, this can include checking exam and midterm score distributions, results of missed exam question analyses, and evolving absenteeism patterns. In such situations, intuition can help instructors create a holistic interpretation of the numeric data based upon their experience so as to be leery of results that run counter to their sense of the norm, of what is right, or what is typical (Burke and Sadler-Smith, 2006). As do corporate counterparts who report using intuition when making hiring decisions (Burke and Miller, 1999), I have also utilized intuition as an important check when creating, completing, and examining quantitative rubrics used in faculty hiring situations. Certainly, there can be important candidate attributes that just fail to be quantifiable in selection rubrics.

In my former department chair days, one of my primary tasks was creating semester class schedules that worked not only for faculty but served our student population's needs well. As any corporate professional would do, I invoked software to ease my task. I created a color-coded, multisheet template in Excel, complete with all the class times we offered, days of the week, courses in my department, and comprehensive listing of full- and part-time faculty and adjuncts. Core classes were formatted one way, and elective courses another, to ensure effective distribution yet avoid ineffective "competition." During construction of the schedule, I checked off the courses and instructors as they were aptly slotted into the spreadsheet to ensure a proper array of morning, afternoon, and evening classes as well as Tuesday/Thursday, Monday/Wednesday, and Monday/Wednesday/Friday classes across all the time slots offered. I would also make special efforts to ensure students in the major could get as many courses "in" as possible and avoided offering critical courses at the same time/day. Common prerequisites for the major needed special care so that high volumes of students could secure the prerequisite at various points during the week. Each professor was slotted for the same number of courses (unless an adjunct who only taught one section), and I also tried to allot an equivalent number of course preps to each professor.

Structured and seemingly formulaic, this template was a great start for approaching this task, but it was certainly not sufficient for generating the best schedule. That is, before, during, and after the schedule was complete, I planned for and made numerous adjustments based on a multitude of experiences with instructor preferences, student feedback, room limitations, curriculum innovations, new programs, dean or program director strategies, and so on. No matter how much time I put into structuring the template and quantifying simple yet important attributes, the process greatly benefitted from overlaying my personal experience and knowledge of multiple relevant variables.

6.6 Conclusion

Intuition is built upon experiences and lessons learned by immersion in the social setting of practice (Burke and Sadler-Smith, 2006); hence, the academic context is no exception. In this chapter, multiple cases were discussed where I have used intuition in the academic context, including as an instructor in the classroom and as an administrative head of an academic department.

Future research could also explore the use of intuition by academics in their role as researchers. For example, I have likely invoked my intuition when I sense a coauthor is getting off track and needs guidance, when I "read between the lines" as I scour editor reviews of submitted work, or when I have very narrow windows of time to respond to editor, reviewer, or coauthor concerns about an impending article. However, although intuition is the culmination of knowledge and experiences that managers, professors, and others rely on throughout the working day, often we are unable to articulate or explain such use easily or readily (Gregory, 2000). As such, research methods that appropriately tap subjects' recall, thick descriptions, and richness are needed.

References

Agor, W.H. (1989). *Intuition in Organizations: Leading and Managing Productively*. Newbury Park, CA: Sage.

Burke, L. and Miller, M. (1999). Making intuitive decisions: Demystifying the process. *Academy of Management Executive*, 13(4): 91–99.

Burke, L. and Sadler-Smith, E. (2006). Extending intuition in the educational setting. *Academy of Management Learning and Education*, 5(2), 169–181.

Gregory, G. (2000). Developing intuition through management education. In T. Atkinson and G. Claxton (Eds.), *The Intuitive Practitioner: On the Value of Not Always Knowing What One Is Doing*. Buckingham, UK: Open University Press, pp. 182–195.

Hogarth, R.M. (2001). *Educating Intuition*. Chicago: University of Chicago Press.

Klein, G. (2003). *Intuition at Work: Why Developing Your Gut Instincts Will Make You Better at What You Do*. New York: Currency Doubleday.

7

CAPITAL DECISIONS IN THE RETAIL INDUSTRY

DENISE CHENGER

Mount Royal University

Contents

7.1 Evolution of Decision Making

I spent my twenties traveling, working in retail, and completing a degree in business. I was almost 30 by the time I settled into my first corporate position and landed a job as an area manager with responsibility for approximately 30 retail sites for a large national retailer. Although I held over a decade of retail experience, this particular position was within the oil and gas industry and was a higher level of management than I had held in the past.

The scope of responsibility for the position included everything from safety to sales to sourcing and recommending new sites and opportunities within my geographical region. In a short period of time, I learned and applied all the key requirements of the job. In just over a year, the retailers and I were achieving or beating all sales and customer service goals; in essence, we had developed into a very high-performing team. For the next four years, the region remained in the top five (of 25) regions and had caught the positive attention of senior management.

A key aspect of the position was to ensure a high level of brand consistency across the retail network. This meant each retail property site needed to be cleaned and maintained on a regular basis. Of equal importance was ensuring equipment at each site was always in good working order. This could include replacing a furnace, fixing a leaky roof, or adding new gas pumps to a station. A large pool of funds was available for all area managers to draw upon. These funds allowed each of us to ensure site repairs and minor renovations could be carried out. I was only one of ten area managers who heavily relied upon this budget; however, each year I managed to utilize between 40–60% of the total available maintenance dollars. I had quickly realized after my first year with the company that a little financial analysis and the ability to justify why the funds were required was all that was needed to beat my peers to the available capital.

For larger projects, such as a site rebuild or expansion, the area managers were required to compile a fairly comprehensive business case justifying the large capital investment. The business case would advance through each of the various levels of management until eventually the senior vice president (SVP) would sign off on any project deemed worthy of investment. Poorly justified projects (or just bad projects) would typically only progress a level or two before being turned down. I was proud that each of my business cases moved through the levels of management rather quickly, where my peer's business case often took weeks to months to seek approval and often with revisions. My business degree seemed to be paying off versus most of my peers! In addition, my retail managers were thrilled with the money I was able to use for repairs at each of their sites.

A couple of years into the role, my retail company began a major rebranding effort where new retail sites were being acquired and developed, old ones demolished, and some existing sites renovated and rebranded. Each one of these projects required a similar business case for management's review. However, there was more at stake given the substantial retail networkwide investment, and therefore sites needed to be carefully chosen. This required experience in understanding the whole network because sites were chosen in part based upon their strong street appeal and the desire to create a bang in the industry when relaunching the new brand image to consumers.

Because the rebranding initiative affected the entire network, my company was working with an outside firm that specialized in retail site modeling. This company had built a comprehensive program that could estimate store sales following the completion of renovations at any particular site in our network. The formula in their program took into consideration a number of inputs and included criteria such as all the competitor sites within a geographic area, an associated brand value with each competitor, and information about our proposed site (i.e., square footage, product offering). I was required to use their "scientific" program as a basis of my financial analysis and include this as part of my business case to rebrand and build each of the new sites. At a few sites, management had requested that I tweak the scientific numbers provided by the expert modeling company. In essence, I was being asked to embellish some of the numbers slightly in order to ensure these projects met the company rate of return for capital projects. This step in the process was confusing and perhaps a bit frustrating, not to mention it made me feel very uncomfortable; after all, why had my company hired experts to assess the proposed sales if we were not going to incorporate their analysis into the business case? But as requested, I proceeded to adjust the numbers until the estimated sales were high enough to meet the company hurdle rate and the project would be approved and sanctioned by senior management. Exactly what did my supervisor and his supervisor know versus a consulting company that was equipped with a highly specialized modeling program? It baffled me. Surprisingly, each of the new sites did very well.

Eventually, I moved from Canada to the United States in a similar role but with a US company. This time I had moved up a level and was now responsible for approximately 80 retail sites. It was a fascinating experience to learn and uncover what industry characteristics held from my familiar Canadian marketplace and into the United States. I continued to grow, learn, and became familiar with the key attributes that supported a highly desirable location. In essence, over the years I had developed a mental database consisting of the attributes associated with the hundreds of sites I had seen. For example, the database of preferred site characteristics included: a specific preference for one particular corner at an intersection; traffic flow in and around the site; the ingress and egress for site and property access; total size of the property; product offering at the site (i.e., car wash); demographics and the size of the population making up the surrounding community; whether the site was patronized by the community or commuters; other fuel brands within a certain geography; and the distance between competitor sites.

These were just some of the many criteria used to evaluate the quality of the "dirt" as it was called in this industry. In addition, there were numerous guiding principles or rules of thumb to follow. For example, one site needed a general population of approximately 3,000 homes to support one gasoline station (i.e., a community of 10,000 should have three gas stations). Or never select a property located in the middle of a long street; instead choose a busy intersection with good in/out access. Woiceshyn (2009) describes how these guiding principles are the result of "integration by essentials"; where a decision maker incorporates new information and can quickly evaluate it against existing knowledge.

Each principle combined with other principles could literally produce hundreds of potential combinations of what made for a good piece of dirt in the retail gasoline industry. Combining this with other industry challenges and changes that were occurring simultaneously (i.e., large grocery stores entering the retail gasoline industry) produced an interesting matrix of information to consider with all capital decisions. Each decision needed to be determined on a site-by-site basis; there was no magic formula to follow by which to choose a site.

Another piece of knowledge contributing to my database of information was the focus and attention this particular company placed on reviewing the total sales for every single one of these sites. This was done on a weekly basis. This process forced the cross-referencing of sales versus my mental recall of each site and the community each site served.

Volumes of data, week after week, year after year, went into understanding what made for a good retail site in the gasoline industry. In essence, I had built a very similar mental database of the key attributes one would focus on to build a new site. This was very much like the scientific model used by the site modeling company referenced above and the very same model that had baffled me years before.

A few years later, I moved on to another company and into a senior leadership role where I held responsibility for over 600 retail assets located across the country. It would be impossible to intimately know anything about any particular site much less the demographics and information about each community every one of those sites operated within. Yet, when an area manager would submit a proposal to invest capital dollars into a site, it was surprisingly easy to make a decision whether to approve the project. Their proposals contained current (or projected) sales, community information such as the existing demographics, other existing brands in operation, and future plans for the community such as proposed schools, or commercial or shopping centers. Site photos were also included as part of the proposal. Each piece of information helped to build a mental picture and a business case as to whether the proposal should be approved and granted the capital, or whether the proposal should be reworked or rejected outright. Although the format varied slightly from company to company, the general principles for determining the viability of a proposed capital project within the retail oil and gas industry held constant whether in Canada or the United States.

On certain projects, I soon found myself repeating the words I had heard years before, "Adjust the input numbers to push this project through! This is a good project!" Exactly what made it a good project could not be easily explained or understood but seemed to be relatively straightforward to those of us who held similar experience in the industry. The discussions at this new senior level of management were different than they were a decade before as a green area manager. Years before, I would become excited at the prospect of just about any project and always hoped for new sites to be added to my region. A decade later I understood finding good dirt was very rare. The ability to provide a positive return on capital invested when constructing a new site was generally deemed to be extremely difficult, especially without either good planning (purchasing dirt and waiting for a population to grow into a new community which could take over a decade) or a bit of luck. However, when a good site did come along, there was a sense of knowing and genuine excitement. Some examples of decisions made in my senior role follow below. Note, there would have been some financial analysis done with any and all of the examples cited, but in general we all knew the approximate cost to build a green-field site in this industry. Past experience allowed us to guesstimate whether a particular piece of dirt would be able to generate enough in annual sales to ensure a return on capital invested. The step of completing a formal financial analysis would only serve to fine tune the expected return, plus ensure the due diligence required as a publicly traded company had been done, but it certainly wasn't required for any of our decisions whether to proceed.

7.2 Role of Experience in Decision Making

My company had been approached about a new strip mall being built. The proposed strip mall was to be located within a suburb close to a large city. This immediately suggests most of the residents would be commuters, which indicates residents would already have their traffic routes and favorite stops to make en route to their workplace. The proposed site was to be located within a strip mall, which is generally deemed to be not as desirable a location versus a corner lot within a busy intersection. All indicators meant it would not be an "A" site. However, as time progressed and we became privy to the other proposed tenants who had agreed to locate within the strip mall it instantly made the site much stronger, as these brands would collectively help to reroute existing traffic patterns and make the proposed new site much stronger and lucrative. The convenience store sales would be strong and the gas sales reasonable, but collectively a strong site.

Contrast this with a fairly isolated community where there were no existing fuel stations and all residents were commuting a much longer distance to a larger center than the example cited above. A developer was proposing to construct a large retail and commercial project at the edge of the community. The development was also located along the highway and was expected to have easy access in and off the property. In addition, there were already a few strong anchors (large retail brands) committed to the project. The developer had approached my company as a first choice to build a new gas facility within the development project. It was an exciting opportunity and we were all on board. It was an "A" location. Again as time progressed and late in the negotiating process, we learned that one of the new anchors had decided to exercise their right to add retail gasoline to their site. It instantly became a deal-breaker for me. Intuitively, I knew that with the high cost of construction at the time, it would not be enough to provide the required return on investment for the site. Although the site had great access on/off the highway and fantastic visibility and proposed signage, because I was the person who held responsibility for providing a return on capital, the financial return would not be there within the timeline my company required. If the construction costs had not been as high as they were at that time, or if the property had been available a few years before or after, the site would have been a great addition to the network.

Although brand or customer service is generally a strong reason to entice or push customers to return to a site, convenience will often play a stronger role. One particular site was located along a long major artery (road) with numerous traffic lights and side streets. The city had decided to remove many of the exit points along the busy road because each one affected the flow of traffic and because of the many accidents occuring along the route due to the stop and go of traffic. It just so happened that one of these required changes by the city was at an intersection where my company had a high-performing site in our network. I knew in an instant it would affect the high-volume site. It would be very difficult for customers to backtrack and regain access to the lights following the proposed changes. The city's proposal made sense from both a safety and a traffic flow perspective, but the long-term impact to our site was obvious. Experience suggested current customers would never circle around to regain access but rather, most customers would redefine their traffic routes and find another site with easier access. Generally, in retail gasoline, no brand is that strong that any customer will add time and frustration to their day to reach a particular site. This became the key negotiating point with the city: to try to explain what would likely happen to the site (we knew from experience). Negotiations with the city proved futile and the changes were to proceed. Traffic slowed during construction and within months the fuel volume had dropped to almost half of what it had been.

7.3 Learning Stages for Decision Makers

Dreyfus and Dreyfus (2005) provide a roadmap of five learning stages that suggest how an individual might move from a beginner to an expert status on a subject. They term the first stage as novice. During this stage, information is decomposed so that the novice can understand what is required of him or her without actually doing the activity. For example, this would have been my introduction to the area manager role, company processes and culture, and the industry itself. The second stage, termed advanced beginner, occurs once the learner gains experience through practice. For me, I learned how to construct a business case for new capital projects (yet I was confused when certain projects would be forced through or rejected). Stage three is termed the competence stage. This occurs when the learner determines which elements in the domain are relevant in order to make a good decision. For me, as I gained more experience, I began to recognize which key attributes pertinent to a retail gasoline site made one site more desirable over another. Stage four occurs when intuitive responses begin to replace reasoned responses. With over a decade of experience in one single industry, I was able to quickly call upon multiple guiding principles stored from memory, and connect them in order to produce a decision. The fifth stage is termed the expert stage. This occurs when the person immediately sees what needs to be achieved and decisions are made quickly. In my senior role, I no longer had to be intimately involved with a particular site; I could make a reasonably good assessment based on limited but relevant information submitted in the form of a business case and then be able to reject or approve a project.

It is reasonable to assume that over a decade in the industry I had evolved from a novice status to what Dreyfus and Dreyfus termed expert status. I had a positive history of making solid capital project decisions. The decisions were based on numerous data points that had been learned and tested over time and through experience with hundreds of projects with which I had been involved. For me, these decisions had become relatively straightforward and did not require a financial analysis to indicate whether to proceed.

7.4 How Capital Decisions Are Made

After a few years in my senior role, I began to wonder how others might make similar decisions within their respective industries. Furthermore, I questioned what factors would go into a major decision, such as a large acquisition, where the decision maker could not possibly have acquired previous experience as I had over the previous decade. It would be fair to suggest that most executives could only be involved in a couple of major decisions throughout their entire career. Exactly how would those individuals build experience (intuition) to make such a large decision when realistically, it appeared they would not have had the opportunity to acquire that experience?

This question became the foundation for my PhD dissertation: how does an executive make a major capital project decision? Interviews were conducted in Calgary's oil and gas industry with numerous CEOs and senior executives. These individuals were chosen based on their high profile and public projects. I aimed for large unique projects relative to the current size of their company: actual revenue versus the cost of the capital project. This should have made it next to impossible for each of those individuals to have gained specific experience within their respective careers given both the uniqueness and size of these major projects.

The assumption made prior to conducting the research was that all major decisions were likely conducted by the whole executive team. For example, determining how to spend the available capital the following year was a team decision based upon reviewing a portfolio of proposed projects.

The results suggested that only one individual, the CEO, made all major capital project decisions. Sometimes it was the CEO and CFO, or the CEO and chairman of the board; but it was always led by the CEO. Although these decisions may appear to have been made impulsively, the findings suggest that these intuitive decisions were based on years and years of relevant and valid experience. Their decisions were well thought through by each of the individuals I interviewed.

Four clear paths emerged with respect to how the CEOs made their decisions, one of which is related to this discussion. This first path, which I termed opportunistic, revolved around how the CEO made an acquisition decision. The research participants noted they received, on average, five acquisition opportunities per week. For a CEO to review every single one of those opportunities, she or he is in essence creating a similar database to that which was discussed previously. This process builds decision-making experience in an individual and would be termed by Dreyfus and Dreyfus as an expert. Therefore, although the CEO may only enter into a couple of large acquisitions over the course of his or her career, constantly reviewing numerous industry-related acquisition opportunities builds exposure and experience. Each of the CEOs had a feeling of intuitively knowing when the right opportunity presented itself. The following are CEO quotes from the research (Chenger, 2012):

> … [Y]ou know right from the beginning I went "ya, I like this one a lot."… We quickly just start circling the wagons cause you get one every week. You got someone trying to sell to us. And obviously most of them are "No! That is not consistent with the type of equipment we want to buy or where we want to take the company."

... [I]t was a combination of things. At any one day we are looking at maybe 10 different opportunities. Maybe I'll say 5 corporate opportunities at any day of the week. And then, and usually they are too expensive, and usually they, there's issues. ... Um, or maybe not quite the right strategic fit or whatever. So all the stars lined up vertically on this one. Where it was a strategic fit. Where it was an extremely good valuation. ... And of course the financial ability to do it. And the financial ability to execute on the [opportunity] once we had done the acquisition.

Common to all four decision-making paths was the executive's intuitive approach to making a decision. This included a decision that was made by one individual. It was also noted that at the decision-making stage, no financial or risk analysis had been completed. Their decisions were based on years and years of experience within an industry. Similar to my decisions on determining which piece of dirt was valuable and desirable enough to build a retail site upon, these CEOs used the same principles to make a major capital project decision based on information unique to their own industry.

7.5 Conclusion

The novice builds a database of knowledge and experience over time, years and years of experience, with feedback, and by closely following those tedious but required company processes. No one could have explained to me when I first started my career in retail oil and gas why I should "embellish the numbers to make the project appear feasible;" this knowledge and skill could only be gained over time. However, having clearly defined corporate processes and receiving specific and timely feedback certainly aided in my ability to build clear guidelines and principles required to make a good decision. What started out as purely rational decisions early in my career eventually became intuitive decisions over time. One key factor that supported the ability to be a good decision maker included building experience at numerous retail companies, three of which were solely focused on the oil and gas retail industry. Furthermore, experience was acquired across two large countries where I was able to apply previous knowledge and learning into new situations and cultures. One final noteworthy point on this topic relates to my research: the majority of the participants made their major decision within their geographic foundation of experience in their respective industries. In other words, they did not acquire experience in one country and then make a major decision in another. It was unusual for any of them to make a major decision in a geography where they lacked experience or at least exposure.

In summary, this chapter proved to be a challenge to write. How does one attempt to describe all the decision-making points and factors that go into a very quick and rapid decision? It challenged me to go back to the very foundation of when the skills and competencies were first introduced and developed in order to unravel the numerous data points that go into a decision that can now be made quickly and without much consideration. In order to understand the years of experience and insights that combine to make an intuitive decision, the bulk of this chapter required that I focus on bringing the reader along my 20-year journey in order to fully appreciate everything that went into these quick but significant capital project decisions.

References

Chenger, D.T. (2012). "Executive Level Capital Project Decision Making: Rational or Rationale? DPhil, The University of Calgary, Calgary, AB. Retrieved from http://www.collectionscanada.gc.ca/obj/thesescanada/vol2/002/NR91100.PDF (20132126346)

Dreyfus, H.L. and Dreyfus, S.E. (2005). Expertise in real world contexts. *Organization Studies*, 26(5): 779–792. doi: 10.1177/0170840605053102

Woiceshyn, J. (2009). Lessons from "good minds": How CEOs use intuition, analysis and guiding principles to make strategic decisions. *Long Range Planning*, 42(3): 298–319. doi: 10.1016/j.lrp.2009.05.002

PART II

PRACTICE TRACK

8

INTUITION AND CRISIS LEADERSHIP

ERIC J. MCNULTY,
LEONARD J. MARCUS, AND
BARRY C. DORN

*National Preparedness Leadership Initiative
Harvard School of Public Health and Harvard's Kennedy
School of Government Center for Public Leadership*

Contents

8.1 Introduction

Forty years ago, Russell Ackoff cautioned against equating analysis with thought (Ackoff, 1973). Although his talk was given long before today's pervasive data analysis and even before most of us had ever interacted with a computer, his understanding of the limits of reductionist mechanistic thinking that characterized the Industrial Age is at the heart of the battle between data-driven and intuition-based decision making. Do we make the best decisions by breaking the whole down into ever-smaller parts at ever-greater speeds—tasks at which data analytics programs excel—or by comprehending the whole in which those parts are assembled and connected, something to which the human is well suited?

Data-driven, analysis-based decision making, sometimes referred to as analytics (Davenport and Harris, 2007), has become increasingly relied upon. As the world moved online, vast troves of data were created and technological advances made it possible to analyze those data ever more quickly and in greater detail. This increasingly scientific approach to decision making was popularized by the book *Moneyball*

(Lewis, 2004), which chronicled the transformation of the Oakland A's, a team with a relatively low budget for player salaries, from an also-ran into a consistent winner by substituting the sophisticated use of statistics for gut feelings and folkloric rules-of-thumb. The Boston Red Sox used this numbers-driven approach to win the 2004 World Series and end the 86-year "Curse of the Bambino" (Shaughnessy, 2005). By 2012, being a data scientist was called "the sexiest job of the 21st century" (Davenport and Patil, 2012).

8.2 Distinctions between Analysis and Intuition

To paraphrase Mark Antony, we come neither to bury data-based decision making nor to praise it; rather we come to argue that both intuition and analysis-centric decision making have their place. The challenge for leaders, particularly in crisis, is to employ intuition and analysis at the right times; it is no more useful to use a hammer to cut wood than to use a saw to bang a nail.

According to the Merriam-Webster *Online Dictionary* (n.d.), analysis is "an explanation of the true nature and meaning of something" whereas intuition is "something that is known without proof or evidence." Analysis involves learning about something through the study of "its parts, what they do, and how they are related to each other." It is driven by evidence. Intuition, on the other hand, is defined as "a natural ability or power … that guides a person to act a certain way without fully understanding why." In this description, it has a somewhat ethereal quality. Intuition should not be confused with wishful thinking; that I am feeling lucky does not mean that my odds of winning this week's lottery are better than in any other week. Meaningful intuition arises from experiences where one can have both successes and failures through which recognizable patterns can be accumulated.

In the end, both analysis and intuition are ways of knowing. Both can be right or wrong. The former offers the seeming certainty of logical reasoning; numbers provide a definitive count of what is being measured. The latter tenders only the comfort that something feels right or not.

To better understand when best to rely on analysis or intuition, it is useful to visit the Rumsfeldian realm of knowns and unknowns (Rumsfeld, 2002): in any situation there are known knowns, known unknowns, unknown unknowns, and one essential to intuition that

Rumsfeld did not include, unknown knowns. If one is dealing only with known knowns (observed phenomena and hard data), even a rudimentary algorithm will generally outperform an intuition-based "best guess" (Kahneman, 2011). The rapidly evolving tools and techniques that have come to be known as Big Data (Davenport, Barth, and Bean, 2012) can perform remarkable feats with known knowns.

Known unknowns—questions one thinks to ask but to which answers have not yet been found—are subject to bias in the assumptions made about those unknowns; these derive from cognitive bias (Konnikova, 2013; Eagleman, 2011), cognitive illusions (Kahneman, 2011), and hidden cultural bias (Banaji and Greenwald, 2013). Again, algorithms likely have the edge when they can correct for bias over time, as they are informed by and evolved through robust feedback mechanisms that exceed those available to any one individual through his or her personal experience. However, poorly constructed or employed analytical models can mislead, sometimes with enormous consequences (Davenport, 2008).

Unknown unknowns—questions that one does not think or know to ask and the answers for which are also unknown—are not better served by either approach, as neither a data scientist nor individual employing intuition will factor them into thinking or action. These are potentially the most dangerous as they lead to true surprises.

That leaves unknown knowns and this is where intuition has a distinct advantage. Unknown knowns are those bits of data, patterns, and experiences that sit in the unconscious mind yet of which one is not consciously aware. The brain accumulates vast amounts of this information and it informs a great deal of an individual's thinking (Konnikova, 2013; Eagleman, 2011; Kahneman, 2011). One knows without knowing that one knows; psychologists generally agree that "much of human judgment and behavior is produced with little conscious thought" (Banaji and Greenwald, 2013). Intuition is what we call tapping into this valuable resource. As explored in greater detail below, unknown knowns can be critical to crisis leadership and high-stakes decision making.

8.3 Crisis Leadership

At the National Preparedness Leadership Initiative (NPLI), a joint program of the Harvard School of Public Health and the Center for Public Leadership at Harvard's Kennedy School of Government (www.hsph.harvard.edu/npli), we train executives from the public, private, and nonprofit sectors in crisis leadership. These are people who must make high-consequence, at times life-and-death, decisions often with incomplete or conflicting information and under extraordinary time pressure. Our teaching is informed by traditional academic research as well as through firsthand observation of leaders during crisis situations or in their immediate aftermath. For example, we deployed during the responses to the Deepwater Horizon oil spill and Superstorm Sandy and have been involved in extensive interviews in the aftermath of the Boston Marathon bombings. We were involved in these as well as the responses to the H1N1 pandemic, Hurricane Katrina, and other events.

Our teaching is built around a framework we call meta-leadership (Marcus et al., 2012). Its dimensions are: (1) the person, (2) the situation, (3) leading down, (4) leading up, and (5) leading across. Intuition and analysis manifest themselves in each of the dimensions, although they are discussed here largely in the context of dimension one; learning the "person of the meta-leader" requires an understanding of both intentional and intuitive thinking and action. Intentional means both being purposeful and taking the time for careful and considered analysis. Intuitive means thinking and acting rapidly, in almost automatic fashion. We argue that one can and should be intentional about building one's intuitive capacity. How is this done?

Psychologists generally agree that the human brain has two "systems" for thinking, one fast and one slow (Konnikova, 2013; Kahneman, 2011). The fast brain system is in use most often and is the home of intuition; the slow brain is where complex thinking and problem solving occur. As applied to crisis leadership, we further refine these distinctions and utilize a three-zone metaphorical model to help individuals better understand their physical and psychological function under stress. Zones one and two correspond to the fast brain: the first zone contains instinctual and involuntary functions such as breathing, heartbeat, and, most important for crisis leaders, the freeze–flight–fight response to threat. The second zone contains learned patterns and behaviors that can be accessed and exercised with minimal mental effort, those things that become stored in the brain as a result of exercises, training, and experience. The distinction is important because one cannot easily alter what happens in the first zone, what has been called "the basement" by Freud (Prochnick, 2012) and others (Ashkenazi, 2007; Marcus et al., 2012), whereas one can purposefully build a rich repository of patterns and tools in the second zone, the part of the fast brain system that we call the "workroom". This is where intuitive capacity can be built and stored. The third zone, the research and development laboratory in our terminology, is home to idea generation, innovation, and novel and complex problem solving; it correlates with the slow brain in the psychologists' model.

Neither intuitive nor analytical function is optimal when one is "in the basement," reacting to real or perceived threats. The "minimize threat, maximize reward" response has been called "the fundamental organizing principle of the brain" (Rock, 2009). At its extreme, this response results in an "amygdala hijack" (Goleman, 1995) that triggers a panicked freeze–flight–fight response. The amygdala, an "almond-shaped cluster of gray matter in the anterior extremity of the temporal lobe" (Merriam-Webster, n.d.), helps the brain process emotions. It was useful to our ancient forebears threatened by saber-toothed tigers. In the face of a perceived threat the amygdala fires and stimulates the body's survival responses. First, one freezes as animal predators initially detect their prey through its motion. In a wild setting, freezing would be the best defensive response. If detected, one would flee as avoiding an encounter with the predator is the next best chance of survival. Finally, if a confrontation were unavoidable, one would fight for survival as the only option.

In this hijack or basement state, the amygdala is animated with an increased flow of blood and oxygen. Simultaneously, the prefrontal cortex, the R&D lab, experiences a decrease in blood and oxygen that can cause one temporarily to lose the equivalent of 10 to 15 IQ points (Nadler, 2009). Deliberative decision making and other cognitive functions are impaired by the brain's forced concentration of mental and physical resources for survival. Research has shown that people experienced an amygdala hijack when exposed to threatening stimuli even when the exposure was so brief that it did not register in their consciousness (Kahneman, 2011). There is no need for analysis; this automatic response is intuitive, honed over eons of evolutionary development. The unconscious knows and spurs action before the conscious brain registers that the knowledge is available for processing. This is one example of an unknown known.

Although one no longer needs to fear prehistoric predators, the amygdala hijack is embedded in brain function. This is evident when people under stress say and do things they later regret. Rock (2009) has cited research that demonstrated that negative social interactions are processed by the brain similarly to physical pain. When one is excluded from a group, one will experience a descent "to the basement." The same reaction occurs when one's boss issues a stern and unexpected call to come to her office. An explosion or other loud noise can trigger the triple-F response. Once one becomes aware of the basement phenomenon, one recognizes that it occurs regularly. It becomes a known known.

In order to engage in analytical thinking and problem solving, one must get out of the basement. Like a staircase running through a building, the climb to the R&D lab must traverse the intervening level of the workroom. A measure of relative certainty can be restored by employing a tool from the workroom; demonstrating basic competence at a function is one way to reset the brain and abort the amygdala hijack. This can be done with a trigger script such as the timeworn advice of counting to 10 before responding when angry, or by engaging in the practiced steps of a learned protocol such as a fire alarm evacuation. These actions reassert some control in a situation that may otherwise seem chaotic. Initially, this must be done intentionally. Eventually, recognition of the descent to the basement and activating the mechanism for rising become so deeply ingrained that the process becomes intuitive, particularly in the face of threats one has trained for or experienced previously. Once firmly in the workroom, with balance even somewhat restored, it is possible to begin the ascent that makes it possible to engage the prefrontal cortex of the R&D lab. Thus, even if analytical reasoning is ultimately the best tool to meet a challenge, an intuitive response provides the fastest path to be able to gain access to this resource.

Once the leader rises out of the basement, the leadership task is to ensure that others are out as well. Rock (2008) has shown that the threat response can be triggered by threats to status, certainty, autonomy, relatedness (or inclusion), or fairness. A leader can enhance perceived social safety and help people counteract the triple-F response by giving them jobs to do; followers are able to calm their amygdalae by demonstrating competence and making productive contributions.

We are often told by participants that the lessons about brain function and the amygdala hijack are among the most useful takeaways from our executive education program.

As demonstrated by the studied response to a basement trigger and quick ascent, we subscribe to Simon's contention that "intuition is nothing more and nothing less than recognition" (Simon, n.d. as cited by Kahneman, 2011). One recognizes a cue which triggers stored information that can be used to formulate a response. The amygdala hijack is not the only context in which learned intuition is useful in crisis leadership. Intentionally building up the stock of tools in one's workroom can speed decision making and action in situations where seconds count. Intuitive "hunches" are essentially fast brain activity that uses emotional tagging to help the brain expedite pattern recognition, including in situations with a large number of variables (Waytz and Mason, 2013). Konnikova (2013) asserted that "accurate intuition is really nothing more than practice" to replace one set of heuristics with another that is more disciplined to correct for and overcome common biases as well as retrieve unknown knowns. This is central to her assertion that one can learn to think like Sherlock Holmes, the fictional detective renowned for his ability to perceive clues missed by others.

In this vein, expertise is sometimes thought of as the ability to call upon a vast mental storehouse of knowledge and experience to solve complex problems quickly. Anthropologist Dr. Robert Deutsch conducted a study on expertise. He interviewed cosmologists, then at the cutting edge of the exploration of abstract challenges, chief fire fighters, experts in concrete challenges, and auctioneers, domain experts who must know both that which they auction and how to read an audience. Each of these occupations employs both analytical and intuitive thinking. They deal with all of the knowns and unknowns. Deutsch found that these experts had four things in common: they understood that their knowledge had limits and were open and curious to push the boundaries; they asked questions. They thought metaphorically and brought in off-topic information to catalyze their thinking. They were playful with ideas and open to different ways of looking at them. Finally, they were more concerned with problem structuring than problem solving; they were confident that they would get to an answer (Robert Deutsch, personal communication,

August 6, 2013). These activities can all be seen as ways to build intuition and enable unknown knowns to bubble to the surface. Similarly, Konnikova (2013) described how Holmes would take steps to let his brain's unconscious process information until an insight emerged in his consciousness. At times this was contemplating a "three pipe problem" in his easy chair; at others it involved spending extended time at a crime scene simply sitting.

Thus we teach would-be leaders to expose themselves continually to new experiences, reflect and keep a journal, ask questions and challenge orthodoxies, and practice seeing situations through the perspectives of others. We suggest that they evaluate their decisions and the resulting outcomes through all five metaleadership dimensions. Each of these techniques is designed to increase the store of knowledge and problem framing devices on which the leader can draw in a crisis. During the stress of a high-stakes, high-pressure situation, it may not be possible to construct an algorithm and test its validity. Decisions must be made and action must be taken. Honing one's ability to trust what feels right or wrong is essential to an effective crisis response. One must be able to draw upon the unknown knowns.

For example, in the first days of the H1N1 influenza pandemic in 2009, there simply were not enough data to determine the nature of the virus definitively, yet political leaders and the public demanded to know, "What is going on? How bad will it be? What should I do?" Dr. Richard Besser, then Acting Director of the Centers for Disease Control and Prevention and an alumnus of the NPLI, could not provide the authoritative analysis on which a science-based agency prefers to base its policy advisories. Without the data, he and other CDC leaders were able to share only the opinions of top scientists. Although at first it required some effort, CDC scientists learned to rely on intuition: first to elevate the initial cases to the attention of the White House; then to be transparent with the public and the media about the known knowns, the known unknowns, and the unknown unknowns; and then to take steps to prepare the agency for a long-duration response. Besser struck a balance between analysis and intuition; he used the science where it was solid and drew on his intuition, honed through experience with other epidemiological events, to make the best possible decisions.

More recently, we have interviewed many of the first responders, political officials, and medical personnel involved in the aftermath of the bombings at the Boston Marathon on April 15, 2013. There were many examples of courage … and of intuition in action. Consistent with the terms of those interviews, the stories shared here protect the identities of the individuals involved.

At 2:49 p.m., an improvised explosive device was detonated near the finish line. Twelve seconds later, another ripped through the crowd (*Globe* Staff, 2013). Several interviewees used expressions such as "a war zone" to describe the carnage. Many recounted trips "to the basement"; for some the ascent was almost immediate as they intuitively called upon their years of experience and well-rehearsed protocols for a terrorist attack. For others it took a cue from a colleague to reset the brain. Several bystanders, unguided by any training or planning, stepped up to help the injured rather than fleeing the scene. Their intuitive reaction to assist others saved lives.

One of the more dramatic stories involves a Boston Police superintendent who was assisting the injured. He soon realized that all of the available ambulances had been dispatched to hospitals. There were still many more people requiring immediate evacuation for emergency medical attention. He had to make a quick decision that could both save lives and cost him his job. Procedures, certainly developed through careful analysis of both risks and rewards, required that only ambulances be used to transport the injured. Police vehicles were strictly prohibited. Something—an unknown known—told him that these people could not wait. He countermanded the protocol and directed that police vehicles transport the injured until more ambulances became available. Some of the injured were in critical condition where minutes, and even seconds, could be decisive for treatment. The result: all of the injured who were taken from the scene of the bombing survived (Dr. Eric Goralnick, personal communication, April 26, 2013). Again, intuition saved lives.

8.4 Crafting the Balance

One should not see the choice between data-driven analysis and intuition as an either–or distinction; it is more useful to put them in the context of "and." Crisis leaders must balance rigorous analysis alongside experienced intuition. We find ourselves in a time when we are fascinated by analytics and many technological tools are easily accessible; it can be easy to shun intuition.

Barriers to calling upon one's unknown knowns can result from the formal structures that favor evidence-based choices as well as the fear to trust one's gut. Accepting the legitimacy of intuition in certain circumstances is the first step to empowering oneself and others to draw upon the rich store of subconscious knowledge. Legitimate concerns about the reliability of intuition can be overcome through intentional cultivation of meaningful intuition so that it is called upon where it is most appropriate, integrating the intuition of multiple individuals, and fostering a professional environment where truth-to-power is both spoken and heard.

Leaders must be honest and transparent about the domain in which they are operating: data-based analysis or intuition. This must be as clear as possible up and down within their hierarchy and across to other stakeholders in order to inform the expectations and calculations of those parties. Data should not be ignored when they are available, robust, and credible. However, leaders at times cannot fail to act because data are unavailable or their robustness and credibility are in question. The human mind and our computers can each produce extraordinary outcomes. Crisis leaders and those they lead are best served when they call upon the exceptional, and complementary, capabilities of both.

References

Ackoff, R. (1973). Science in the systems age: Beyond IE, OR, and MS. *Operations Research*, 21(3): 661–671.

Ashkenazi, I. (2007, March 9). *Psychology & Actions of the Crisis Leader*. Presentation at the National Preparedness Leadership Initiative, Harvard University, Cambridge, MA.

Banaji, M. and Greenwald, A. (2013). *Blindspot: Hidden Biases of Good People*. New York: Random House.

Davenport, T. (2008, September 25). *Is This an Analytics-Driven Financial Crisis?* HBR.org. Retrieved October 2, 2013 from http://blogs.hbr.org/2008/09/is-this-an-analyticsdriven-fin/

Davenport, T. and Harris, J. (2007). *Competing on Analytics: The New Science of Winning*. Boston: Harvard Business School Press.

Davenport, T., Barth, P., and Bean, R. (2012, Fall). How 'big data' is different. *MIT Sloan Management Review*. Retrieved September 30, 2013 from http://www.stevens.edu/howe/sites/default/files/MIT-SMR%20How%20Big%20Data%20is%20Different.pdf

Davenport, T. and Patil, D. (2012). Data scientist: The sexiest job of the 21st century. HBR.org. Retrieved October 2, 2102 from http://hbr.org/2012/10/data-scientist-the-sexiest-job-of-the-21st-century/

Eagleman, D. (2011). *Incognito: The Secret Lives of the Brain.* New York: Pantheon. *Globe* Staff (2013, April 28). 102 hours in pursuit of Marathon suspects. *The Boston Globe.* Retrieved October 2, 2012 from http://www.bostonglobe.com/metro/2013/04/28/bombreconstruct/VbSZhzHm35yR88EVmVdbDM/story.html?event = event12

Goleman, D. (1995). *Emotional Intelligence: Why It Can Matter More Than IQ.* New York: Bantam.

Kahneman, D. (2011). *Thinking, Fast and Slow.* New York: Farrar, Straus and Giroux.

Konnikova, M. (2013). *Mastermind: How to Think Like Sherlock Holmes.* New York: Penguin.

Lewis, M. (2004). *Moneyball: The Art of Winning an Unfair Game.* New York: W.W. Norton.

Marcus, L., Dorn, B., Ashkenazi, I., Henderson, J., and McNulty, E. (2012). Crisis preparedness and crisis response: The meta-leadership model and method. In D. Kamien (Ed.), *The McGraw-Hill Homeland Security Handbook.* New York: McGraw-Hill.

Merriam-Webster (n.d.). *Merriam-Webster Online Dictionary.* Retrieved September 30, 2013 from http://www.merriam-webster.com/dictionary/

Nadler, R. (2009, July). Handling the hijack: What was I thinking? *Business Insider.* Retrieved on September 30, 2013 from http://www.psychology-today.com/files/attachments/51483/handling-the-hijack.pdf

Prochnick, G. (2012). *Putnam Camp: Sigmund Freud, James Jackson Putnam and the Purpose of American Psychology.* New York: Other Press.

Rock, D. (2008). SCARF: A brain-based model for collaborating with and influencing others. *Neuroleadership Journal,* 1(1): 1–9. Retrieved October 1, 2013 from www.davidrock.net/files/NLJ_SCARFUS.pdf

Rock, D. (2009, Autumn). Managing with the brain in mind. *Strategy+Business.* Retrieved October 1, 2013 from http://www.strategy-business.com/article/09306?gko=5df7f

Rumsfeld, D. (2002, February 12). DoD news briefing: Secretary Rumsfeld and Gen. Myers. US Department of Defense. Retrieved October 1, 2013 from http://www.defense.gov/transcripts/transcript.aspx?transcriptid=2636

Shaughnessy, D. (2005). *Reversing the Curse: Inside the 2004 Boston Red Sox.* New York: Houghton Mifflin.

Waytz, A. and Mason, M. (2013, July–August). Your brain at work: What a new approach to neuroscience can teach us about management. *Harvard Business Review,* 91(7/8): 102–111.

9

INTUITION

The Competitive Differential
for Successful Leaders

SUSAN K. NEELY

American Beverage Association

Contents

9.1 Introduction

Ask the former governor of the seventh largest state, the CEO of the largest independent soft drink manufacturer, or the COO of the nation's largest business advocacy organization if you can be a great leader without using intuition, and the answer is a resounding "No." Although the three leaders use different words to describe intuition and how they use it, all agree that intuition has provided the competitive differential for many of their major successes. Having worked with all of them at some point in my own career in both the public and private sectors, as well as in politics, I can attest to their skilled use of intuition to make decisions. In my own experience running the trade association that represents the $140 billion US-based non-alcoholic beverage industry, I am in complete concurrence with their assessment of the value of intuition to effective leadership.

For all of us, it's not a question of whether data has value and a role in decision making. It does. Our view is that you just cannot rely exclusively on data or you risk missing an opportunity or making a mistake. Far from being a panacea, data constitutes only one factor that should be used in decision making.

Intuition can give you the courage to make a higher-risk choice that in turn pays larger dividends for your organization. Use of your intuition is often the key to finding other factors that provide a more complete picture from which to make a major decision. That same intuition can even mitigate losses that might occur when you follow the data and experts but they prove to be wrong. Although the four of us whose experiences are shared in this chapter would acknowledge that our intuition is not foolproof, we believe intuition is essential to successful management of complex organizations. We all believe that leaders cannot be effective without using their intuition.

9.2 Taking Higher Risks

As a cabinet secretary, six-term member of Congress, and two-term governor of Pennsylvania, Tom Ridge says that his intuition allowed him to take higher risks that yielded greater benefits to his constituents. He argues that leadership by mathematical equation doesn't make a lot of sense, particularly in elected office when that may mean making a decision based exclusively on what is popular in the opinion polls. His intuition helped him stick to his principles, because he could gauge what voters would accept beyond what they were saying in the polls, particularly if a decision were explained properly. As governor, he proposed a major transportation bill to overhaul the state's aging highway system. Everyone on both sides of the aisle agreed on the need to address the problem. However, the point of controversy was how to pay for it. Although even those of his own political party were gravitating toward a $4 billion bond issue as the least contentious means of financing, Ridge thought this approach was a cop-out that would merely pass the burden on to future generations. His gut said that Pennsylvania voters who use the roads would accept a modest per gallon tax increase along with an increase in the fees to register passenger cars. His intuition was right. The transportation bill including the gas tax and registration fee passed with bipartisan support.

Ridge also used this combination of taking a stand on principle and then calling on his intuition to explain his position to voters the first time he ran for governor and faced a Republican primary.

He was serving in Congress and the vote on the assault weapon ban was scheduled to occur the week before the primary. The National Rifle Association has significant influence in Pennsylvania and the poll data among Republican primary voters was unequivocal: a majority did not support a ban on assault weapons. On moral grounds, Ridge disagreed with them. Having served as a staff sergeant in the Vietnam War, he thought anyone who needed to carry that kind of weapon should be in the military. Despite the dire warnings of electoral consequences from his closest advisers, Ridge voted in favor of the ban. Arguably an act of political courage, Ridge said that his intuition told him that because he had served in the US Army, he could explain his vote to his constituents. Ridge was sufficiently persuasive not only to carry the primary, but to go on to win the governorship.

The president and CEO of the 125-year-old Polar Beverage Company, Ralph Crowley, agrees with Ridge that intuition helps you see where there may be opportunity. Domiciled in Worcester, Massachusetts, the Polar Beverage Company was founded by Ralph's great-grandfather and is now the nation's largest independent manufacturer of soft drinks. Crowley says that data tells you about the past, but intuition tells you about the future. One of the most vivid examples in his experience is his decision to invest in a virtually unknown company called Glacéau that invented a brand called **vitamin**water®. Crowley noted that when Glacéau's founder, Darius Bikoff, first talked to him about an investment, the company was only two-thirds the size of Polar Beverages, and less profitable. **vitamin**water® had been around for 10 years, but had not taken off. Based on the data, Crowley was skeptical that Glacéau, and **vitamin**water® had a path for growth. Bikoff, however, was passionate about the brand's prospects and had a compelling vision for where it could go. Crowley himself had made an early bet on the future of flavored seltzer water because he saw consumer tastes trending in that direction, and was producing it in his own company. His gut told him to give Bikoff—and **vitamin**water®—a shot, and he agreed to buy a modest number of shares at $14 each in 2005, doubling down on his investment a year later. This turned out to be the smart bet. Glacéau and its flagship product were purchased in 2007 by The Coca-Cola Company for $330 a share, an amazing total of $4.1 billion.

9.3 Unlocking the Process to a More Complete Picture

Whether governing a state or making a major investment, the experiences of Ridge and Crowley illustrate how intuition can lead to a decision that may involve higher risk, but also yield higher rewards. Likewise, the process of using intuition can lead to a more complete analysis of choices, with data as just one factor that is considered. David Chavern is chief operating officer of the US Chamber of Commerce, the $250 million organization that advocates on behalf of both small businesses and large corporations from around the country. Chavern believes that intuition is the way to measure what cannot be measured. He says that there are only a limited number of things that can actually be quantified, and leaders can be fooled if they try to rely exclusively on data. He likened it to the old tale about the man who lost his watch on one side of the street, but looked for it on the other side. When asked why, the man said, "There's a street light over here, and I can see better." According to Chavern, managers who are too obsessed with data may be clustered around the light, but not looking for the watch where it actually is.

He cites the development of the Chamber's online engagement as an example of how he avoided such a pitfall. The most often used measurement for the success of a website or social media program is how many "eyeballs" they attract, along with duration of visit, click-throughs, and number of "shares" or "likes." The caution, he said, is that the strategies used to capture visitors and build engagement typically involve anger, gossip, sex, or sports. The choice presented to him was whether the US Chamber should strike an angry tone in its online political communications to attract more public participation.

He ultimately rejected the use of such a tone for the Chamber's program. Even though this approach could help achieve the Chamber's objective of building a larger online community to advocate for business, it would undermine the organization's reputation as a leader for the private sector that does not sling rhetorical mud, but actually solves problems. If it advocated in a tone that was too harsh, it would alienate the core of the Chamber's membership and could even prompt some of them to stop paying dues. Ultimately, he determined that having a smaller set of e-advocates was preferable to devaluing the Chamber's brand. Chavern said that leaders should not be dragged around by data, as the data never shows the complete picture.

As a leader of an organization like the US Chamber that is focused on policy and advocacy, I think it is essential, as Chavern says, to seek solutions where the light may not necessarily be shining. The use of intuition can trigger a process that is a more complicated form of analysis than one based exclusively on data. When I was hired in 2005 to run the American Beverage Association, the industry was beginning to face challenges to its "flagship brands" from activist groups. Among those were a collection of prospective plaintiffs who threatened to bring a class action lawsuit against the major manufacturers over the sale of their products in schools with the charge that soft drinks were causing childhood obesity. Legal counsel from both inside and outside the companies assured us that the litigation would eventually fail. However, my board of directors was understandably reluctant to engage in what was sure to be a public battle of some duration. At the same time, no one beyond the activist litigants thought there was any problem with children enjoying a product that had been safely consumed by all ages for more than 100 years.

Rather than focusing solely on the litigation, I started a search for a different path. As a mother myself, my intuition said we should seek advice from parents of schoolchildren to hear firsthand what they thought we should be selling in the school channel. As a result of qualitative and quantitative research, as well as many informal discussions, we learned that parents wanted two things: more limited beverage choices for their younger children, and fewer calories in the choices provided to their high-school-age children. These two insights from one of our most critical consumer segments showed us how to proceed. Ultimately, we entered an agreement with President Bill Clinton's Foundation and the American Heart Association to change what we sell in all elementary, middle, and high schools across the country. Over the course of three school years, we removed our full-calorie soft drinks from all schools. Water, milk, and juice remained, with more lower-calorie and smaller-portion beverage options, such as sports drinks and teas, in high schools only, but subject to portion and calorie caps. In the end, no litigation was ever filed. The industry effort to change the school beverage landscape resulted in a whopping 90 percent reduction in the calories from our products sold in schools. And, the entire initiative continues to be lauded by parents and policymakers throughout the country.

9.4 Intuition Is Not Foolproof

Although all four of us—Ridge, Crowley, Chavern, and I—attest to the value and critical nature of intuition in our leadership styles, we all agree there is no guarantee that every decision will be successful. Ridge cites the example from his days as governor when he tried to interconnect public financing for four new professional sports stadiums to privatization of the state-run liquor stores. The four owners of the Steelers, Pirates, Eagles, and Phillies all had approached him at the same time about public financing to build new stadiums. His intuition had guided him well on how to engage the owners. He gauged their price point, and brought them to the table together to discuss the amount and terms of state support. He knew that as soon as one owner accepted the terms, there would be more pressure on the other three to do the same. Ultimately, all four agreed to accept public financing that was less than a third of the overall cost of the project. Ridge believes that his state funded four venues for less than the Commonwealth of Massachusetts had for just one, the stadium for its New England Patriots.

To cover the state's share of the stadium construction, Ridge thought he saw an opportunity to kill two birds with one stone. The Republicans in the legislature had historically been opposed to privatizing the state-run liquor system. Given the popularity of the plan to build new sports stadiums in Pittsburgh and Philadelphia, Ridge's gut told him that the time was finally right to convince those Republicans to support privatization, and to use the proceeds from the sale to finance the state's share of the stadium deal. Ridge says that privatization was rejected by conservative legislators almost immediately. To this day, Pennsylvania remains one of only two states that still owns its liquor stores. Although Ridge continues to believe that the state system should be sold, he acknowledges that his intuition about what legislators would accept then, or even now, was wrong.

9.5 Mitigating the Negative Consequences

Although intuition is not foolproof, it can mitigate the negative consequences of decisions based more on data than the analysis of trusted advisers or experts. In the mid-1980s, Crowley was approached about investing in a real estate development and country club on Cape Cod. The timing of the project was right, and also fit the criteria that his company had identified for possible investments. The bank that was involved in the proposal gave the green light to proceed. However, because of the discomfort he had with the individual leading the effort, Crowley's intuition kept raising questions about the project's viability. He ultimately was persuaded by the data, as well as advice of others who he respected, to support the development. However, because of his instinctive concerns, he scaled back the size of his company's investment. When the country club project failed, the losses that his company sustained were less significant.

Like Crowley, I have been in situations where I was convinced to move ahead on a course of action in spite of lingering intuitive doubts about its viability, because the data and opinions of people I trusted were leading in that direction. After the American Beverage Association had successfully delivered on its commitment to change the beverage mix sold in schools, the board of directors began discussing other initiatives of similar significance that we could undertake as an industry to demonstrate our ongoing commitment to the health of our consumers. President Barack Obama had been elected in 2008 and shortly after taking office, First Lady Michelle Obama announced her intention to focus her time and energy on the fight against obesity. This confluence of agendas provided an opportunity for the industry to once again show leadership, and I convened a strategy group of my senior staff and experts from the major beverage companies to develop a proposal to support her efforts. Data from the public opinion research with the same parents and others whom we had consulted about schools revealed interest in a program that would label bottles, cans, and vending machines with the word "Go." What made the idea edgy and potentially compelling was that placed next to the word "Go" would be the amount of time necessary to be active physically to burn the number of calories contained in that beverage. There was something about the "Go" campaign that did not feel right to me; however, as a leader, I did not want to discourage unconventional, potentially breakthrough ideas from gestating. The trusted team that was developing the proposal was excited about it, and I allowed it to be presented to the board of directors. The board's conclusion was that the labeling scheme would not produce the desired action. Far from helping consumers think about balancing calories with physical activity, they instead would be confused by the specificity of the amount of required exercise as well as how it related to all of the calories they consumed throughout their day. As a result of my reservations, we had presented the "Go" campaign not as a firm recommendation, but as an option. I wanted to avoid a straight up or down vote that might stall the board's collective thought process. Even though the "Go" campaign was rejected, the discussion around its pros and cons inspired creative thinking and established an imperative for action. The process and leadership of the board led the industry to put a standardized, clearly visible calorie label on the front of every one of its cans, bottles, and packs. This program, "Clear on Calories," was welcomed by consumers and seen as significant by policy leaders. When Mrs. Obama launched her *Let's Move!* initiative in 2010, we were the only sector of the food industry to join her. Intuition tempered the level of both Crowley's and my commitment to an opportunity. Crowley's intuition helped mitigate the fallout from what proved to be the wrong direction. In the case of the beverage association, intuition framed the decision making in a way that led to the best outcome.

Each of the leaders who are featured in this chapter believes that the use of intuition is critical to effective decision making. It is the faculty that allows us to navigate complicated scenarios and find the most successful path for our organizations. Put another way, intuition is the start of a process to a more complicated form of analysis that takes into account a variety of factors, among them data; experience; assessment of individuals' personalities and strengths; marketplace or other external trends; and the opinions of customers, members, or voters.

Governor Ridge's intuition showed how he could advance a more controversial but fiscally responsible way to finance a major overhaul of Pennsylvania's highways. His gut also allowed him to stick with principle on a vote that put him in the crosshairs of a powerful advocacy group. Crowley's intuitive read of another leader gave him the confidence to ignore the data and make a high-risk investment that yielded extraordinarily high returns. Chavern used his intuition to trigger a more comprehensive analysis that involved factors far beyond the data. It was a gut feeling that caused the beverage industry to consult parents, not prospective plaintiffs, on what beverages it should sell in schools. The end result for both the US Chamber and the American Beverage Association was more productive than if only data had been used to make the decision.

All four of us acknowledge that there are times when our intuition has not been foolproof. Sometimes intuition puts you ahead of where customers, members, or an electorate may be. Your intuition also may give you a false sense of confidence in a direction. Ridge's intuition was wrong when it told him that the Republican legislature was ready to accept privatization of the state-run liquor system as a means to pay for new stadiums. In Crowley's situation with the investment in a new development, and mine with a novel campaign, we allowed the data and smart advisers to persuade us to proceed. In the end, the negative impact on Crowley's company was reduced because of his nagging doubts that prevented him from a total commitment.

Those who claim that data trumps the gut of a good leader are only looking where the light is shining. Intuition is the competitive differential for successful leaders. Rather than the incremental progress that an exclusive reliance on data may yield, analysis triggered by gut instinct can lead to breakthrough ideas, and ultimately the kind of gains that allow private or public sector organizations to really flourish. The use of intuition in decision making helps leaders find the opportunities that return better, and more powerful, results for their organizations.

10

GIVING VOICE TO INTUITION IN OVERCOMING MORAL DISTRESS

LYNN PASQUERELLA

Mount Holyoke College

CAROLINE S. CLAUSS-EHLERS

Rutgers, The State University of New Jersey

Contents

10.1 Introduction

The term "moral distress" was coined in 1984 by philosopher Andy Jameton (1984, 1992, 1993) within the context of nursing ethics. Moral distress refers to situations in which institutional and organizational cultures coerce individuals into acting in ways that go against their ethical principles. Within the literature, the concept of moral distress has been conceptualized as the situation individuals face when they make "moral judgments about the right course of action to take in a situation, and they are unable to carry it out" (McCarthy and Deady, 2008, p. 254). Alternatively, the individual may decide to pursue the course of action he or she knows is wrong (McCarthy and Deady). Judgments "about the rightness or wrongness of an action may be understood as evaluating an action from the perspective of a particular set of moral values" (McCarthy and Deady, p. 254). The literature has discussed choices made in circumstances of moral distress as being influenced by

131

individual characteristics (e.g., poor decision making) or institutional realities (e.g., lack of resources). Since Jameton's (1984) description of the concept of moral distress, the phenomenon has been applied to a variety of organizations and institutions, including higher education.

Some of the most frequent instances of moral distress in academia occur when a college or university's written or unwritten policies and practices go against what a decision maker believes is in the best interest of the individual and promotes justice. In such instances, the question becomes how much individual injustice should be countenanced for the sake of long-term organizational reform. This chapter discusses the role of intuition in ethical decision making in academia through analyzing cases that appeal to intuition as applied to exercising leadership that upends existing institutional practices. This discussion concludes with strategies to promote the use of intuition in overcoming moral distress situations on campus. Suggestions for future research are also provided.

Ethics, in its most general sense, is the study of the correct conduct—an examination of those actions that are right and those that are wrong (McCarthy and Deady, 2008). Right actions are those done in accordance with certain moral principles. Wrong actions are those that violate these same principles (Starkey, 2006). Thus, the major challenge for moral theorists is to determine what principles are the correct ones to guide behavior. This is the task of normative ethics: the attempt to arrive at and defend certain norms, standards, and principles such that any act done in accordance with these is correct and any act going against them is incorrect.

There are two broad categories of normative ethical theories: deontological and teleological, or consequentialist (Akaah, 1997). The difference between these two types of theories can be seen in how they respond to the question, "Are there certain actions that are right or wrong regardless of the consequences, or, is the rightness and wrongness of acts wholly dependent upon the consequences?" For deontologists, the correctness of actions can be determined independently of their consequences. Instead, actions are considered correct if and only if they are done out of a sense of duty to certain principles. In contrast, teleological ethical theories are based on the notion that the rightness and wrongness of acts is wholly dependent upon their consequences. The most common form of teleological ethics is utilitarianism, whereby the rightness and wrongness of acts rests on whether they promote the greatest good, or the least amount of bad, for the greatest number of people (or for everyone involved).

Ethical dilemmas, by their very nature, are such that no matter what course of action one takes, some ethical principle or norm will be violated (Clegg, Kornberger, and Rhodes, 2007). Whether a decision maker appeals to deontological or teleological principles in attempts to resolve an ethical dilemma, the result may be contradictory conclusions, depending on the nature of the dilemma. Some of the most challenging dilemmas arise when deontological principles that dictate a duty to justice and fairness conflict with teleological principles that take into account the likelihood of lasting reform of the organizational culture through the sacrifice of individual rights. The following paragraphs provide examples of how such dilemmas might play out on college campuses.

10.2 Examples from Higher Education

Consider, for instance, the case of the student whose financial circumstances have changed dramatically since entering college.[*] She has one major course left to complete to fulfill her graduation requirements and is a semester away from graduation. She has used the maximum financial aid for which she is eligible, but can meet the requirement through an online course at another institution. The chair of the department of which she is a member refuses to waive the rule that all required courses for the major be taken on campus. Without this option, the student is unlikely to finish. Although the college is committed to enhancing its retention and graduation rates, the academic appeals committee is unwilling to overturn the decision of the department chair regarding the integrity of the program. Both the dean and the president are approached by the student for help in resolving the matter.

In this case, even if the dean and the president believe that principles of justice and fairness, respect, and dignity are being violated by not allowing the student to take an online course, there may be broader consequences to consider. Suppose, for example, that the decision takes place within the context of a culture that has struggled to demonstrate

---

[*] Identifying information has been changed and/or omitted to protect confidentiality.

practices of shared governance. Overturning a chairperson's decision with respect to the requirements for an academic program may not only have an impact on morale by undermining leadership at the departmental level, it may have a ripple effect with respect to perceptions of top-down administration. Yet, college officers have fiduciary responsibilities that extend beyond those of the department chair. Although faculty and staff have a shared responsibility for the retention of students, the chair is not accountable to the Board of Trustees for graduation rates or student success in the same way as the administrators.

In wrestling with dilemmas such as these, the course of action administrators take often relies on moral intuition (Rooney, 2009). Although moral intuitions are, by definition, noninferential, this does not preclude their being informed by experience. Chassy and Gobet (2011) review defining characteristics that reflect theoretical approaches to intuition. These include: "rapid perception and understanding of the situation at hand, lack of awareness of the processes involved, holistic understanding of the problem situation, the fact that experts' decisions are better than novices' even when they are made without analytical means, and concomitant presence of emotional ['coloring']" (p. 199).

Recent research has shown that decision making is often made in alignment with emotional values (Chassy and Gobet, 2011). Emotions influence cognitive processes that, in turn, influence intuition. The research contends that emotional values draw the individual to the cognitive chunks deemed most relevant in a problem situation. The process that connects emotional values to specific cognitive thoughts thus directs the decision maker to specific problem-solving strategies (Bechara et al., 1996; Chassy and Gobet, 2011). The individual's intuition acknowledges that the problem-solving strategy he or she is led to through this process is the right action to take.

The case where an administrator is convinced that the chair's decision should be overruled is one such example. Here the decision may result from an intuition arising from a deep and abiding commitment to the principle that the institution's primary goal is to educate students to provide them with opportunities necessary to meet the nation's historic mission of promoting participatory democracy. The administrator may have learned from addressing similar types of cases, that when upholding the institution's rules or standards comes into conflict with serving the best interest of the student, if there is no fault on the part of the student and the harm to the institution's principles would be minimal, it is warranted to override a judgment that goes against the student's interest.

Of course, assessing the level of harm due to bending the rules is the sticking point. Indeed, this dilemma raises the question of whether the harm that occurs to a segment of the institution through the reversal of a policy or practice violates fundamental principles or is simply a way of carrying out principles that could be achieved through other means. Yet, even if there is no other means of protecting principles, such as departmental autonomy that would speak in favor of conformity with the rule, in the end, the harm that would follow might be overridden. Thus, the administrator's appeal to moral intuition in going against the department chair's ruling can be grounded in the principle that, under these specific circumstances, an individual human being's educational success is worth more than any particular rule or uniformity with respect to that rule.

Still, despite the administrative decision maker having a moral intuition that the student should be accommodated, institutional and organizational factors may prevent the implementation of that decision. This is where moral distress arises (Kälvemark et al., 2004). Moral distress is different from the anxiety that comes from simply facing an ethical dilemma. It is the continual overriding of what one regards as the correct moral principles that leads to moral distress. For instance, we often hear as a justification for denying appeals by students with unique circumstances that if we allow an exception in one case, then a dangerous precedent will be set. This response fails to take into account that slippery slope arguments are notoriously weak in assuming that we have no control once we start down a particular path.

Decision makers are capable of discerning circumstances that distinguish one case from another and can act on these distinctions. Yet, undermining the authority of those who believe that rules must be followed at all costs, otherwise the flood gates will be opened, can take a toll on morale. It can also hamper the ability of a leader to achieve lasting reform through a shared commitment to certain institutional objectives such as students getting an education. The dynamic at play is reflected in recent research that suggests moral distress occurs not only as a result of institutional constraints, but also on an individual level where the individual follows his or her moral decision and is confronted with backlash from policies or legal regulations

(Kälvemark et al., 2004). These studies suggest that increasingly, moral distress needs to be understood within the context of ethical decision making (Kälvemark et al., 2004). Giving voice to intuition invites an exploration of specific environmental variables that influence the status of the situation from which moral distress arises.

Suppose, for instance, that the dean disagrees with the ruling of the faculty member in refusing to accommodate the student's desire to take an online course to be able to continue working, and thus pay for her education. Nevertheless, she feels compelled to go against her intuition that the decision should be countered because she considers having department chairs who feel empowered, valued, and respected is critical. Her actions are constrained by an organizational and institutional culture that reflects values she does not share. At the same time, she recognizes that in the long run, she might be able to accomplish cultural reform by gaining the trust of her colleagues.

If the chairs rally around reviewing and revising policies that would prevent these types of cases from occurring in the future, consequentialist or teleological principles could lead one to the conclusion that team morale takes precedence over the educational needs of one student. After all, many other students will be helped by a policy change, a change that could be preempted if the focus is on resistance to change that intends to send a message to the dean from those who feel professionally undermined. The dean's moral distress results from the fact that, in the end, her intuition tells her she should act to protect the student, but she does not feel empowered to do what she believes is ethically correct. Here the context of the moral distress situation occurs within a system of policies and practices that counter the dean's moral choice and the intuitive processes that led her to it. Moral distress is given voice while moral intuition is silenced.

10.3 Campus Strategies and Directions for Future Research

Given that administrators are enjoined to make ethical decisions with the full understanding that no one has a lock on moral rectitude, what are the ways in which moral intuition can be informed and moral distress curtailed? Although moral distress can occur in any institutional setting, there are some approaches we can take to overcome it.

1. *Train people to identify moral dilemmas as the source of their distress.* The nursing profession provides a model of training that focuses on awareness of moral dilemmas and how they contribute to distress. Research highlights the complexity of moral distress within the healthcare system. It was found, for instance, that staff across disciplines often followed their moral intuition only to experience moral distress when their moral choice went against organizational regulations (Kälvemark et al., 2004). Providing access to ethics training in higher education settings is a strategy that promotes learning how to navigate these types of complexities (Kälvemark et al., 2004). Training can include opportunities to discuss case studies or forums where the resolution of moral distress situations are explored. This type of training can "help professionals to understand better their own process of ethical decision-making and create a greater readiness for related situations" (Kälvemark et al., 2004, p. 1083).

2. *Establish forums such as ethics committees to make sure that ethical dilemmas and their resolution continue to be at the forefront of public discussion and private debate.* Having a campus ethics committee contributes to an infrastructure that acknowledges and supports the importance of ethical practice. An ethics committee can also provide training through seminars about moral distress situations that may arise in different aspects of campus life such as student well-being, education financing, educational access, grading, research, and campus housing, among others.

3. *Inventory the obstacles within one's institutions that might prevent people from coming forward with dilemmas, and implement policies and practices that reward voicing concern.* A survey can provide insight about the fears campus constituencies have with reference to expressing ethical concerns. Identifying these perceived threats provides campus leadership an opportunity to encourage voicing moral intuition when confronted with moral distress.

4. *Create a culture where people are expected to do the right thing, so that individuals do not feel at risk by raising ethical issues.* Clegg, Kornberger, and Rhodes (2007) critique how ethics can be broken down by organizations into rules and administrative protocol. In their approach, Clegg, Kornberger, and Rhodes (2007) look at ethical decision making in organizations

as being "non-rule based," or, as they state, "an ethics that involves freedom" (p. 394). Campus leadership can model a commitment to a culture where ethical decision making is considered an opportunity to express freedom and democracy.

5. *Gain the support of superiors.* When an organizational culture has become so well formulated that it overrides a written code of ethics, strong leadership is required to achieve reform and provide a model of change.

6. *Assess the support of staff to nurture and cultivate reform.* As mentioned, research on moral distress in the healthcare system indicates that it occurs among staff at all levels. Similarly, it is important to explore the impact of moral distress situations across campus constituencies (e.g., students, faculty, staff, administrators, alumni, board of trustee members, parents, and the surrounding community). Implementing a survey to assess impact, as mentioned in the third strategy, gives voice to each of these campus partners.

7. *Develop a long-range plan based on role modeling.* Through the aforementioned strategies, higher education leaders can serve as role models that encourage ongoing discussion and deliberation about complex ethical issues. Leaders from different institutions can meet regularly to discuss how their respective leadership styles influence this change.

8. *Develop a sense of self that allows for clear role definition and the understanding that the professional roles we play are just one facet of our lives.* It is important that higher education leaders seek to make institutional decisions that uphold the values of the organization. Having other facets of life allows the leader to experience a sense of value in different ways. As such, the hope is that decisions will be based on an intention to pursue the best interest of the institution, even if leadership backlash is the result. Because the leader has other areas of life that support him or her, there is less risk that a decision will be made to bolster a sense of worth or popularity at the expense of the institution and its values (Horrigan, 2011).

These strategies suggest several areas for research focused on voicing intuition in campus moral distress situations. Recommendations for future investigation are largely based upon research conducted in the healthcare setting that is relevant for higher education practice. Higher education has gone through, and continues to experience, great change. Research can explore the nature of moral distress in higher education settings and the processes used to cope with this experience (Kälvemark et al., 2004; Musto and Shreiber, 2012). Are there themes associated with moral distress in higher education? If so, what is their impact on campus stakeholders? What are the connections between campus moral distress and retention among constituencies? How does having a positive ethical climate promote retention (Bell and Breslin, 2008)? These are but a few directions for future research.

10.4 Conclusion

The higher education realm is changing rapidly. Stakeholders across campuses face increasingly complex instances of moral distress. Campus dynamics, a lack of institutional resources, and even administrative policies may confound the individual's ability to engage in decision making that reflects his or her moral choice. Acknowledging and supporting the use of intuition is one over-all strategy when confronted with such situations. This process can be encouraged by efforts to train individuals to identify the nature and source of their moral distress, establish an infrastructure that promotes discussion of ethical practice, create an environment that supports ethical decision making, garner support for institutional reform from superiors and colleagues, and have a clear sense of self that does not depend upon the institution as the sole source of self-worth and sense of value. Through a combination of these efforts we seek to give voice to intuition and bring transformation to campus life.

References

Akaah, I.P. (1997). Influence of deontological and teleological factors on research ethics evaluations. *Journal of Business Research*, 39(2): 71–80.

Bechara, A., Tranel, D., Damasio, H., and Damasio, A.R. (1996). Failure to respond autonomically to anticipated future outcomes following damage to prefrontal cortex. *Cerebral Cortex*, 6: 215–225.

Bell, J. and Breslin, J.M. (2008). Healthcare provider moral distress as a leadership challenge. *JONA'S Healthcare Law, Ethics, and Regulation*, 10(4): 94–97.

Chassy, P. and Gobet, F. (2011). A hypothesis about the biological basis of expert intuition. *Review of General Psychology*, 15(3): 198–212.

Clegg, S., Kornberger, M., and Rhodes, C. (2007). Organizational ethics, decision-making, undecidability. *The Sociological Review*, 55(2): 393–409.

Horrigan, J. (2011, February 18). SUNY New Paltz candidate: Leaders need not be loved. *Times Herald-Record*. Retrieved from http://www.recordonline.com/apps/pbcs.dll/article?AID =/20110218/NEWS/102180368/-1/rss01

Jameton, A. (1984). *Nursing practice: The ethical issues*. London: Prentice-Hall.

Jameton, A. (1992). Nursing ethics and the moral situation of the nurse. In E. Friedman (Ed.), *Choices and conflict*, pp.101–109. Chicago: American Hospital Association.

Jameton, A. (1993). Dilemmas of moral distress: Moral responsibility and nursing practice. *AWHONN'S Clinical Issues*, 4(4): 542–551.

Kälvemark, S., Höglund, A.T., Hansson, M.G., Westerholm, P., and Arnetz, B. (2004). Living with conflicts—ethical dilemmas and moral distress in the health care system. *Social Science & Medicine*, 58: 1075–1084

McCarthy, J. and Deady, R. (2008). Moral distress reconsidered. *Nursing Ethics*, 15(2): 254–262.

Musto, L. and Shreiber, R.S. (2012). Doing the best I can: Moral distress in adolescent mental health nursing. *Issues in Mental Health Nursing*, 33: 137–144.

Rooney, C. (2009). The meaning of mental health nurses experience of providing one-to-one observations: A phenomenological study. *Journal of Psychiatric and Mental Health Nursing*, 16: 76–86.

Starkey, C. (2006). On the category of moral perception. *Social Theory and Practice*, 32(1): 75–96.

11

ACTIVELY LISTENING TO BETTER RESPOND TO HEALTH AND DEVELOPMENT NEEDS

TARA M. SULLIVAN

Johns Hopkins Bloomberg School of Public Health
Center for Communication Programs

Contents

11.1 Introduction

Working in low- and middle-income settings such as sub-Saharan Africa and Southeast Asia brings unique challenges not readily solved by data alone: resources are scarce, infrastructure can be weak, and systems and cultural practices are unique. Consequently, I relied on intuition and lessons learned from my experience and some failures as a Peace Corps volunteer in sub-Saharan Africa in order to forge a more fruitful work experience five years later on the Thailand–Burma border in Southeast Asia. Among the many lessons I learned in the Peace Corps was the value of using intuition and active listening to understand better the needs and context of the people with whom I worked. The concept of "Big Data" does not easily translate into action in community-based cross-cultural settings. In these settings, observation and dialogue are often more effective methods for collecting data points to inform decision making and subsequent action.

11.2 Sub-Saharan Africa: Budding Intuition

Serving as a Peace Corps volunteer (PCV) was a dream of mine. As an undergraduate, I studied anthropology and yearned to travel the world and make a difference. Full of passion and conviction, but little experience, I was delighted when I was offered a position as an environmental education volunteer in Botswana. Peace Corps marked my first experience abroad. However, as volunteers, we were thoroughly trained before we went to our posts. We were taught Setswana, we received technical training for our jobs, and we were introduced to local customs. For example, we were taught to shake hands with our right hand while the left hand clasped the right elbow and how to address our elders respectfully. In short, we received basic competency to do our jobs.

The pinnacle of Peace Corps training is the "home stay," in which volunteers are placed alone or in pairs with a host family for several months. The goal is for volunteers to gain a better understanding of the culture and to practice the local language. My roommate and I stayed with a single mother who had three beautiful young children. Chickens grazed in the yard by day, and roaches flew across the walls by night as we took our bucket baths by candlelight. Our host mother quickly realized that the name we used for cockroach was "gross." We rapidly learned about and tested popular foods such as pap (thick sorghum) and morogo (leafy greens) but not seswa (stewed meat) because we were both vegetarians. As environmental education volunteers, our training extended to a trip into the Kalahari desert where we investigated hornbill nests, termite mounds, birds, animal tracks and dung, and different species of acacia trees.

Armed with these basics, I embarked on my volunteer assignment as an assistant game warden at the Department of Wildlife and National Parks (DWNP). I worked under the game warden and with other DWNP officers at a small game reserve stocked with ostriches, rhinos, warthogs, zebras, a variety of antelopes, and towering termite mounds. The assignment was both daunting and exciting: to engage members of DWNP to enrich an existing environmental education program.

Some describe intuition as much more than just a "gut feeling." Rather, intuition is the culmination of many years (and data points) of experience that allow us to develop heuristics or rules of thumb that we apply unconsciously and instantaneously to make decisions. As a young professional, you might say that my intuition was "under-developed," although all of my preparation up to the point of being sworn in as a volunteer had taught me several rules of thumb:

- Respect local knowledge and experience
- Build mutual trust
- Actively listen and observe
- Go slow
- Use a participatory approach

Initially, I heeded my inner voice, accepting the slow pace of government work. Together we taught busload after busload of schoolchildren about why male ostriches dance (mating) and why termites take flight at night (mating again). We coordinated workshops training primary school teachers how to incorporate environmental education into the curriculum. We even worked with a local production company to develop an environmental education video, writing the script, casting schoolchildren, and even acting out key lessons in front of the rhinoceros paddock.

All went well for the most part, but at certain points I became impatient with the process, got ambitious, and moved ahead by myself. World Environment Day (WED) was one such time; it marked both a high and low point for me. On the surface, it was a great success: for the first time ever, the country held a nationwide event. However, I lost sight of my rules of thumb and acted alone instead of with the team. I chaired the WED General Committee and National Essay Contest Sub-Committee, raised funds, and recruited numerous organizations to plan WED events, including a national essay contest, national cleanup day, environmental fair, panel discussions, radio shows, and nature walks. In the planning phases of the event, I worked with other organizations, including my counter-parts in some of the meetings, but also moved ahead without them. I pushed my agenda forward and was the prominent representative from the DWNP. As a result, although the event was by all accounts a success, at the end of that day there was no triumphant rallying cry of, "We did it!" None of my teammates said anything directly, how-ever, I knew I had acted more or less alone, and it had come at a cost.

Immediately following WED, I walked alone to the game reserve and worked alone for much of the coming week. I realized that I had inadvertently alienated my coworkers. I needed to make amends to re-establish trust. So, I went back to my rules of thumb. I slowed down, I listened, I observed, and I slowly built back trust.

11.3 Southeast Asia: Using Intuition[*]

I left Peace Corps with many fond memories, but I had a lasting sense that I could have done better. So, when I embarked on a second long-term overseas assignment five years later, I vowed to stay true to my rules of thumb. My assignment in Southeast Asia was quite different: to work with a clinic on the Thailand–Burma border to strengthen the capacity to monitor and evaluate programs and to help improve the quality of reproductive health care. As part of the assignment, I gathered and analyzed all types of data: both routine data on family planning visits; antenatal visits; postnatal visits; number of deliveries; and data on patient knowledge, attitudes, behaviors, and satisfaction with the services they received. Although these data helped set priorities and assess quality at the clinic, it was intuition that guided my day-to-day work.

The clinic plays a unique and crucial role in the community. For many, the clinic is a place not only where community members can receive affordable healthcare (most services are free), but, more important, it is a health setting where they were treated with respect and spoken to in their own language. Clients often travel from Burma and distant areas in Thailand to seek healthcare services at the clinic despite security problems and other barriers. Because of the quality and array of services provided at the clinic, it has a lead role in offering healthcare services to this community.

It was called a clinic based on its modest beginning, however, the facility was really more like a small hospital. Serving a catchment area of approximately 150,000 people, the clinic had an inpatient department, outpatient department, reproductive health department, child health department, eye clinic, surgery and prosthetics for landmine

---

[*] This section draws from Sullivan, T. M., Maung, C., and Sophia, N. (2004). Using evidence to improve reproductive health quality along the Thailand-Burma border. *Disasters*, 28(3), 255-268.

survivors, and training programs. At the time, the staff included 5 doctors, 80 healthcare workers, 40 trainees, and 40 support staff. The clinic had very basic equipment and amenities. The staff provided the best care possible with limited resources. For example, women gave birth on raised wooden beds in a bright and airy room.

Safety and trust were big issues among clients. Most people who sought care at the clinic were unrecognized refugees, internally displaced people from Burma, or migrant workers. Migrant workers who accessed services at the clinic live illegally in Thailand. Without proper documentation, these people feared fines, arrest, and possible deportation from Thailand. People often crossed the border to receive services at the clinic due to lack of health facilities and outreach services, low quality of care, and high prices in Burma. Health workers continuously patrolled the border of the clinic grounds to keep the health workers and the patients secure. An added complication on the border was the sheer number of nongovernmental organizations (NGOs) and international nongovernmental organizations (INGOs) seeking to assist in a variety of ways, but with their own health and human rights agendas that did not necessarily coincide with what the local ethnic groups needed or wanted.

The head of the clinic during my tenure there was an amazing doctor from Burma who viewed her work through the lens of health and human rights. When she taught, she set a tone of mutual respect from the outset by saying, "I look forward to how we can learn from each other." She carried this tone of respect with her as she talked with patients at the clinic, looking beyond the disease to see the whole person who is part of a family and community. Although I had come to the situation with a clear scope of work, it was equally clear that the local team, reflecting the tone set by the clinic director, was eager to work as a team and learn together. With that in mind, I tried to stay true to my intuition: actively listening, observing, and playing a supporting role behind the scenes.

While I was at the clinic, there were many tasks to accomplish. Together we worked on improving the quality of care in reproductive health (RH). We conducted participatory evaluation activities to improve quality of services including baseline and follow-up assessments, intervention activities, and other quality assurance methodologies. The clinic director, my counterpart (who was the head of the RH department), and I taught the reproductive health team to use evidence for decision making, document program results, and present findings in papers and conference presentations. We also co-taught monitoring and evaluation, survey design and implementation, data analysis and interpretation, and results presentation courses to other departments to strengthen capacity clinicwide. With newly secured funds to improve emergency obstetric care services, the team designed a new inpatient facility, purchased emergency obstetric equipment, developed management and supervisory systems, and implemented training programs.

At the clinic, we used a participatory approach to strengthen the clinic's monitoring and evaluation capacity. Together, we created an evaluation design, objectives, indicators, and instruments to measure quality. I worked closely with the head of the RH department, an extremely intelligent woman who facilitated the process and explained the technical concepts to the team in the local language. Although the project was meant for one department, the clinic director decided that it was important to build the capacity across the senior-level providers at the clinic. This senior team took part in all aspects of the evaluation: data collection, data entry, data analysis, and data dissemination. This team further took ownership of the process by presenting the results to the entire RH team to determine how the data could inform future training and implementation. For example, the team found weaknesses in the area of infection prevention and subsequently arranged training to improve infection prevention techniques.

Using a participatory approach to monitor and evaluate reproductive healthcare quality was important for the success and sustainability of the program. The RH team initially viewed evaluating the quality of reproductive health services as a threat. However, by including the entire reproductive health staff in the process, the RH team was able to identify those areas they wanted to measure. Because the RH team was in charge of the process, they were invested in gathering information on their strengths and areas for improvement, and they were motivated to use the results to make positive changes.

The program was fairly successful, but there were some bumps in the road. Monitoring and evaluation concepts were new for the team. So although the team was well versed in clinical areas such as antenatal care, postnatal care, family planning, and delivery, monitoring and evaluation terms and concepts were not easily translated into the local language. Teaching and training about monitoring and evaluation were quite time consuming. So, although the new skills ultimately served the reproductive health team, in the short term, they drew important resources away from provision of health services to clients.

By using a participatory approach driven by the local team, we achieved great results with lasting benefits. When I left the clinic, the reproductive health team planned to continue to hone their skills in monitoring and evaluation and to use data to inform decision making. The RH team also planned to continue weekly quality assurance meetings to assess quality of services and use checklists for multiple areas including antenatal care, family planning, delivery, postabortion care, and neonatal care.

Through these two different experiences, I learned a lot about the value of using my intuition. In both cases quantitative data were available to guide the work at hand but intuition was my compass for daily interactions. In Botswana, I did not pay attention to my budding intuition and I paid the price: I let myself down and disappointed the DWNP team. On the Thailand–Burma border, I was truer to my intuition and had a much more satisfying and successful experience. Today, intuition and active listening continue to play an important role in my work on the Knowledge for Health (www.k4health.org) project where our vision is a world where healthcare workers and program managers have the knowledge they need to feel empowered, respected, valued, and trusted in their daily work. By using intuition, active listening, and participatory approaches, complemented by data, I believe we can attain this vision.

12

INTUITIVE AND ANALYTICAL
DECISION MAKING

DONALD S. ORKAND

DC Ventures and Associates, LLC

Contents

12.1 Introduction

W. Edwards Deming (1950) in the preface to his historic book on statistical sampling theory noted that "The intuition, like the conscience, must be trained." This chapter argues that intuitive decision making can be improved if the decision maker has some knowledge and appreciation of analytical methods, and that this is true despite the fact that critical senior-level decisions must often be made without explicit quantitative models or relevant data.

We are often faced with the need to rely on intuition and experience, and rigorous analytical thinking can help in formulating the decision questions and issues. It also helps avoid fads and fallacies and points the way to future data collection efforts. Examples include business planning, merger and acquisition decisions, operational modeling, and estate planning. A final section discusses, at more length, a bid decision at a critical stage in the growth of a company the author headed.

12.2 Some Examples

12.2.1 Business Planning

Far too many business plans begin by defining a large market (for which there is a mass of substantiating data), extolling the virtues of their new product or technology (which depending on the year is either a paradigm shift or a disruptive application), and declaring that this will enable the business to capture a significant share of the large market. Such plans can be characterized harshly but accurately as suicide notes, not business plans. What are the fallacies here and how could some analytical thinking correct them?

First, that superficial mode of planning ignores the likelihood of competitive response, an issue that is appropriately identified and highlighted in even a rudimentary exposition of game theory. Competitors can respond in myriad ways including accelerating the introduction of a newer technology, acquiring a startup that owns a more advanced product, lowering prices, intensifying the efforts of a marketing force that is already in place, or claiming patent infringement, real or bogus. Raising the issue of possible competitive responses should trigger some serious analytical thinking about potential threats and countermeasures from other firms in the market.

The analysis of possible competitive responses can begin with an assessment of their current strengths and weaknesses including products, marketing force, R&D efforts, and other factors. Information about these factors can usually be obtained from industry sources and public documents. The more difficult question is assessing the actions competitors might take in responding to a new challenge. Here the analysis becomes far more judgmental and intuitive and may, out of necessity, rely more on speculation about corporate directions and leadership. (The reader who is familiar with military threat analysis will recognize the above as the capabilities and intentions components.) In any case, the most dangerous assumption is that competitors will stand idly by while another firm takes market share from them.

Second, business plans are often based on the mindless extrapolation of past trends, particularly when those trends are positive. Past growth is extrapolated not only into the future but also the hereafter. The projection of ever-increasing housing prices to justify home equity loans, and the resulting financial damage, is another example.

Serious efforts at statistical forecasting should take account of the difficulty of identifying inflection points and limits as well as the possibility of low probability outcomes with enormous consequences. The black swan may be hovering overhead (Taleb, 2007).

Finally, business plans often ignore the possibility that things may go wrong. Every business plan should address the questions of what can go wrong, how will we know it has gone wrong, and what will we do then or earlier to avoid or fix the problem. Technology may take longer to develop, a key business partner may go bankrupt, or a star employee may leave during a critical project phase.

The analytical reader will recognize that this simply means that we live in a world of probabilities, not certainties and plans; schedules and budgets should reflect that reality. It is quite true that the above issues may seem obvious from both intuitive and analytical perspectives, but how often are they addressed in business plans? Even in formal securities offerings a long list of risk factors is included (primarily for legal reasons) but the second and third issues are ignored.

12.2.2 Mergers and Acquisitions (M&A)

During any period of intense M&A activity there is a tendency for rational analysis to be ignored. Intuitive reasoning can be biased by exuberance and by the fact that an acquisition can appear to offer an easier route to increased revenues and earnings than the hard work needed to achieve organic growth.

In that environment, the term "synergy" comes into vogue as a justification for risky or overpriced acquisitions. Synergy is often defined as the whole being greater than the sum of its parts; that is, $2 + 2 = 5$. Systematic analysis, however, might well show that the whole might be equal to considerably less than the sum of the parts, as many companies have discovered during the integration phase that follows an acquisition. Cultural differences, diversion of management attention, systems incompatibilities, and many other factors make it difficult to get back to 2 + 2 = 4, to say nothing of any positive effect.

The author was once faced with a proposed acquisition in which the pro forma profit and loss (P&L) statement included a projected profit increase of several million dollars due to "unspecified synergistic" effects. Clearly, this is an instance in which a comprehensive and rigorous analysis is required to inform and discipline the intuition. Such an analysis would, at a minimum, look at the specific benefits that might be realized, discounted appropriately, and offset by the costs and risks of achieving them. The analysis should be quantitative to the degree possible but comprehensive in identifying even the variables that cannot be quantified precisely.

Another issue in the mergers and acquisition arena is the pricing or valuation of the company from the perspectives of both the buyer and seller. In a common but flawed strategy, the buyer may decide to offer a low-ball price whereas the seller may ask for an inflated price. In his brilliant work, Daniel Kahneman (2011) notes that "Because negotiators are influenced by a norm of reciprocity, a concession that is presented as painful calls for an equally painful (and perhaps equally inauthentic) concession from the other side." An effective countermeasure to these tactics is to prepare for negotiations with a realistic analytic evaluation of the market and company and then simply walk away from an unrealistic offer so that it does not become a reference point in the negotiations. (The same applies, of course, in buying or selling a house and in other negotiations.)

12.2.3 Operational Modeling

Other examples in this chapter deal with cases in which the decision process is improved by blending intuitive and analytical thinking. This example is one in which the problem was clearly defined and all of the data were available to calculate an optimal solution. It was a fairly early application of the linear programming model to business problems.

The author (Orkand, 1957) was part of a team assigned to work on a purchasing and shipping problem dealing with the purchase of raw materials from five suppliers to supply 25 manufacturing locations. The objective was to minimize purchasing and shipping costs subject to the constraint that each supplier be allocated a fixed proportion of the business.

The problem was solved using the transportation method and minimizing total cost subject to the constraints of meeting the requirements of each manufacturing location while maintaining the desired allocation of business among the five suppliers.

The IBM 650 computer, featuring vacuum tubes and punch card input, was used to compute the solution which, although state of the art at the time, limited the range of alternatives that could be considered.

The solution was counterintuitive to some of the purchasing executives who identified apparently inefficient purchase/shipping combinations. We convinced them of the validity of our solution by inviting them to change any of the individual combinations that appeared incorrect and then change other combinations as required to meet the constraints. The consequence, of course, was an increase in total cost. As a result, the recommendations and linear programming model were implemented successfully.

Because this problem was relatively low level and well defined with all relevant data available, the purely analytical solution yielded better results than an intuitive or judgmental approach. The role of management judgment in this instance was the setting of the allocation percentages that constrained the solution. We could have done more to inform those judgments by calculating the total cost of an unconstrained solution or one based on more flexible constraints, that is, by performing a sensitivity analysis. Although conceptually simple, that step was precluded by limited computer time and capability.

12.2.4 Estate Planning

This example is taken from a very different domain than the preceding cases. The purpose is to show that sloppiness in formulating a decision or action issue can lead to serious and unfortunate consequences. Anyone who has worked with developing analytical models or systems is aware of this danger but it is, nonetheless, difficult to avoid.

In this instance, the author was afforded the dubious pleasure of listening to an estate planning presentation that began with "If, God forbid, you should die...". Two things are wrong about that opening: First, "God forbid" implies some link between estate planning and the religious belief in the possibility of life after death. That belief is shared by many and should be respected. The tax code and estate law admit to no such possibility; however, the legal and tax clocks start ticking when you are pronounced dead. Second, the phrase "if you should die" implies that there is a question about whether that event will occur. In fact, the only question is when it will occur.

The only formulation that is useful as a guide to decision making and action is, "when you die." The initial formulation encourages inaction and leads to one of the most common errors in estate planning, dying without a will or with an outdated will that no longer reflects your wishes. Hence, although the initial formulation sounds softer and kinder it may well work to the detriment of those whose inheritance is left to the tender mercies of the tax authorities and courts. The second formulation may sound harsh but is kinder in reality because it leads to necessary and timely action.

The takeaway in this and in other instances is that analytical discipline need not be complex or quantitative to be useful. Straightforward but rigorous critical thought will often yield substantial improvements in decisions and action in situations where emotions and intuition may lead the decision maker astray.

12.3 Case Study: A Critical Bid Decision

12.3.1 Decision Issue

The author was the founder of an information technology company where he served as CEO for 34 years. In the early years of the company's growth, our major client was a government agency. Several other contractors, some large, worked for the same agency performing similar work. For reasons of its own, the agency decided to combine all of the work into one contract. It was assumed that one of the larger firms would serve as the prime contractor with the other contractors relegated to the role of subcontractors. A larger firm that planned to bid as prime contractor offered us the chance to join them as a sub with the inducement of allocating a percentage of the award to us.

The implicit threat, later made explicit, was that if we did not sign on with them they would ensure that we would receive no work should they win. Because they were considered the leading contender, the threat was not a trivial one.

At first glance, the analysis of alternatives seemed simple, if not particularly pleasant. We could sign on as a subcontractor and be guaranteed a portion of the work with higher probability. Alternatively, we could bid as the prime contractor and go for all of the work but with a lower win probability. As we evaluated the alternatives, the analysis turned out to be far more complex.

Because of the proposal deadline, it was necessary to reach a decision quickly, but the importance of the decision required a serious evaluation of the alternatives. In short, we needed a thoughtful and complete analysis done quickly. Because our management team combined both analytical capabilities and a deep knowledge of the business environment, conducting such an analysis within several days was entirely feasible.

12.3.2 Assessing Win Probabilities

The first step in the analysis was to estimate the probability of winning as a prime contractor and compare it to the win probability of the other bidders with and without us as a subcontractor. We were aware that if we didn't sign on as a subcontractor one or more of the prospective primes would, as a competitive response, recruit other firms to fill the role planned for us. Thus, we needed to assess multiple possible configurations of competitors.

In evaluating our win probability, it was essential to avoid the bias that results from believing that the client perceived our firm as distinctly superior to others, a bias sometimes expressed as "the client loves us." It is a bias that often leads to fatal bid decisions. As a safeguard, we examined the evaluation criteria specified by the government agency and ranked all of the contenders using those criteria. We also set up a red team of individuals not assigned to the current contract to do the same.

Obviously, we had precise and quantifiable information regarding our own wins, losses, and strengths but, of necessity, we had to rely on public information, industry knowledge, and our judgment to complete our assessment of our competitors. When completed we believed we had a reasonable estimate of the probability of a win given, of course, that our proposal would reflect all of our comparative strengths and that the reviewers would follow the stated evaluation criteria.

A by-product of the exercise was the identification of areas where we believed we were stronger than our competitors measured against the evaluation criteria. This formed the basis for the formulation of the winning themes to be presented in our proposal, that is, the features that would differentiate us. The identification and presentation of such themes is essential to developing winning proposals but that aspect of proposal development is outside the scope of this chapter.

12.3.3 *Estimating the Expected Return*

The expected return that results from winning as a prime can be estimated with reasonable accuracy from the levels specified in the government's request for proposals, even though the actual revenue levels may ultimately be modified because of budget constraints or other factors. Thus, we could estimate the revenue that would result from the award of a prime contract simply by multiplying the contract value by the win probability.

In contrast, the estimation of the revenues that we would receive as a subcontractor is not as simple. Earlier, we mentioned that one of the prime contractors had promised us a fixed proportion of the resulting work as an inducement to sign on with them. Such commitments are usually documented in teaming agreements. For a variety of legal and operational reasons, teaming agreements are difficult to enforce and many prime contractors choose to ignore them after the initial year of a multiyear contract.

Thus, the revenue to be received as a subcontractor had to be estimated by using the joint probability of the prime contractor winning the award and then subcontracting the agreed-upon proportion of work. Based on industry experience and our judgments, we discounted our estimates of potential revenue as a sub sharply after the initial contract year, which narrowed the gap between our expected return as a prime contractor and that as a subcontractor even allowing for the higher win probability in the latter role.

12.3.4 *Nonquantifiable Benefits*

It was also important to take into account the nonquantifiable factors that entered into this decision. They include the ability to control the quality of work delivered as a prime, the resulting client and staff satisfaction, and the ability to work directly with the client. All of these enhance the ability to win future work with the existing client as well as from new clients. All of these intangibles pointed in the direction of bidding as a prime and gaining more control of our corporate destiny with serious long-term strategic implications.

12.3.5 *What If We Lose?*

Earlier in this chapter, we noted the importance of identifying the things that can go wrong, the indicators that they have gone wrong, and the actions that will be taken at that time or perhaps sooner. In this case, the loss of the contract award would require one or more contract wins to compensate for the revenue loss and enable the company to survive and grow. It was particularly important to make this assessment because in highly competitive situations with a number of qualified bidders it is difficult to imagine a situation in which the probability of a win reaches or exceeds 0.5, that is, a situation in which one has better than an even chance of winning.

In this instance, we examined our pipeline of proposals outstanding and marketing efforts and checked to see if the assigned win probabilities were still valid, that is, conservative. The projected yield summed over the expected value of the ongoing procurements was sufficiently high to justify a reasonable confidence that we could replace the lost revenue if necessary. This was reinforced by the fact that there were a reasonable number of outstanding proposals with decent win probabilities. As every experienced CEO knows, relying on a few wins (small n) that "we are sure of" is, or should be, terrifying.

Overall our analysis showed that bidding as a prime was not the "bet the company" decision that many outsiders and some insiders perceived it to be.

12.3.6 Happy Endings and a Cautionary Note

As it turned out, we were awarded the prime contract and earned the full estimated value in revenue. Equally important, the nonquantifiable benefits were also achieved. We were able to deliver a level of technical quality that energized our staff and strengthened our reputation with our government client and prospective clients. This win also validated our corporate strategy of focusing only on prime contracts. Ultimately, when we were acquired by a multibillion-dollar public company, we were able to command a higher valuation because of our status as a prime contractor.

Focusing on this happy outcome, however, can be misleading. As noted earlier, we operate in a universe in which random events can drive outcomes. We could have lost this contract because of a last-minute change in the source selection panel, a project mishap during the evaluation process, or an employee who violated some regulation. The key point is that even had we lost, our analysis showed that we could survive and eventually regain our growth trajectory.

There is an understandable tendency in writing about corporate history to highlight the decisions that turned out to be successful. Perhaps it would be more instructive to discuss the decisions that turned out badly and how the company survived them.

12.4 Conclusion

Decision making can be enhanced by blending intuitive insights with analytical methods and logic rather than pursuing an either–or approach. The appropriate mix for a given decision question will depend on the degree to which the problem and variables can be defined and quantified. For higher-level decisions, it is often the case that relevant data are not available and that judgments are needed to fill the gap. In any case, analytical methods and insights can serve to discipline and train the intuition and avoid the fads and fallacies and biases that distort our decisions. Analytical thinking can also identify the types of data that are needed for future decisions. Equally important, it can help stem the flow of irrelevant data to management, a flow that is computer generated and all too often untouched by human thought.

References

Deming, W.E. (1950). *Some theory of sampling*, New York: Dover, p. viii.

Kahneman, D. (2011). *Thinking, fast and slow*, New York: Farrar, Straus and Giroux, p. 305.

Orkand, D.S. (1957). "Some Theory and Applications of Mathematical Programming," thesis presented to the faculty of the Graduate School of Business Administration in partial fulfillment of the requirements for the degree of Master of Business Administration. New York University, pp. 28–66.

Taleb, N.N. (2007). *The black swan*. New York: Random House, pp. xviii–xx.

QQQ—Delivering Success through Integration of Quantitative and Qualitative Models or "None of Us Is as Smart as All of Us"*

JOHN L. JACOBS

The NASDAQ OMX Group, Inc.®

Contents

13.1 Introduction

Frank G. Zarb, chairman of the National Association of Securities Dealers, Inc.® (NASD®), rang the opening bell on the American Stock Exchange® (AMEX) on March 10, 1999 to celebrate the launch of the NASDAQ-100 Index Tracking Stock® or QQQ®. It was a milestone in a project that had already evolved significantly from the original concept, and would eventually trigger a series of events and outcomes that no one would have been able to anticipate at the time. With seed capital from Susquehanna Investment Group® of $14.49 million, first-day trading volume of 5,232,000 shares, and an opening price of $51.13 (split adjusted),†

---

* Ancient Japanese proverb.
† Securities Exchange Commission®, The NASDAQ OMX Group, Inc.

it grew to be one of the most heavily traded and popular products in the world. On the QQQ's 15th anniversary, assets under management (AUM) would total $47 billion at a closing price of $90.61 on March 10, 2014, with 2014 year-to-date average daily volume of 37.5 million through March 10, 2014.* In addition, kicking off with notional value of $500M on day one and growing to over $1 trillion today,† the growth and success of the NASDAQ-100 Index family of products is evident. More important, the QQQs put exchange-traded funds or ETFs on the map for retail investors in the United States and launched an index business for NASDAQ OMX. The QQQs became the model of how investors, traders, arbitrageurs, and hedgers would utilize indexes for trading and investing strategies encompassing a suite of products from ETFs and funds to sophisticated derivatives that dominate the industry today.

This story follows a path, sometimes highly structured, sometimes highly intuitive, that can be very instructional as a case study in applying strict financial and business modeling versus utilizing intuitive, experiential, and observational inputs. Let's start at the beginning, which precedes that first opening bell 15 years ago. It actually dates to early 1997 with the kick-off of the strategic planning process of The NASDAQ Stock Market® or NASDAQ® (part of the NASD at the time). NASDAQ's strategic planning was not a designated staff position as it is today in The NASDAQ OMX Group (NASDAQ OMX®), but rather a function that was assigned to a line officer to execute in addition to his or her daily responsibilities. The concept was to keep the planning close to those responsible for execution and to those with the best access to the people, information, data, and analyses that were most relevant to the area of study. In 1997, Mark DeNat, vice president of NASDAQ Operations, was given the responsibility to lead the strategic planning process surrounding NASDAQ's tactical and near-term response to changes—both current and possible—in exchange market structure. I, NASDAQ's vice president of institutional and investor relations at that time, was given the responsibility to lead the team exploring international and Internet developments and our organization's tactical and strategic response.

---

* The NASDAQ OMX Group, Inc.
† The NASDAQ OMX Group, Inc.

Mark was chosen due to his pivotal role in the organization at the intersection of NASDAQ trading systems and NASDAQ technology. My role at the time was equally opportune in that I led NASDAQ's efforts with buy-side traders and portfolio managers as well as being part of the combined issuer services and marketing group. That placed me at the center of our brand building, listed company services, and investor and trader services. This would prove significant to the success of the project. As team leaders, we were given carte blanche to pick our team members and had access to a consultant (McKinsey & Co.) to facilitate the process. Our outstanding team included Adena Friedman (now CFO of the Carlyle Group), Ann Neidenbach (current SVP of global software development at NASDAQ OMX), and Robert Power (now in the NYSE Listings Group); these individuals had top-notch skills and expertise and represented a broad cross-section of the organization.

13.2 Background

The strategic planning process led to fundamental shifts in NASDAQ's thinking regarding our Internet strategy, international strategy, market structure (the SuperMontage® platform grew out of the DeNat team's efforts), and our strategy and tactics to engage the individual or retail investor directly. The relevance of the retail investor to NASDAQ at this time needs to be put into context. Between 1990 and 1999, L. Brian Holland, EVP and chief marketing officer, had embarked upon a multiyear, multimillion-dollar campaign to build awareness and change the perception of the NASDAQ brand. When Brian took the helm as NASDAQ's first CMO, awareness of NASDAQ by retail households in the New York metropolitan area, with household income over $50,000 that executed three or more trades a year, was 26%. The over-the-counter or OTC market was 32%, the AMEX was 79%, and the New York Stock Exchange or NYSE was over 90%.[*] NASDAQ, which at the time was the second largest US equity market and the third largest global equity marketplace (behind the NYSE and the Tokyo Stock Exchange), did not even have a level of awareness among individual investors in the financial capital of the world on par with the OTC market. This lack of visibility was clearly a challenge

---

[*] The NASDAQ OMX Group, Inc.

for NASDAQ's listing business. At the urging of our largest listed companies, NASDAQ set aside tens of millions of dollars over the next decade in an historical and award-winning advertising and brand-building campaign that encompassed every aspect of the programs, products, and services that NASDAQ provided to its listed companies.

As a member of Brian's team from his first day on the job, I had a ringside seat to this multifaceted and innovative program. As part of the strategy process, my team was looking for other ways to directly influence the individual investor. The challenge at the time was that NASDAQ only interacted with individual investors indirectly, either through our listed companies or through our market-making firms with retail businesses. For example, Microsoft had hundreds of thousands of shareholders, but we interacted with Microsoft as a listed company. Merrill Lynch® (now Bank of America/Merrill Lynch®) had tens of thousands of retail customers, but again, we interacted with Merrill Lynch as a market maker or an underwriter. One of the primary influencers on the NASDAQ brand is individual investors (along with institutional investors, managers, executives, and professionals, MEPS for short) and it was hard to influence perception without direct interaction.

After studying the marketplace and looking at all the ways that organizations interact with investors, we came across a fairly new product that had only been in the marketplace a few years and was still not widely known, the Spider® or SPY®. SPY was the very first product in what is now the huge and fast growing segment of ETFs, although no one called them ETFs back then. The product was invented at the AMEX by a team led by Nate Most. It was an index share that tracked the S&P 500® Index like an index mutual fund, but was constructed to allow it to list and trade continuously all day long on an exchange.

In creating the SPY, the AMEX team filled a great need in the market that came out of the Crash of 1987. Program trading took a lot of heat as a primary contributor of the crash. Traders and investors of all sizes were utilizing electronic program trades in a widespread fashion for the first time. Essentially a program trade is a preset order that triggers the buying or selling of a predesignated basket of securities when certain conditions are met. For example, an investor might arrange for several million dollars' worth of all the stocks in the S&P 500 Index to be sold if the S&P 500 Index drops to a certain price. The computer automatically triggers the sell order when the index value is reached.

Multiply that action by thousands of similar actions and you can see how in a rapidly declining market, electronic program trades can further exacerbate the situation and create more downward pressure on stock prices and therefore indexes, triggering more program orders to sell. The problem wasn't caused by the buying and selling of a basket of stocks at one time; it was with electronic program trading.

The AMEX team, under Nate Most, studied the events of 1987 and the subsequent market break in 1989 and came up with a new way to trade a basket of shares, through an exchange listed and traded index fund, the very first ETF. The concept was that retail and institutional investors and traders would trade the product on the open market like a share of stock during regular market hours. However, the truly innovative and unique characteristic was the invention of an in-kind, postclose, creation and redemption process that made the whole thing work. There was now a way to execute basket trading, while the market was open, without triggering the massive buy and sell orders we saw as a result of historical program trading. It was revolutionary and spawned an entire industry by paving the way for investors and traders—big and small, sophisticates and novices—to invest in and trade the S&P 500 Index in real time.

13.3 The Plan

When our team studied this product we decided that the best way to interact directly with investors was to create a financial product that allowed them to buy, sell, hold, short, flip, or execute any strategy they wanted on "The NASDAQ." After the strategic planning process wrapped up, I started planning the launch of the "NASDAQ Spider," as we referred to our project. As I began to outline the steps to go from concept to launch, it was clear I would need assistance. I brought on board Steven M. Bloom, PhD as a consultant. Steven was a former SVP and chief economist at the AMEX and a key member of Nate Most's team that had developed the SPY. There was no one better qualified in the industry to help me navigate the issues of product design and structure. The next addition to the team was David Mahle of Jones Day as legal counsel. Internally, Lisa Chaney, Leslie Bosch, and Kate Mitchel were assisting on the business side, as well as Joel Wolfson, Sara Bloom, and Josh Wymard on the legal side. None of us was working on this full-time, and our goal was simply to create a NASDAQ-branded financial product so that investors and traders could participate directly in one of the most widely followed benchmarks in the world. Millions of times a day, investors and traders asked the question, "How is the market doing?" and one of the answers was always "The NASDAQ was up (or down or flat) x number of points and volume is heavy." For the first time, instead of just being a leading market barometer, NASDAQ was about to become a financial instrument accessible to the individual investor.

We sketched out a preliminary timeline and basic budget, although the timeline had one unknown factor. Up until this point in 1997, all index share products like SPY (by year end there would be 19 in total; Investment Company Institute, 2006) were listed on the AMEX. We were NASDAQ and we were certainly not going to list our product on a competing marketplace. Therefore, we knew we needed to develop listing and trading rules for NASDAQ and have them approved by the Securities and Exchange Commission (SEC), which would take an as-yet-to-be-determined amount of time, energy, and legal fees. The budget process was straightforward, as the products were, in essence, just a new twist on the standard mutual fund and all fell under the rules of The Investment Company Act of 1940. Therefore, we knew that the product would be built with a total expense ratio or TER that defined how much the fund would be able to spend on expenses such as marketing, administration, legal, accounting, trustee fees, and license fees. A fund's expense budget is determined by the TER expressed in basis points and multiplied by the assets under management or AUM. Although we would need to budget for the start-up legal, consulting, and other costs to get the product launched, we planned for the NASDAQ SPY to be self-funding over time (that would turn out to be an understatement). Working with the marketing, trading, and listing groups, we sketched out a plan to create, launch, and list the new product on NASDAQ by the third quarter of 1998.

13.4 Wildcard

On March 18, 1998 the NASD issued an official press release titled "NASD and AMEX to Combine to Create a Global Market of Markets," confirming the rumors that the NASD was going to buy the AMEX.* This was a huge paradigm shift for the NASDAQ Spy project. If we merged before launch, the listing market would be the AMEX; if we launched before the merger became effective, then the listing market would be NASDAQ. There were a few voices suggesting we slow down the project until this issue resolved itself and the thinking was that the project could become a pawn in the negotiations. We chose to follow a different path or rather two paths. We would proceed with bifurcated plans. Plan A was to list on NASDAQ with multiple market makers and Plan B was to list on the AMEX with a single specialist. The wildcard turned out to be highly beneficial for us. It gave us enhanced credibility to engage in discussions with both traditional AMEX specialist firms such as Spear Leeds® and Susquehanna Investment Group (something difficult to justify as a dyed-in-the-wool NASDAQer) and traditional NASDAQ market-making firms including Goldman Sachs and Morgan Stanley. Indeed, these meetings would lead to the "aha moment" that forever turned the project from a pure brand-building play to become the cornerstone of a new business. By now, most of the key players were locked in. Jones Day as counsel, E&Y® as auditor, Bank of New York® as trustee, ALPS® as distributor, and Winston Strawn® as counsel to the trustee. In addition, the myriad SEC filings and agreements were all under way in various work streams. We had, by this time, decided to launch index options on the index, and options on the actual fund simultaneously with the launch of the NASDAQ SPY. That tripled our work flow, but feedback from the market was so strong that we felt it was the right action to take.

The ultimate goal of the Global Market of Markets touted in the NASD press release was to make AMEX be the listing venue of ETFs and Options, and NASDAQ be the listing venue of equities. We did not know this at the time, but this decision ultimately decided that the QQQs would list on the AMEX.

13.5 "Aha Moment"

Steven Bloom and I were highly focused on all the issues surrounding the creation of the fund, seeding capital, market making, trading, listing, and postmarket operations. Because the intent to merge with the

---

* The Financial Regulatory Authority®.

AMEX was official and public, we had the freedom to broaden our conversations among market participants. We picked six NASDAQ market-making firms and six AMEX specialist firms to engage with through a series of in-depth working sessions. The specialist firms clearly had more experience because all products were AMEX listed, but the NASDAQ market makers knew how to trade NASDAQ stocks, and this basket was going to be all NASDAQ stocks. The first decision we made as a result of our first round of discussions was to use the NASDAQ-100 Index (NDX®) instead of the NASDAQ Composite Index® (COMP®). The COMP was deemed too broad a basket and the NDX contained a concentration of highly liquid names. It would also be more effective to create options products on a limited number of securities.

The sets of meetings were very different; the more experienced specialist firms wanted to discuss very practical questions. What was in the basket? Who was going to get the fund specialist allocation, the index option specialist allocation, and the fund option specialist allocation? Unlike the NYSE allocation process, the listed company or fund in this case had some input into the specialist allocation process. The NASDAQ market makers, being less familiar with the product, wanted to know what names were included in the basket, and how they were weighted. In addition, they wanted to walk through the postclose, in-kind, creation and redemption process. We met with six of each type of firm—floor specialists and market makers.

The turning point meeting for us occurred when Steven Bloom and I visited the equity trading floor of Goldman Sachs, a leading NASDAQ market maker and underwriter. We met with Joe Della Rosa, head of trading, to talk about the product. After walking through the concept, he stopped us short and said, "What's in the basket?" We gave him the list of the 100 stocks in the NASDAQ-100 Index, with their corresponding weight, and told him roughly how many shares of each would make up a basket equal to 50,000 shares of the index fund. He called over his NASDAQ trader (at the time they ran two desks, NASDAQ and Listed) gave him the sheet and told him, "Put together this basket and come back." We continued our discussion and about seven minutes later, the NASDAQ trader returned. Joe asked him, "How long?" and the reply was, "I can put the top 80 or so names together instantly, but it takes another 3 or 4 minutes to get the rest of the basket in size." We all looked at each other until Joe broke the silence and said, "You are going to give me instant liquidity in the top 100 stocks on NASDAQ that takes 3 to 4 minutes to compile today?" We said, "That's the plan," and added that we were launching options on the index and options on the basket at the same time. He replied, "Sign us up. Goldman Sachs will make a market in this no matter where you put it, AMEX or NASDAQ."

It was the "aha moment" when the NASDAQ SPY went from being a brand-building project to a financial product (with the benefits of brand building). The reception was just as strong at all 12 meetings. There was unanimous support for the product. The specialists wanted it on AMEX, of course, but the market makers were equally passionate that these vehicles should trade in a multimarket maker environment on NASDAQ. Their reasoning was completely sound. "We already trade each and every name in the basket and we can certainly trade the basket side by side with the stocks themselves." We now knew the product would trade and be liquid and would get seed capital, but what we didn't realize was how fortuitous our timing would be.

13.6 "The Trend Is Your Friend"*

There is a long-term saying on Wall Street that "The trend is your friend." It usually continues on with a few endings such as "until it isn't" or "until it ends," and so on, but the sentiment is the same. Do not fight conventional wisdom and when the street is going headlong in one direction, take advantage of it. John T. Wall, the president of NASDAQ International® and the long-term NASDAQ veteran who put together what is the genesis of modern NASDAQ, pulled me aside one day to check in on our progress. We were diligently going over every arcane detail and John listened patiently for a while, occasionally asking a question or two and then stopped us. He said he felt very comfortable that all of the blocking and tackling was being handled efficiently and effectively. He had drilled into me my entire career working for him that the "devil was in the details." John wanted us to step back and look at the big picture for a moment. John said we were at a unique time in the securities industry and we should spend some time studying everything

---

* Conventional Wall Street wisdom.

that was happening in the industry and the economy to figure out what that meant to our work. John's advice turned out to be spot on.

To assess the big picture, I began a series of interviews across a broad swath of people and disciplines. Because I was part of the Issuer Services and Marketing Group and had previously run the New Listings/IPO team, I knew the best place to start was with Brian Holland. Brian defined "big picture thinking" and viewed branding and marketing as strategic functions first and foremost. He had spent nearly a decade building the NASDAQ brand to the point where it had become a household word. Brian pointed out to me that the 1990s had so far been marked by tremendous increases in the equitization of companies through the public offering process. (see Table 13.1) For example, 4,408 companies went public between 1990 and 1998 in the United States[*].

Furthermore, over 900 of those IPOs were technology companies[†] (see US Technology IPOs, Table 13.2) and the percentage of technology companies versus nontechnology companies was rising each year. The total number of public companies was growing rapidly as well[‡] (see US Public Companies, Table 13.3), and most were listed on The NASDAQ Stock Market.

These facts clearly pointed to several fundamental shifts: (1) companies were accessing the public markets in numbers never seen before; (2) technology companies were going public at astonishing rates,

Table 13.1   US IPOs

US IPOs			
YEAR	ALL US	NASDAQ	% NASDAQ
1990	125	91	73%
1991	311	249	80%
1992	393	292	74%
1993	614	445	72%
1994	580	443	76%
1995	569	480	84%
1996	842	708	84%
1997	613	469	77%
1998	361	269	75%

---

[*] The NASDAQ OMX Group, Inc.
[†] The NASDAQ OMX Group, Inc.
[‡] The NASDAQ OMX Group, Inc.

Table 13.2   US Technology IPOs

US TECHNOLOGY IPOs			
YEAR	ALL US	NASDAQ	% NASDAQ
1990	19	18	95%
1991	46	44	96%
1992	48	43	90%
1993	91	90	99%
1994	94	92	98%
1995	177	171	97%
1996	217	203	94%
1997	136	129	95%
1998	105	96	91%

Table 13.3   US Public Companies

US PUBLIC COMPANIES			
YEAR	ALL US	NASDAQ	% NASDAQ
1990	6,760	4,132	61%
1991	6,083	4,094	67%
1992	6,202	4,113	66%
1993	6,557	4,611	70%
1994	7,030	4,902	70%
1995	7,369	5,127	70%
1996	8,032	5,556	69%
1997	8,113	5,487	68%
1998	7,679	5,010	65%

reflecting the growth in demand for computers and telecommunications and supporting industries; (3) more companies were public in the United States and listed on NASDAQ than at any other time in history; and (4) NASDAQ had become the home for new companies, growth companies, technology companies, and the innovative forward-looking visionaries that would dominate the American economy.

Another shift was the growing participation in the market of individual investors and traders (including day traders) as reflected in the rapidly growing trading volume[*] (see US Average Daily Volume, Table 13.4).

This trend was mirrored by the growth of individuals owning mutual funds in the United States. In 1990, there were 61,948,000

---

[*] The NASDAQ OMX Group, Inc.

Table 13.4 US Average
Daily Volume

US AVERAGE DAILY VOLUME	
YEAR	ALL US
1990	288,009,229
1991	342,970,931
1992	392,584,733
1993	528,491,682
1994	586,156,100
1995	748,065,444
1996	956,254,242
1997	1,172,200,156
1998	1,473,173,765

fund shareholder accounts and by the end of 1998, the number had swelled to 194,029,000 (Investment Company Institute, 2008). These two statistics represented an undeniable wave by investors and traders of all shapes and sizes participating in the US capital markets, either directly through buying and selling of stocks, or indirectly through the ownership of mutual funds, in levels never experienced before. Within these numbers was also a somewhat hidden trend, the growing use of index investing and derivatives trading.

To further explore the growing world of derivatives trading, Rick Ketchum, NASD president, suggested I spend some time with Eric W. Noll, currently CEO of ConvergEx and formerly EVP of Transactions US and UK at NASDAQ OMX, but managing director of Susquehanna Investment Group (SIG®) at the time. The world of derivatives was very new to me and SIG had extensive derivative and specialist platforms on NYSE, AMEX, and the Philadelphia Stock Exchange® or PHLX®. Eric patiently walked me through the mechanics of index options and said that I should be viewing the NASDAQ SPY not through the eyes of an equity fund, but rather through the lens of futures and options. Eric pointed out that the explosion in equity trading was actually even more pronounced in the options and futures worlds. He said the success of the product would be driven in the derivatives markets as much as the equity markets. This became the essence of the value proposition that SIG put forth later in the formal allocation process to become the specialist for the fund.

If "The trend is your friend," what does it mean when you have eight trends, all heading in one direction? We were witnessing: (1) the birth of modern basket trading, (2) the equitization of the US markets, (3) the growing participation by individual investors and traders, (4) the rise of NASDAQ, (5) the IPO boom, (6) the technology boom, (7) the growth of indexing, and (8) the explosion of derivative trading. We realized we should accelerate our efforts and planned to launch in the fall of 1998; however, we were held up by the impending merger of NASD/NASDAQ with the AMEX. By now, it was clear that the merger would receive regulatory and DOJ (US Department of Justice) approval and it was in the hands of the organization's members.

We had formerly named the product "The NASDAQ-100 Index Tracking Stock" and had filed to list it under the ticker "Q" with "QQQ" as a backup. The merger closed on October 30, 1998 and we decided to launch in the following spring. We had to rebalance the NASDAQ-100 Index in the fall of 1998 to meet the Regulated Investment Company (RIC) diversification test because the market capitalization of both Microsoft and Intel had increased significantly compared to their peers in NDX. We wrapped up our allocation process to pick specialists for the Qs (one of the many nicknames of the product) and the options programs. SIG was picked for the Qs and Bear Hunter® for the options. We had also started work with Rick Redding, vice president of Index Products, at the Chicago Mercantile Exchange® or CME® to develop a new NASDAQ-100 e-mini future® on the index to complement the Qs and the options. This product launched in June of 1999, three months after the other products, and completed the product set.

By every measure, the launch of these products has been a tremendous success. In the 2013 annual earnings release of NASDAQ OMX, one can see that the Global Index Business has an annual run rate of revenue of $100 million, with over 40,000 indexes and 150 Exchange Traded Products licensed.* It all started with the Qs, the options, and the e-minis. More important, we can make the case that modeling needs to be quantitative and qualitative. The very best and well-thought–out assumptions and targets must be challenged

---

* The NASDAQ OMX Group, Inc.

and looked at from a variety of angles. The Q's success was the result of a lot of work and input from a large group of people. Each and every one contributed an insight or a suggestion that we could put to use as we designed and rolled out the products. There have been many times that market and economic forces have aligned like we witnessed in this case, but the key is to be able to look above the spreadsheets and models and assess the trends and act on them.

Under CEO Bob Greifeld, NASDAQ OMX has formalized both the strategy process and the process for internal strategic initiatives. They reside together in our organization and have full-time permanent positions dedicated to the efforts. We look at them as two halves of the whole: strategy (including M&A) and organic growth initiatives. The GIFT Council (Growth Innovation Forward Thinking) is the program where we solicit ideas from across the company in our Idea Room and also where ideas are turned into formal initiatives. There is a very disciplined and objective approach with models, projections, and detailed analysis, but that is not the goal of the process. If that were the case, one could merely fill out a form or application like a loan or a mortgage to get funding. The key word here is council. When a team is ready to present their idea to the organization, they actually are meeting with a group of their peers and all of the EVPs and the CEO. Our goal is not only to review the quantitative models, but also to understand the environment and market opportunities. The Council is there also to provide insight and advice. It is rarely a straight go/no go decision, but rather an iterative process as various inputs and results will alter the course of a project until it either graduates out of the program and into a business unit or is tabled.

As with QQQ, it is hard to predict where every idea will go and how successful it will be. The challenge is balancing between the absolute requirement of a disciplined, quantitative, and objective process without missing the bigger picture, and killing an idea for the wrong reason or too early, just because it didn't follow a linear path. There wasn't a financial model at the time that we could have utilized to accurately quantify and predict the results of the QQQs. We thought we had found a need in the market and had the solution to the need, but our intuition told us we had much more. The success of the QQQs is an absolute embodiment of the ancient

Japanese proverb that "None of us is as smart as all of us" and that the path to success is rarely a straight road without turns, bumps, and roadblocks.

References

Investment Company Institute. (2006). *2006 Fact Book*. Washington, DC.
Investment Company Institute. (2008). *2008 Fact Book*. Washington, DC.

14

Appendix Named Filipe

MARTA SINCLAIR

Griffith Business School
Griffith University, Australia

I don't know when it actually started. Really. The first time I remember, it was a week or two after I finished first grade. There was this weird tingling feeling on the right side of my abdomen: two inches straight from my belly button, then two inches south, to be precise. It wasn't painful or tender, just kind of tensely awkward. You know, something like if you look down from a twentieth floor balcony and your tummy gets queasy, your thighs become rubbery, and your calves are tense. This time it was just my tummy, not the calves or thighs. And again, it wasn't painful I assured our family doctor who my Mum took me to see and who was ready to operate. He was concerned that my funny feeling was nothing else but an inflamed appendix.

When I asked Doctor Craxton what an appendix is and what it's good for, he wasn't sure. "It has absolutely no purpose," he said. How could it be, I wondered, thinking that God didn't create anything without a purpose, but the doctor just shrugged his shoulders. "That's the way it is with appendix." Then, complying with my request, he drew it on a piece of paper. It looked like a curled worm.

This time, my Mum saved me. "Let's put an icepack on it," she suggested to the doctor, "Then we'll see." So we did. And it stopped. Because in my family everything had a name, our radio, gramophone, even trees, not just our two dogs and two cars, I remembered what my bohemian granny once told me, and named my appendix Filipe. You see, ever since I was a small child, I was told I had some wit about me. Nana, who was full of wisdom and mysterious proverbs, assured me in her heavily accented English that I have "Filipe." She didn't know who he was or where he resided. But I did. He was my invisible friend who, grandma said, was very smart and, as I always knew, lived in my belly.

Then on Friday, 10 days after Ms. Golding, my math teacher said there's going to be a test next week, Filipe started tingling again. Math was not my favorite subject and Ms. Golding not my favorite teacher. And she knew it. I sat at our kitchen table quite dazed but unperturbed, for I already knew what I was going to do. I took an icepack from the fridge, told Mum I was going to study for my Wednesday test, and went upstairs to my room to talk to Filipe. I felt high.

"What's going on, Filipe? Why such fuss again? That's the math test, isn't it?" and I started leafing through the textbook. Slowly. When I came to page 157, I could feel a little choke. You know, something like when a nurse takes your blood pressure. The mercury goes up and, on the way down when it reaches your maximum or systolic pressure point, makes this warbling sound; then it repeats its funny giggle at your diastolic low. My math diastolic low was at page 221. Three full chapters of math.

I sat there like I was nailed down. The entire weekend. On Wednesday I aced the test. It never happened before. Me, a solid C+, got a full 100. Ms. Golding usually glorified anyone who ever got an A+, but not me. She just wondered aloud, quite maliciously, whether someone told me what will be on the test. So I answered quite truthfully: Filipe. Then she complained to my Mum at the PTA meeting that I was quite impertinent, even though my math somehow improved beyond her understanding. Mum didn't ask me who Filipe was, concluding that he must be one of the boys I knew.

Once, after listening on one of the late TV shows to a highly accredited medical doctor with impeccable credentials from Yale and psychiatry residence at Mass General who explained intuition as the link into our subconscious mind, I came to an irreversible conclusion that my vermiform friend is nothing else but an antenna for receiving messages. That Filipe could be actually somewhere else and my appendix is like one of those hi-tech, snowflake-shaped antennas on modern laptops, helping me get in touch with him. I never said anything about Filipe to anybody. I treated the existence of my special friend as a secret, like all those people who have seen a UFO but refused to be ridiculed by the official government policy.

When I was 18 and about to graduate, my neighbor and friend, Johnny Walker, a first-year med student, invited me to go climbing with him in the Rockies. I liked Johnny because he was a nerd. He was into science, regular or weird, and I was sure if I could talk to someone about my predicament, it would be him. I just had to get him out of his regular zone. The Rockies would do fine. I planned my soul-opening spiel for the last day of our climb.

We slept in some kind of a hut, nothing much, no beds, just wooden planks one above the other, but our sponge mats made the hardness of the wood bearable. It would have been a gorgeous morning if I didn't feel Filipe. This time he wasn't just tingling with some kind of regular anxiety, he was positively rattling. You know, something like high-voltage wires behind the farmhouse of my Aunt Eli, in Liberty, New York. Oh my! This was unusual. I just couldn't ignore it but, for an unknown reason, I wasn't quite forthcoming in telling Johnny what it was about. Don't ask me why. It is an irritated appendix, that's for sure, he said. We have to go back. You don't want it ruptured over there, and he pointed way to the rocky top covered in snow. That's what I wanted to tell him anyway, that we should turn back, but I knew when a man takes an idea as his own, it's much better. And so we went.

The weather changed in the midpoint of our descent. Dark, ominous clouds roughed up by powerful wind rolled in from nowhere. When we came back to our hotel, we could see it was a vicious snowstorm up there. Then, the next day we heard that the winds had triggered an avalanche that swept a few people in its deadly path. Of course, my appendix miraculously healed. That evening, Johnny Walker, sipping his favorite brand of scotch, joined a heated debate about the inclement weather that stopped us from achieving our planned goal. Pointing at me, he pronounced loudly in the bar for everybody to hear that "It looks like her goddamn appendix saved our goddamn asses." And on that auspicious day, as a mission from God, I decided to take intuition seriously.

* * *

I do not much like third-world countries. Not just because I am a perfectionist and they are every perfectionist's nightmare, but it eludes me why all those rich folks from Australia, Europe, and North America go to India to seek so-called enlightenment in some kind of ashram, when the owner, the "very famous guru" sits in her palatial residence in California. I guess because after they scrub floors and holler their chants for two weeks, they write a bestseller on how they got their stripes of enlightenment, whatever that is, and become rich. That's why.

To fly for a week to Bali was my husband's idea of a romantic birthday gift. Since he stopped flying gliders, I reasoned, he needed an occasional slight fix of a third-world danger. So Carl said we were going to Bali, and that it's his shout. That I need a break. But I knew better. He gave it to me knowing very well that I'd prefer to take the bullet train between Osaka and Tokyo or the TGV from Paris. That's the way my husband is. He gives presents he'd like to get. As a teenager, I was told by my mother-in-law, he once gave her an LP of the Stones for Christmas. When the imperturbable Mary, who accepted graciously Mick Jagger's much repeated complaint that he can't get no satisfaction, gave Carl curtains for the living room for his birthday, he was about as satisfied as Mick in his signature song.

The Indonesian island of Bali is an Australian playground. It is because it's "close by," just around the corner, a mere eight-hour flight. And also because it's exotic, beer is decent, and the lore says you can buy drugs there cheaply. I wouldn't know. I wondered why Carl, who was so affected by the bombing carnage at Kuta 10 years ago, wanted to go there. He isn't into drugs or beer, and short-legged brunettes aren't his type. At least, I insisted, we are not staying anywhere near Kuta. Too many drunks. So he booked us into a villa nestled in the rice fields, 10 miles away from Ubud.

A couple of days after our arrival, I assessed the entire Bali scene as a large exotic village full of poor people who, wherever you walk, are trying to sell you something. Someone told me that the government offered a scooter to any young male willing to undergo a vasectomy. It could be a rumor. Nevertheless, millions of two-stroke, testosterone-driven scooters are buzzing around Bali. This makes you wonder whether the rumor is true. You can't drive there. It is too dangerous. You need to hire a local driver because of the heavy flow of scooters. One more thing, it is hard to walk on the sidewalks in Ubud. Too many holes trying to entrap your shaky ankles. You are better off walking on the road.

For four fun-filled days we ate, prayed, and loved all those gold-painted temples and rice paddies. We lay down on the rim of the volcano where supposedly, while still available, virgins were thrown in to assure a plentiful harvest. When our most competent driver named Wayan Apple learned about my family furniture business, he took us to a factory where they make amazing furniture out of bamboo.

Today was the day of relaxation. I decided to enjoy our open-space villa. It was my time to meditate. But the only thing that came to my mind and I couldn't get rid of, was one of my PhD students, Dani Kandi, a "self-acknowledged psychic." When I told her about our trip, she came to me the next day with "mortal danger" written all over her little face. Now, as I was meditating on world peace, I could hear her voice again: "There will be danger. Maybe scorpions, spiders, snakes, or malaria-bearing mosquitoes." Well, "We've been here for four days and haven't seen one of those. So, shut up, Dani." I tried to silence her harangue as if she were a campaigning politician. But Dani was right. Only that mortal danger came from a completely different angle. Thank God, Filipe was vigilant.

It was a very slow morning as we slept in. Carl was in and out of the shower, as usual, and I went right after him. I liked the bathroom. It had large marble tiles on the floor, a few mirrors around, a bidet next to the commode, and, peculiarly, an open-air shower where you could see the stars. Although the tub was still inside the bathroom, the high-powered shower was mounted on the volcanic peripheral wall, outside. The ceiling was missing. Moving around as fast as a feeding koala, I watched the passing clouds above my head and enjoyed the high-pressured stream of rainwater, heated by the morning sun. Then, as I stepped out, I announced to my waiting husband that because the restaurant closed for breakfast at 10 already, it would be better if he went first and ordered for both of us. I would need another 15 minutes to dry my hair. He looked at me funny and smiled. My 15 minutes would be at least half an hour, he knew. As he left and I reached for the hairdryer, I could feel Filipe buzzing me. I stopped cold, noticing that the beautifully polished marble floor was quite slippery. "Is that the problem?" I asked Filipe, walking into the bedroom with the hairdryer in my hand. Standing there, I looked for a plug. Just before I plugged it in, about to sit down in front of the bedroom mirror, Filipe's annoying buzz turned to an angry rattle. I couldn't fathom why. But I should have known better.

When the hit came, I thought it was a terrorist bomb. After all, this is Bali. The shock of pain hit me at the same time as blackness. It went through my arm, shoulder, head, and buckled my knees. I don't remember much except for the acute pain zipping through my body. When I finally opened my eyes, I felt quite paralyzed. Lying on my left side, neck twisted, my eyes trying to focus on the texture of the carpet. I couldn't move and had a hard time breathing. The darkness slowly dissipated and so did the horrible pain. My right arm was out of commission. I tried to figure out what had just happened, or maybe not just. I had no idea how long I was laying there. Using my left arm, I tried to move my knees under my body and lift myself up. It was a useless struggle. My paralysis wouldn't go away. I stayed curled in a fetal position, happy to breathe, thinking: "What is going on?"

When I finally regained mobility and my senses, the smell gave away the culprit. No bomb and no terrorists. It was a faulty hairdryer. A tiny little bit of wire with missing insulation touched my perspiring wrist and the current of 240 volts, otherwise confined to a copper wire, did exactly what it is supposed to do: it ran wherever there was an auspicious opening. A little peephole and right into my wrist. Nothing personal, girl, just business. I checked the clock. I must have been out of commission for 10 minutes. Then the anger set in. How dare! And with wobbly knees and shaky legs, I proceeded to find the GM of the resort. By the time I found him, I was livid. As I waved the faulty hairdryer at his face, full of passion to get my justice like a Goddess of Vendetta herself, he looked genuinely scared. Then I slammed the door of his office and went to look for my husband. The show was not over yet.

Carl was already out of the restaurant, on the concrete path, in search and rescue mode. I was an hour late, at least 30 minutes later than usual. When he saw me looking wrought, pale, yielding the hairdryer like a lethal weapon, he knew that something horrible must have happened. After I told him about Filipe buzzing me to get out of the bathroom and me thinking I could slip on the wet floor and injure myself, I pointed to the hairdryer which I smartly kept in my possession as corpus delicti. His response was as swift and fearsome as I hoped for. With red sparks flying out of his aura, he dragged me back to the manager's office, and if I was bad, he was awful. He gave him hell about lack of due diligence, usually punishable by court. In his eyes was mortal fear and in his harangue was molten lead. This was not just any simple accident involving scratched insulation on a 240-V wire, but quite a successful attempt to kill his beloved wife and put him in the Kerobokan jail.

There I stood, quite pleased with his fierce defense of myself but rather disturbed by his argument. Why the hell would *he* be thrown into jail, in that awful abode where a prisoner is responsible for his own food, toothpaste, soap, and all the rest of provisions civilized people use, that much I knew. As we walked out, I could see he was beyond pissed. He was in primordial fear, shaking fiercely. "Did he love me really that much?" I asked.

"You dummy, this is Bali," he spat out. "You are guilty unless proven innocent, but the onus is on you! Capish? If you can't prove yourself innocent, you are guilty. Remember Chapelle Corby?"

"Of course I do," I said indignantly. "Who doesn't?"

"Well, what happened to her?"

"She was bringing a bag of grass to Bali in her boogie-board and the Customs found it."

He hissed, "Exactly!" Then with an unctuous disposition, slowly and patiently as he would talk to a retarded child, he explained: "They never proved it but she couldn't prove her innocence either. There were no fingerprints on that four-kilo bag of vacuumed grass. Thank God you listened to Filipe and stepped out of that puddle I left behind. He and the bedroom carpet saved my arse! Good boy, Fil," he said and patted me on the right side of my belly.

I stood there flabbergasted. "Saved *you*?"

"Sure! If you stayed in the puddle, you'd be dead now like Brendan Nelson's wife."

"What about her?"

"She took her hairdryer while showering. The good doctor got away unscathed because he wasn't at home, and his home was Brisbane, not Bali."

"And?"

"If I went up to the villa after eating my and your breakfast and found you an hour dead, lying on the floor with a smelly hairdryer," he said with the utmost disdain, "those local police morons, because of your life insurance and me being your beneficiary, would find me guilty that very hour."

"Why would they?"

"Like Chapelle, her fingerprints weren't on that bag and the police didn't even bother to look for them. So, the unfortunate girl got 20 years on the basis of circumstantial evidence. The term 'without reasonable doubt' that we in the West value so much, local justice doesn't care for."

Now it became clear. It wasn't me my husband was so fiercely defending.

"Is this why you were—I could see—so scared? Is it what triggered it?" There was a long and awkward pause. I could feel my husband coming out clean.

"There've been many predictions my mother made and, as far as I can remember, all came true," he said hesitantly. I could see that he was struggling but I also knew that he was right. Mary was a regular Cassandra of NYC. "Once, while swimming at Rockaway Beach in New York City, a wave flipped me over like a burger and slammed me onto hard sand. There was no more than two feet of water but I had no idea what was up and what was down. I almost drowned. When I came home, I told my mother. Without a drop of kindness or pity, she proclaimed coolly: 'You should have known better and trust your mother, dearest. Remember what I always told you?' I couldn't believe what I was hearing.

"That for me is—the gallows? That I die being hung by rope till dead? That was one of your sick jokes, Mum!" I said, walking out of the kitchen, not really anxious to hear her acerbic rebuttal that she was so good at.

"That's why I was so scared, darling. Your unusual appendix saved me. But getting life and being locked up in that hell-hole," he sighed, "without you—that'd be the worst." Then he touched my tummy again and said with complete sincerity: "Thank you, Filipe."

I was flabbergasted. "Do you think anyone will believe it?" I asked my grateful husband after a protracted silence.

"Believe what? That you almost got electrocuted by a hairdryer?"

"No. That my appendix is an antenna to some 'other' world?"

Carl looked me with cool detachment. Then he assured me in his peculiar, unique way: "Remember Dan Quayle?"

"The VP of Bush Sr.?"

"Yes, that's the one. He once said: 'The ridges on Mars mean that once upon a time, there was water.'" My husband, former engineer on the space station project, looked at me quizzically. "Do you know what happened after that?"

"Yes. The entire world laughed how stupid he was."

"Even NASA. But," Carl paused, "they aren't laughing any more. It's time, darling, that you tell the world what the appendix is really good for."

* * *

And that's how it all started. I figured out, because the appendix has no known physical function, its only possible function is ethereal. This was my hypothesis which I set about to test. My problem, of course, was not only to get ethical clearance but how to recruit willing participants. So I decided to study myself. I based my methodology on Gail Ferguson who, as a sole subject, sorted out her own intuitions into neat categories and wrote a whole book about it. I could not quite foresee any Nobel Prize coming my way, even if my rigorous research would prove true. And rigorous it was. In my diary, I recorded meticulously any minute reaction in my belly, then noted whatever happened to me. I kept score of Filipe's hits and misses, looking for a significant variable. I felt like a UFO observer who is unwilling to go public. So for the time being, I decided my personal data collection has to stay in the closet. Let a medical doctor get my glory one day.

In the meantime, weird studies started popping up, giving credence to my original idea. A researcher in Sydney monitored her patients' brain waves, only to find out that intuition-related parts of the brain were active when the patient got emotionally in sync with the therapist. So, I reasoned, this connection could make the transfer of feelings and even thoughts between two people possible. Quantum physics has been hinting at the existence of "nonlocal intuition" for quite some time. Then a PhD dissertation from Melbourne came across my desk, suggesting that we register our intuitions not only through emotions, as the Damasio-led team has been implying for years, but also through our senses. Here we go, the same thing I suggested in our intuition training book. So why wouldn't it be possible to use for the same purpose, and maybe more, our appendix? Rest assured, my little project is going on.

Recommended Reading

Bradley, R. (2011). Resolving the enigma of nonlocal intuition: A quantum-holographic approach. In M. Sinclair (Ed.), *Handbook of Intuition Research*. Cheltenham, UK: Edward Elgar, pp. 197–213.

Damasio, A. (1994). *Descartes' Error: Emotion, Reason, and the Human Brain*. New York: G.P. Putnam.

Ferguson, G. (1999). *Cracking the Intuition Code*. Chicago: Contemporary Books.

Künding, B. and Sinclair, M. (2012). *Intuitiv richtig: Wir wissen mehr als wir denken* [*Developing Intuition: We Know More than We Think*]. München: Windpferd.

Otto, J. (2014). "The Development of an Intuitive Cognitive Style Process Model." PhD dissertation. Melbourne: Monash University.

Sinclair, M. (2010). Misconceptions about Intuition. *Psychological Inquiry*, 21(4): 378–386.

Sinclair, M. and Hamilton, A. (2014). Mapping group intuitions. In M. Sinclair (Ed.), *Handbook of Research Methods on Intuition*. Cheltenham, UK: Edward Elgar, pp. 199–217.

Stratford, T., Lal, S., and Meara, A. (2012). Neuroanalysis of therapeutic alliance in the symptomatically anxious: The physiological connection revealed between therapist and client. *American Journal of Psychotherapy*, 66(1): 1–20.

15

MANAGING PROJECTS AS THOUGH PEOPLE MATTERED

Using Soft Skills and Project Management Tools for Successful Enterprise Transformation

DAVID F. RICO

University of Maryland University College

Contents

15.1 Introduction

Project management has a long and rich history stretching back thousands of years. Large public works of historical significance were only possible using project management techniques. It doesn't take much imagination to recall some of the great project achievements of humankind. These are often known as the wonders of the ancient world. Some of them include the Tower of Babel, Great Pyramids, Roman Aqueducts, Great Wall of China, Nazca Lines, or perhaps even Noah's Ark or Solomon's Temple. More recent examples include the Taj Majal, Panama Canal, Hoover Dam, Golden Gate Bridge, Empire State Building, Eiffel Tower, and Suez Canal. The great engineering feats of World War II were also remarkable, including aircraft carriers, long-range bomber aircraft, submarines, radar, V-2 rockets, jet engines, and atomic bomb. Aerospace projects included

Mercury, Gemini, Apollo, Skylab, Voyager, Space Shuttle, Hubble, Space Station, Opportunity, Curiosity, and so on. The Hadron Collider, Chunnel, Dubai Tower, Akashi Kaikyo Bridge, and Syncrude Tailings Dam are modern wonders. How about large information technology projects such as the Internet, Facebook, Amazon, eBay, iTunes, Microsoft Windows, Linux, and the like? Even large multimillion-member organizations qualify as projects, such as the US DoD, China's People's Liberation Army, China Railway Corp., Walmart, and McDonald's, among others.

What do all of these projects have in common? First, they required enormous resources to construct in terms of money, time, and manpower, that is, billions of dollars, decades or centuries, or thousands of workers. What else do they have in common? Well, they required visionary leaders, careful planning, meticulous designs, careful project execution and control, and extremely high technical performance. Their functional and performance requirements were orders of magnitude beyond anything imaginable in the past, present, or future. Their structures reached to unprecedented heights that could be seen for miles or even from space. They consumed enormous volumes of materials that boggled the imagination. They held large volumes of resources such as people or water, they traveled at enormous speeds and distances, they required multigenerational budgets, and they caused enormous damage to their victims. Twentieth century projects necessitated new tools, which included the program evaluation review technique (1956), critical path method (1957), work breakdown structure (1962), cost/schedule control systems criteria (1967), theory of constraints (1983), earned value management (1989), and critical chain project management (1997). Many organizations were formed including the International Project Management Association (1965), Project Management Institute (1969), Association of Project Management (1972), and American Academy of Project Management (1996). The crowning achievement of project management included the Project Management Body of Knowledge (PMBOK) in 1986 and its 10 major pillars (i.e., project integration, scope, time, cost, quality, human resources, communications, risk, procurement, and stakeholder management). Today, millions of project managers are certified to the PMBOK.

But what is the point of all of this formality, structure, ceremony, professionalization, certification, and exactitude? The basic theory is a project's scope can be discerned, documented, translated into a written plan, and controlled within a 5 or 10% margin of error. For example, let's say one wants to build the world's tallest skyscraper. Then, the scope would include requirements discovery, conceptual modeling, and estimation of resources such as people, materials, capital, land, equipment, tools, and time. These boundaries are then translated into a work breakdown structure or hierarchy of deliverables and activities, and a detailed schedule measured in years and decades, which is tracked using cost and schedule measures. The latter is known as *earned value management*, which assumes frequent measurement of a project's resource utilization rate should be made to ensure resources are not consumed too quickly or slowly. Expending resources at a planned rate is believed to enable completion of the skyscraper at a preplanned date. There are three major assumptions upon which this paradigm is based: First, this is the way that humankind consumed vast quantities of resources, constructed enormously complex structures, and created the timeless wonders of the ancient world. The second is that 100% of a project's scope is knowable, definable in a project plan, and can be reduced to simple arithmetic to achieve scope, time, and cost constraints. The third is that the 10 pillars of project management are the critical success factors behind complex twenty-first–century projects and systems.

The mathematical tenets of project management appeal to left-brained, analytical scientists, mathematicians, and engineers. However, project managers have always admitted that soft tools are just as important as hard ones. These include people skills, motivation, trust, communications, relationships, instinct, intuition, camaraderie, morale, dignity, and respect for one another. We have to credit the early organizational sociologists, psychologists, and behavioral researchers from 1925 to 1965. They had the audacity, vision, and courage to challenge scientific management that reducing tacit knowledge to a simple set of repeatable and measurable processes was not the only key to performance improvement. Scientific management advocates argued for division of labor, specialization, measurement, and "one-best-way." Early human behavioral researchers argued that power should be shared with workers, motivation could be optimized through empowerment, and small autonomous work groups should be used. They also argued that decision making should be decentralized, conflict should be managed, and individuals should master the principles of sociology and psychology to improve organizations. This was a far cry from the industrial revolution and scientific management era efforts to enable mass manufacturing, economies of scale, and the treatment of humans as machines or automatons by reducing their work to a set of mathematical routines using statistical process control.

However, the breakthrough came from the systems theorists who discovered complex new products and services are triads of people, processes, and technologies. These elements were not to be treated equally, but that the lion's share of the complexity lay in the people side. That is, the answer to successful projects was not in economic optimization, but in understanding and mastering psychology and sociology, as the early human behaviorists had discovered. These included Mary Parker Follett (1926), Elton Mayo (1933), Abraham Maslow (1943), Kurt Lewin (1951), Ludwig von Bertalanffy (1951), Kenneth Boulding (1956), Douglas McGregor (1957), John French (1959), Frederick Herzberg (1959), Tom Burns (1961), and Philip Herbst (1962) among others. These giants formed the basis for understanding human behavior, such as ethics, culture, efficacy, motivation, rewards, decision making, teamwork, conflict management, communication, power, organization change, and egalitarian leadership. The study of human behavior has and will take place in three periods: theoretical (1920–1960), implementation (1960–2000), and optimization (2000–2040). The third phase is dominated by right-brained thinking, brain science, emotional intelligence, intrinsic motivation, relationships, trust, collaboration, communication, empowerment, delegation, participation, cognitive bias, visual abstraction, and collaboration. These allude to what today's project managers call "soft, people, communication, and personality skills." That is, treating people with respect and dignity may be more important than scientific management.

15.2 Organizational Theory and Project Management

The field of organizational theory has a long and storied history. Almost any management scholar admits that its roots and tenets are founded throughout history in the great societies, cultures, armies, and structures of the ancient world. Jeremiah received a title or deed for a plot of land he purchased replete with highly legalistic terms and conditions. The Hammurabi Code contained a system of ethics holding builders accountable for the loss of life if their structures collapsed. Span-of-control was used to organize Levitical priests for healing and judging, as well as Rome's legions into a well-defined hierarchy. This was formalized by George Miller of Harvard (1956) in "Miller's limit"; that is, people cannot recall more than seven plus or minus two numbers. Project teams now contain seven plus or minus two people. Adam Smith pondered the division of labor, specialization, and the competitive advantage of nations. Frederick Taylor created scientific management to convert a worker's tacit knowledge into explicit work routines to be measured. He suggested workers could be motivated by "giving them plums." Mary Parker Follett encouraged managers to share decision-making power with ordinary workers and Abraham Maslow pondered the principles of human motivation. It would take another 60 or 70 years to fully decode the secrets of motivation. Late twentieth-century ideas include international culture and customs, advanced motivation theory, teamwork, self-organization, decision making, conflict management, power, politics, egalitarian leadership, organization change, and ethics.

Organizational theory had its detractors and by 1960 scholars asserted there was no unified theory of management. Some claimed it included everything from Taylorism forward. Human behaviorists claimed everything from Mary Parker Follett on forward. Scholars yearned to develop a discipline of management science and insisted upon measurability. Early tenets of organizational theory contained little measurement and were not considered a science. Furthermore, many did not consider psychology, sociology, and human behavior sciences either, because thoughts and feelings could not be easily measured. Thus, human behavior theory was rejected as well. This quandary of mathematics versus human behavior was a gauntlet, resulting in a theoretical deadlock. Scientific management was considered inadequate and psychology was not considered a science. Twentieth-century project management was based on scientific management with a smattering of human behavior. Twenty-first–century versions call for less scientific management and more human behavior. However, this only deepened the divide between proponents of each paradigm. Moreover, twenty-first–century approaches do not have well-developed human behavior theories, exacerbated by the immaturity of organizational behavior. Proponents of scientific management fiercely attack twenty-first–century theories by claiming human behavior is not based upon mathematics and should be rejected outright.

15.2.1 *Scientific Management View*

Adam Smith (1776) called for centralized factories, division of labor, and specialization to enable mass production and economies of scale during the British industrial revolution. Frederick Taylor (1911) created the megatrend known as scientific management in the late American industrial revolution. It consisted of four parts: documenting tacit work routines, selecting qualified workers, motivating workers with simple rewards, and sharing tasks among managers and workers. Taylor is credited with the success of America's manufacturing phase from 1900 to the 1970s. He is considered the progenitor of Fordism and the American system of manufacture, although this is now disputed. His contemporaries refined the early principles of organizational theory, namely Henri Fayol, Max Weber, and Chester Barnard. Scientific management manifested itself in the works of W. Edwards Deming, Joseph Juran, Walter Shewhart, Taiichi Ohno, Peter Drucker, Daniel Koontz, Herbert Simon, Tom Burns, G. M. Stalker, Philip Crosby, and numerous others. Megatrends emerging from this era included total quality management, statistical process control, Toyota Production System, Japanese management, Kaizen, zero defects, root cause analysis, process improvement, flexible manufacturing, Six Sigma, Lean manufacturing, Lean Six Sigma, and Kanban. However, these theories had a central weakness. They focused on converting documented tacit work routines and extracting the most amount of efficiency. Some rested upon respect for people, but didn't say how or to what extent.

15.2.2 *Human Behavior View*

Scientific management was called the "coordination view" and human behavior was called the "cooperation view." This was a euphemism of sorts for scholars who recognized that willingness, motivation, disposition, and agreement were necessary for organizational efficiency.

Managers didn't believe that workers' opinions mattered well into the late twentieth and early twenty-first centuries. This view is still pervasive and workers are considered property. Managers are task-masters, and workers are servants who must perform or be punished. A better name for "cooperation view" would be "equality view," but is too provocative. Organizations have done just about everything they can without declaring managers and workers as equals. Organizations shortened work hours, increased safety, improved working conditions, eliminated child labor, increased pay and benefits, and even granted generous work leave. Today, Western workers are the most productive in the world and none of these efforts involved documenting tacit work routines. Cooperation view became organizational behavior, but scholars stopped short of calling it the "psychological, sociological, or behavioral view." To do so would be to imply organizational efficiency was based in cultivating deeply embedded tacit human behaviors versus codifying them.

Early human behavior scholars understood that businesses were owned by capitalists with formal power, who didn't have patience for half-baked theories of human behavior. Scholars depended upon capitalists for their livelihood, enabling them to perform organizational research. Early scholars treaded lightly in Darwinistic American organizations. Taylorists believed America reached the height of its manufacturing prowess by scientific management alone and they were not going to accept a human behavior perspective of sharing power with workers. Dugald Jackson of MIT began the "illumination tests" at the Western Electric Hawthorne Factory in Cicero, Illinois in 1924, which are credited as the first human behavior studies. Mary Parker Follett (1926) devised the theories of "power with" versus "power over," positing that people should not "give orders," but rather "agree on a common course of action." The next major breakthroughs came with Maslow's hierarchy of needs (1943), McGregor's theory X and Y (1957), and Herzberg's motivation-hygiene theory (1959). Organizational behavior was defined as the psychology and sociology of how and why individuals and groups interact within organizations. It now extends to globalization, international culture, motivation, decision making, teamwork, conflict management, power, politics, egalitarian leadership, organizational culture, and organizational change. However, has organizational behavior gone far enough?

15.2.3 Project Management View

Project management is one of the most dominant undercurrents, trends, and disciplines in modern organizational theory and has its earliest beginnings in the neoclassical period. It can be traced directly to rational planning emerging from Franklin Delano Roosevelt's New Deal (1933). As a result, Karl Mannheim published a book on planning theory in 1940, inspiring Herbert Simon's rational planning model (1946) and Edward Banfield's rational planning model (1955). The program evaluation and review technique (PERT) was created to illustrate project schedules for the Navy's Polaris missile project in 1956, although some say it was never used. However, it did lead to the critical path method (CPM) to determine the longest path through a project schedule in 1957. Both were considered a "revival" of scientific management during the Cold War as Russia launched *Sputnik* into orbit in 1957. Much earlier scheduling techniques included stopwatches (1821), harmonografs (1896), and Gantt charts (1903). A host of project management innovations rapidly emerged, including work breakdown structure (1962), cost/schedule control systems criteria (1967), project management institute (1969), project management body of knowledge (1987), earned value management (1989), and so on.

Note that scientific management and project management share common assumptions. First, scientific management is necessary for project success. Second, tacit knowledge must be converted into explicit work routines. Third, work routines must be measured using time. However, the largest assumption is that humans can be managed like machines or automatons. Innovation studies show over 70% of market and customer needs exist as hidden, inexpressible, tacit knowledge. That is, knowledge, information, data, customer needs, and project scope are in the mind of the beholder. It cannot be spoken, written, or poked, prodded, elicited, cajoled, enticed, threatened, or forced out of a human's head. As a result, over 33% of today's projects fail outright and 70% are behind schedule, over budget, or have breached scope control! Global project failure rates are as high as 50%. Most public sector acquisitions are beyond any hope at all. What happened to the promise of scientific management? Do contemporary approaches offer any hope? We examine this next.

15.3 Case of the Enterprise Lean Six Sigma Initiative

Total quality management (TQM) has a long history in the United States and the world. Joseph Juran, W. Edwards Deming, and Walter Shewhart are the earliest figures in TQM. They were inspired by scientific management, which they practiced at the Hawthorne Works (1920s). Walter Shewhart published a quality control book by 1930 and a statistical quality control (SQC) or statistical process control (SPC) book by 1940. Joseph Juran published *Total Quality Control* by 1950 and W. Edwards Deming started Japan's quality movement in 1950. Shigeo Shingo taught TQC and SPC at Toyota in 1950 and cocreated the Toyota Production System (TPS) with Taiichi Ohno in the 1950s. Japan's Deming Prize was first awarded in 1960 and his "14-points" were immortalized in *Out of Crisis* (1986) when the US Navy changed TQC to TQM at the height of the US TQM movement.

Quality circles also became popular in the 1970s to empower workers to improve organizational processes. Philip Crosby popularized zero defects for squeezing efficiency out of organizational functions. Motorola renamed SPC as Six Sigma, to squeeze manufacturing defects out of its semiconductors in the 1980s. MIT introduced TPS, Lean, and just-in-time practices to the United States in 1990, although flexible manufacturing had been around since 1960. The Baldrige Award was created to exhort US firms to pursue quality, although some went bankrupt because of its high cost. Jack Welch of GE adopted Six Sigma for process improvement in the 1990s. Finally, Kanban, a simple just-in-time system based on TPS, reached its Western peak in 2010. A hidden Japanese tool was the Keiretsu, which is a loose network of firms that combine their resources to give the group enormous leverage based on personal relationships versus contracts.

Executives directed their organizations to transform or reengineer their organizational processes using Lean and Six Sigma when they appeared. Six Sigma maximizes product and service quality by minimizing process variation and increases resources by lowering costs. Lean Six Sigma maximizes customer value, speed, efficiency, and quality by driving out waste, inefficiency, waiting times, and defects to create a just-in-time organizational workflow. Six Sigma uses visual tools and statistical methods, such as cause-and-effect diagrams, check sheets, control charts, histograms, Pareto charts, scatter diagrams, and stratification charts. Lean Six Sigma uses some of the same tools, but focuses on value stream mapping, cycle time, queues, flow, cycle time, WIP limits, and quality. Both Six Sigma and Lean Six Sigma are staffed by teams of black, green, and yellow belts with varied training, education, skills, and experience.

Our executive formed Lean Six Sigma teams (LSSTs) to fix our top organizational issues, one of which was the lack of integration among research, engineering, and operations. These grew to be wholly separate enterprises over the decades, billions of dollars were invested in each function, and we became a loose federation of disconnected operating divisions. R&D was responsible for investigating technologies, engineering was responsible for building systems, and operations was responsible for serving customers. R&D was happy to operate in a vacuum, engineering's projects rarely succeeded due to their immense complexity, and operations cobbled together their own systems to make ends meet. Therefore, an LSST was formed to fix them using value-driven, better, faster, and cheaper tools to help safeguard these investments. However, the LSST was not authorized to fix the enterprise with "cooperation view" principles.

Certified Six Sigma Black Belts (CSSBs) were hired to oversee LSSTs, which consisted of top division managers, and our LSST had six months to fix R&D, engineering, and operations. LSSTs were led by division managers of some importance, and ours had prior success with using consultants, so a project management consulting team was assigned to facilitate our LSST. The consultants were also required to have Lean Six Sigma subject matter experts (SMEs), so the consultants appointed an SME to lead the consulting team. Therefore, our LSST had two leaders, a division manager, and an SME, as well as two teams, other division managers, and consultants. Division managers were a steering committee, and consultants planned and executed the work.

Division managers received Lean Six Sigma training and fed this knowledge into the project planning process, whereas consultants used their own expertise to help fill in the gaps. Project charters, scope statements, work breakdown structures (WBSs), activities, budgets, and schedules were formed and earned value management (EVM) experts tracked the hours used by the consultants to execute the work to devise solutions. External CSSBs provided oversight, although the SME was responsible for providing bottom-up coaching to both the steering committee and consulting team on the use of Lean Six Sigma tools. The SME's first challenge was to gather Lean Six Sigma information, distribute it, and mentor the LSST, which worked as a cohesive unit to devise a roadmap, deliverables, and timelines.

Our LSST's strategy consisted of interviewing key senior managers, who held strategic organizational knowledge and experience. Then, these data could be analyzed using Lean Six Sigma tools and techniques, facilitated by CSSBs to identify recommendations successfully. Our LSST interviewed dozens of senior managers, mostly from within engineering, because this is where the lion's share of the organization's investments lay. The SME coordinated and facilitated the interviews, collected the data, and made them available for Lean Six Sigma analysis. Our LSST filtered the raw data to look for patterns of organizational success. The SME was also an expert in new product development, which is a hybrid of "coordination" and "cooperation" principles.

In one interview, a senior manager described a solution to the issues among R&D, engineering, and operations. In an earlier project, he was placed in charge of solving a key customer need. A field operator had a critical need that came to the attention of our executive. An engineering manager was appointed to solve the problem and he had the foresight to assemble a small cross-functional team from R&D, engineering, and operations to resolve it. Then, they prototyped a new solution based on cutting-edge technology, performed lightweight engineering, and rapidly fielded it to improve organizational performance dramatically. It only cost a few thousand dollars, whereas the typical engineering project cost billions and usually failed.

Unfortunately, our LSST ignored the information, because they were too busy talking over the voice tracks of each senior manager we interviewed. The division managers' egos got in the way and they used the interviews to show off their expertise in order to get promoted. The SME was the only one who seemed to be listening, as it was his job to facilitate the interviews, and he recognized the information as a type of new product development model. The SME was surprised and pleased to hear about the use of coordination and cooperation views (i.e., customer collaboration, adaptive planning, fast incremental deliveries, and small cross-functional teams). The SME politely advised the LSST leader to remind the team to do more listening instead of talking, which was a good opportunity to establish a personal relationship with his customer.

Our LSST leader halved our timeline from six months to only 90 days to focus on getting a new position, which placed enormous pressure on the LSST as well as the project schedule. Hours quickly passed, work accumulated, and milestones were being missed, causing our EVM analyst to lose patience as deadlines approached and EVM measures indicated project failure. CSSBs were not pleased, because Lean Six Sigma steps were skipped to focus on the final set of recommendations, and the LSST had no intention of implementing them to the dismay of CSSBs. Division managers became obsessed with solving the problem individually, bickered endlessly, and fought for power and control to receive credit for fixing R&D, engineering, and operations. Of course, they were relying on their own experience and opinions to devise solutions, as they hadn't taken the time to listen to the voice of the customers who described legitimate alternatives.

Aside from the LSST, the SME was the de facto project champion. He gathered a lot of Lean Six Sigma information, distributed it to the team, and provided coaching. He gathered success stories and developed a business case for the project. He studied the new product development paradigms and organized these data into powerful infographics, which were distributed to the team. He asked some of the world's top experts to consult with the team and created a portal to collect all of the external as well as internal interview data. The portal was a critical success factor, as it served as the central repository of team knowledge, assumptions, priorities, and current focus. He used his expertise to filter the data and ensure the LSST always saw the most relevant data, and he also began seeding a final set of recommendations to the LSST leader and team members.

The LSST lead transitioned to the new role, distanced himself, and pressured everyone to cut corners to complete the project, which undermined the confidence of the consultants. Thus, they began withdrawing from the LSST and assumed responsibility for winding the project down. A new division manager was appointed, who ordered the consultants to terminate the project and undermine the outgoing manager's success, and default on the commitment to our executive. The SME asked the consultants to grant a small amount of time to close the project administratively, which he used to complete the project instead. He negotiated with the CSSBs and communicated the intentions and priorities of the LSST lead, which were to deliver a set of recommendations to our executive using an abbreviated Lean Six Sigma methodology as quickly as possible.

The SME used the remaining time to communicate face to face with the LSST lead multiple times per day, to obtain the team's priorities and communicate personalized strategies. He informed the LSST lead of the sensitivity of the emerging political climate and advised the LSST to walk softly with the various stakeholders who were on pins and needles. He informed the LSST lead that the project was being closed by key stakeholders and suggested tactics for completing the project in spite of these undercurrents. Finally, the SME held a series of capstone meetings to finalize the recommendations, get stakeholder commitment, and motivate the media experts to assemble the executive briefings. He delivered the final recommendations and closed the project, all on the shoestring budget he'd previously requested from the consulting team.

15.4 Summary

This was a case study on using scientific management versus human behavior concepts for diagnosing systemic organizational issues related to R&D, engineering, and operations. These functions became self-serving entities and new products and services did not grow from ideas into engineering and operations in spite of multibillion-dollar investments over decades. As in so many organizations over the last century, scientific management principles were used in the form of Lean Six Sigma and project management to improve organizational performance. Project management is designed to complete new products and services within their scope, time, and cost constraints, while maintaining customer satisfaction, technical performance, and quality. Lean Six Sigma maximizes value by increasing speed, efficiency, and quality of organizational processes by creating a waste-free, demand-based, new product and service delivery workflow.

However, what was the outcome of this organizational transformational initiative? Did scientific management principles in the form of project management and Lean Six Sigma work? Did the LSST fix R&D, engineering, and operations as the organizational executive desired? From the project management perspective, the LSST was a disaster, because the scope consisting of Lean Six Sigma activities and artifacts were not completed to finish the task in only 90 days. The total scope included cause-and-effect diagrams, Ishikawa charts, check sheets, control charts, histograms, Pareto charts, scatter diagrams, value-stream maps, queues, flows, WIP limits, and so on. From an EVM standpoint the schedule and cost performance were nonstarters, because few of the Lean Six Sigma activities and deliverables were utilized. However, the real scope consisting of the recommendations were completed on time and within budget to the executive's satisfaction.

Furthermore, the LSST lead was utterly delighted, which is a benefit of "cooperation view" principles such as relationships, trust, communication, collaboration, shared power, and the like. The LSST lead was young, ambitious, ruthless, cunning, intelligent, merciless, ruled with an iron scepter, and had a well-deserved reputation of being impossible to satisfy, as many on the team experienced. Historically, the LSST lead demanded the use of only the best and brightest consultants with advanced scientific education, sharp technical skills, and rigorous project management discipline. However, the SME used softer people skills, emotional intelligence, instinct, risk taking, and raw courage to establish a close, continuing, and trusting personal relationship with the LSST lead. Armed with cooperation view skills, the SME shepherded this project to a successful end and the LSST lead granted the first-ever formal reward to the consultants because of the SME's efforts.

The executive acted upon the LSST's recommendations and formed a cross-functional project to build the largest and most complex system in the 60-year history of this organization. The SME participated in this new project and was pleased to see the use of cooperation view principles grow every day on this project and many others. The use of cooperation view principles is gaining a foothold throughout industry and the world to readdress both project as well as organizational performance improvement. However, there is still much work to be done.

Further Reading

Banfield, E. C. and Meyerson, M. (1955). *Politics, Planning, and the Public Interest*. Glencoe, IL: Free Press.

Burns, T. and Stalker, G.M. (1961). *The Management of Innovation*. London: Tavistock.

Crainer, S. (1998). *Key Management Ideas: The Thinkers Who Change the Way We Manage*. Harlow, UK: Pearson Education.

Crosby, P.B. (1979). *Quality is Free*. New York: McGraw-Hill.

Daft, R.L. (1988). *Organization Theory and Design*. Mason, OH: South-Western.

Deming, W. E. (1986). *Out of the Crisis*. Cambridge, MA: MIT Press.

Follett, M.P. (1926). The illusion of final authority. *Bulletin of the Taylor Society*, 2(6): 243–256.

French, J. R. P. and Raven, B. (1959). The bases of social power. In D. Cartwright (Ed.), *Studies in Social Power*. Ann Arbor: University of Michigan Press.

George, M. (2002). *Lean Six Sigma: Combining Six Sigma Quality with Lean Production Speed*. New York: McGraw-Hill.

Goffin, K. and Mitchell, R. (2005). *Innovation Management: Strategy and Implementation Using the Pentathlon Framework*. London: Palgrave-Macmillan.

Goleman, D. (1995). *Emotional Intelligence: Why It Can Matter More Than IQ*. New York: Bantam.

Hammer, M. and Champy, J. (1993). *Reengineering the Corporation: A Manifesto for Business Revolution*. New York: Harper Business.

Herbst, P.G. (1962). *Autonomous Group Functioning*. London: Tavistock.

Herzberg, F. (1959). *The Motivation to Work*. New York: John Wiley & Sons.

Highsmith, J. (2010). *Agile Project Management: Creating Innovative Products*. Boston: Pearson Education.

Kozak-Holland, M. (2011). *The History of Project Management*. Ontario, CA: Multi-Media.

Kreitner, R. and Kinicki, A. (2013). *Organizational Behavior*. New York: McGraw-Hill.

Maslow, A.H. (1954). *Motivation and Personality: A General Theory of Human Motivation Based Upon a Synthesis Primarily of Holistic and Dynamic Principles*. New York: Harper.

Miller, G. A. (1956). The magical number seven, plus or minus two: Some limits on our capacity for processing information. *Psychological Review*, 101(2): 343-352.

Ott, J.S. (1989). *Classic Readings in Organizational Behavior*. Pacific Grove, CA: Brooks-Cole.

Pande, P.S., Neuman, R.P., and Cavanagh, R. (2000). *The Six Sigma Way: How GE, Motorola, and Other Top Companies Are Honing Their Performance*. New York: McGraw-Hill.

Pink, D.H. (2009). *Drive: The Surprising Truth about What Motivates Us*. New York: Penguin.

Shafritz, J.M. and Ott, J.S. (2001). *Classics of Organization Theory*. Orlando, FL: Harcourt College.

Smith, A. (1776). *An Inquiry into the Nature and Causes of the Wealth of Nations*. London: Strahan & Cadell.

Taylor, F. W. (1911). *The Principles of Scientific Management*. New York: Harper & Row.

Womack, J.P. and Jones, D.T. (1996). *Lean Thinking: Banish Waste and Create Wealth in Your Corporation*. New York: Free Press.

Wren, D.A. (1994). *The Evolution of Management Thought*. New York: John Wiley.

16

HARNESS COMMON SENSE FOR DECISION MAKING

SIMON Y. LIU

National Agricultural Library
US Department of Agriculture

Contents

16.1 Introduction

Decision making is a cognitive process resulting in the selection of a course of action among several alternative scenarios (Reason, 1990). Every decision-making process produces a final choice. Decision making is at the core of people's daily life and all business activities.

As an individual, you have to make decisions constantly. You have to decide when to get up in the morning, what to have for breakfast, which clothes to wear, what route to drive to work, where to fill up the gas tank, whether to take the stairs or the elevator, which television program to watch, where to go for dinner, who to vote for, and many others. There is just no end to the decision-making process.

As a business person, you have to make numerous business decisions daily. You have to decide who to meet, what to discuss with your customers, what to invest, whom to hire, which company to partner with, when to start or stop a program, and many others. The business decision-making process is getting harder and more complex in the modern world. There are many factors that influence decision making including political, economic, environmental, social, technical, communications, and other perspectives. Common sense is helpful to navigate through these multiple, complex, and rapidly changing environments.

16.2 Common Sense Decision Making

Decision making can be hard. Almost any decision involves criteria, alternatives, conflicts, or dissatisfaction. The difficult part is to pick one solution where the positive outcome can outweigh possible losses. Avoiding decisions often seems easier. Yet, making your own decisions and accepting the consequences is the only way to stay in control of your life, your business, and your eventual success.

16.2.1 What Is Common Sense?

There are many offered definitions of common sense. Wikipedia defines common sense as a basic ability to perceive, understand, and judge things which is shared by ("common to") nearly all people, and can be reasonably expected of nearly all people without any need for debate. *Merriam-Webster's Dictionary* defines common sense as "sound and prudent judgment based on the simple perception of the situation or facts." In a forum titled "How Dangerous Is Common Sense to Managers?" Visotsky stated that "Common sense is defined as beliefs or propositions that most people consider prudent. ..." (Heskett, 2011)

Watts (2011) believed that common sense is "the loosely organized set of facts, observations, experiences, insights, and pieces of received wisdom that each of us accumulates over a lifetime. ..."

Looking at these definitions together, common sense is related to perception, basic understanding, judgment, and intuition. You have learned from past experiences and, as a result, your brain tells you either, "This is common or normal," or, "That seems uncommon or strange." This phenomenon is completely natural; it happens without our thinking about it. For all practical purposes, common sense is a body of rules of thumb for how the world operates.

16.2.2 Common Sense Decision Process

Decision making is a mechanism for making choices at each step of the problem-solving process. There are many methods, models, and techniques for decision making. They include mathematics, statistics, economics, management, psychology, and others aimed at assisting or facilitating people's choice of solutions for various problems.

Common sense allows us to function in the everyday world. As our life becomes more dynamic and less structured, common sense gains more and more recognition as an essential decision-making tool. You may have heard of or witnessed experienced decision makers who are able to recognize directly the best option or course of action in many complex, dynamic, or even tricky situations. The solution just comes to them from somewhere in their subconscious mind, instead of being a result of a lengthy chain of logical derivations or a computer output from a complicated statistical analysis or well-designed simulation.

There are a few common sense decision-making processes (Ponton, 2013; Tanner, 2013). The following six steps have been used in most of these processes. When using this model, each step may be completed quickly, but every step must be considered. It is not necessary to document each step, but it is important to think through every step:

- Step 1: *Identify the problem.* Define exactly the problem to be solved and factors the problem involves.
- Step 2: *Define evaluation criteria.* Establish judgment criteria the solution should meet.

- Step 3: *Explore alternatives.* Generate ideas for possible solutions.
- Step 4: *Select an alternative.* Determine the best alternative based on the evaluation criteria.
- Step 5: *Implement the solution.* Transform the decision into steps for a specific plan of action and execute the plan.
- Step 6: *Evaluate the situation.* Evaluate the outcome of the decision and action. Capture lessons for future improvement.

16.2.3 Strengths and Weaknesses of Common Sense Decision Making

Common sense and intuition can be astonishingly good, especially after they are improved by experience. Savvy poker players are so good at reading their opponents' cards and bluffs that they seem to have x-ray vision. Under extreme pressure, firefighters can anticipate how flames will spread through a building. Doctors or nurses can tell immediately if a baby has a dangerous infection even before blood test results come back from the lab (Arsham, 2013).

Recent research in a variety of fields provides abundant evidence for the existence of universal principles of common sense. According to Steven Pinker (1997), many cognitive scientists believe that the mind is equipped with innate intuitive theories or modules for the major ways of making sense of the world. Pinker's study indicated that the human mind is equipped with a smaller list of core truths and a set of rules to deduce their implications.

Common sense can make you a much more effective decision maker. Decision-making situations where the common sense approach can help most include the following:

- The problem is poorly structured or unstructured.
- Rapid response is required. The circumstances leave you no time to go through complete formal analysis.
- There is a fast-paced change environment. The factors on which you base your analysis change rapidly.
- The criteria, rules, or information you need to take into account are hard to obtain or articulate in an unambiguous way.
- You have to deal with ambiguous, incomplete, or conflicting information.
- There is no precedent.

Yes, common sense can make you a much more effective decision maker. Yet, before you put more weight on common sense, there are a few important points you need to keep in mind. Professor James L. Heskett, professor emeritus at Harvard Business School, elaborates on one of the biggest dangers to strategy makers and managers: their very own experience, intuition, and common sense (Heskett, 2011). A huge body of research has clarified much about how common sense works, and how it doesn't. Here's some of what we've learned:

- It takes a long time to build good common sense. Poker players or firefighters, for example, need years of dedicated study, practice, and experience to assemble a sufficient mental repertoire of patterns or common sense.
- People apply common sense inconsistently. Even experts are inconsistent in dealing with different situations, environments, and other factors.
- Common sense works best in specific environments, ones that provide a person with good cues and rapid feedback. Cues are accurate indications about what's going to happen next.
- People can't tell where ideas come from. There's no way for even an experienced person to know if a spontaneous idea is the result of legitimate common sense or of a pernicious bias.

16.3 Common Sense Development

Common sense provides the ability to know what to do at the right time and in the right place. Common sense sets someone apart from others with the same qualifications and skills. It makes one more marketable because companies prefer to hire people who can solve problems logically, rather than those who constantly need more training. Common sense could include collaborative skills, cultural intelligence, communication skills, emotional intelligence, the ability to connect the digital dots, and others.

Can common sense be learned or developed? Tanner argued that common sense can be learned, it can be developed, and it can be taught (Tanner, 2013; Ward, 2003). It is not conventional learning, such as math, science, or technology. Instead, it is the sum of what we observe, experience, or absorb. In summary, with sufficient practice, people can come to recognize the types of errors the reflective mind makes, and learn to avoid them. One cannot go to school to get this learning, but it can be acquired if one pays attention and proactively seeks it out. Some advice on how to develop common sense is listed below:

- Expand and improve your knowledge by reading, observing, and learning about new and different subjects. This process will give you the confidence to respond when you are in similar situations.
- Proactively seek, try, and experience new things. Grab every opportunity to move beyond your comfort zone.
- Be curious and ask questions to obtain and accumulate knowledge continuously and expand your knowledge base and horizon.
- When presented with a problem, reflect on the situation and break it down into segments before rushing to a solution.
- Arrange a mentor. A mentor can be a big help because the best way to learn new things is through persons with experience. Mentors can help their mentees to develop common sense and cognitive skills through conversation, scenario analysis, table simulation exercises, or other activities.

16.4 Apply Common Sense

Common sense is helpful to navigate faster through much unstructured data and can work around certain gaps and conflicts in the available information. However, it is critical to keep in mind that even when you rely on common sense it is still very important to do your homework. You can greatly increase the quality of your common sense decisions if you include certain elements of the analytical approach. In particular, try to follow the procedure of the rational analysis first. As much as you can, capture on paper the ideas on the main options and the criteria for evaluating your choices. Write down the key facts and factors you need to keep in mind. By having all the important points written in one place, you will also unclutter your mind. At that stage you are much more ready to listen to your common sense. The following two cases illustrate how common sense decision making works in the real world.

16.4.1 *Case I: Making Decisions Based on Future Inevitability—The Common Sense Principle in Dealing with a Future Library Is Simply This: Digital*

To many people, a library probably means a brick and mortar building filled with paper books that anyone can access. At a more abstract level, it's really a repository of information; this could be books, manuscripts, journals, CDs, DVDs, eBooks, and everything in between. Today, libraries around the world are facing financial challenges as governments and academic institutions deal with the aftermath of the recession and budget deficits. At the same time, libraries are facing strong competition. As the Internet has become the primary way people gather information, the traditional "building filled with books" model becomes less relevant to their lives.

Where is the future of libraries? And what should libraries do in the short, mid-range, and long terms to address these challenges? There is much research around the subject of future libraries and proper actions to address these challenges. Some argue that libraries will become increasingly virtual, some argue that libraries will disappear as the world goes to cyberspace, whereas others predict that libraries will become the dinosaurs of the digital knowledge era. Instead of arguing about what makes sense and doesn't, it's very important to look forward into the future to see what the inevitable outcome of the future library will be. There's little doubt that the library of the future is digital.

Digitalization has the promise to transform the library community, creating new opportunities, and helping to achieve operational efficiencies and differentiation that were previously impossible. However, digitalization will challenge the existing business model, channel system, and business processes. It requires libraries to make significant organizational changes and adopt new competencies. Libraries embracing and achieving digitalization will be better positioned to meet next-generation library customer demands for electronic interaction and new library services, and improve user experience management. Finally, digitalization will enable significant long-term competitive advantage for early adopters, which will be a detriment to libraries that are slower to transform.

16.4.2 Case II: Making Decisions Based on Customers—The Common Sense
*   Principle in Dealing with Customers Is Simply This: Listen to Them*

For about 10 years, I worked as a director of information systems for
an information service provider. Because of the thousands of pieces of
interconnected equipment and thousands of customers with various
levels of skill, my organization experienced a good number of customer complaints. Product defects, broken services, system outages,
hardware failures, software bugs, or slow responses were plentiful and
customer complaints were inevitable.

My organization had developed various plans and mechanisms for dealing with these complaints. We also had developed
service-level agreements and matrices that showed the response to
be made for each particular complaint. We even required various
levels of approval just to ensure that my organization responded to
the complaint in the best possible reflection of customer service.
Unfortunately, complaints continued. Furthermore, we had a few
customers who always were very critical and had very specific or
sometimes complicated ideas of how good IT products and services
should be provided.

To address these lingering problems, we decided to add the common sense line of "Ask the customer" when addressing the issue
of dealing with customer complaints. It is proven that the best
way to satisfy customers is to ask them what they want and provide it to them immediately, if possible. No paperwork, no deep
analysis, no judgment, but immediate response. Whenever we
received a negative e-mail or phone complaint from customers, we
would apologize, express our disappointment, and ask, "What can
we do to make this right?" This common sense approach coupled
with other formal customer service tracking and improvement
mechanisms helped to improve customer services and strengthen
customer relationships.

16.5 Conclusion

This chapter has demonstrated that common sense has a long practical, philosophical, and even scientific pedigree, a pedigree that can
help to improve decision making and enrich decision-making science
and management theories.

Common sense is the decision maker's friend when the decision has to be made expediently, in fast-changing environments, with poorly structured, ambiguous, or even conflicting information, and by individuals who have accumulated experience and wisdom. Common sense works well especially when all things are constant and the environment is stable.

Common sense is a grand asset to have. However, you need more than one tool in your box, regardless of how sharp that tool may be. It is the combination of common sense and theory that makes a great leader and decision maker. Use your common sense, but recognize that the situation may include new variables that must be part of analysis. In summary, common sense has its place in combination with formal systems of knowledge, analysis, planning, and management.

References

Arsham, H. (2013). "How to Make Good Decisions." Retrieved from http://home.ubalt.edu/ntsbarsh/opre640/partXIII.htm#rlearngood, October 20.

Heskett, J. (2011). "How Dangerous Is Common Sense to Managers?" Retrieved from http://hbswk.hbs.edu/item/6785.html on, October14, 2013.

Pinker, S. (1997). *How the Mind Works*. New York: Norton.

Ponton, A. (2013). "Do You Remember to Use Common Sense When Making Decisions?" Retrieved from http://thepexstringofariadne.wordpress.com/2013/09/22/do-you-remember-to-use-common-sense-when-making-decisions on October 13, 2013.

Reason, J. (1990). *Human Error*. Cambridge, UK: Cambridge University Press.

Tanner, K. (2013). *Common Sense: Get It, Use It, and Teach It in the Workplace*. New York: Springer Science.

Ward, K. (2003). *Decisions without Mistakes: (Common Sense Decision-Making Strategies for Today's Managers and Leaders)*. Lincoln, NE: iUniverse.

Watts, D. (2011). *Everything Is Obvious, Once You Know the Answer: How Common Sense Fails Us*. New York: Crown Business.

17

TEN COMMANDMENTS OF COMPUTER ETHICS

A Case Study in Intuition-Based Decision Making

RAMON C. BARQUIN

Barquin International

Contents

17.1 Introduction

Let me assure you that I am no cyber-Moses and that any attempt to compare me with that biblical figure is terribly embarrassing to me. Yet it seems like a logical place to start this narrative of how the Ten Commandments of Computer Ethics were written and the role that intuition-based decision making played in the process. First, let us provide some background on cyberethics in general and then we will discuss the Ten Commandments of Computer Ethics, in specific.

17.2 Cyberethics and Need for a Code of Conduct for the Cyber World

Cyberethics or computer ethics can be "defined" broadly as ethics in the context of information technology (IT) systems and addresses the behavior of both developers and owners of IT systems and applications as well as the users of such systems. In today's world, of course, it applies especially to developers, owners, and users of the Internet infrastructure, its websites, and all the social media that operate in cyberspace. Think of the need for responsible "cybersocial behavior" in our virtual world. Should there be any question of how much it is needed, just look at what is happening online today. This is a world where identity theft has reached epidemic proportions;[*] where cyberthieves create fake sites to steal money from your bank account;[†] where cyberbullying has already led to several suicides;[‡] where cyberstalking has resulted in more than one death;[§] where people can be tried on Twitter and Facebook independently of having their actual day in court (Levy, 2013); where billions of hours are wasted every year on unproductive game playing;[¶] where almost three quarters of all Internet traffic is spam;[**] where malware infections or denial of service attacks from criminal gangs or activist hackers cost the global economy hundreds of billions of dollars;[††] and where privacy is basically nonexistent.[‡‡]

---

[*] The Bureau of Justice statistics reports that in 2010, 8.6 million households in the United States had at least one member age 12 or older who experienced one or more types of identity theft victimization. https://www.ncjrs.gov/spotlight/identity_theft/facts.html

[†] One example is the fake PayPal emails used in phishing attacks. Here is what PayPal has to say on how to protect yourself. https://www.paypal.com/us/webapps/helpcenter/article/?articleID=94034&m=SRE

[‡] Although there have been multiple stories on this problem, the recent case of Rebecca Sedwick, in Lakeland, FL, puts it clearly into perspective. See Alvarez (2013). Boschert (2013) provides a clinical view of some of the issues involved.

[§] Most notorious was the Amy Boyer case where a cyberstalker bought information from Docusearch, a data broker, which he used to track, find, and eventually kill Amy Boyer [Electronic Privacy Information Center (EPIC) June 15, 2006. http://www.epic.org/privacy/boyer/default.html].

[¶] In 2003 apparently human players collectively spent 9 billion human hours on the game *Solitaire*. http://news.cnet.com/8301-1023_3-9989480-93.html

[**] The Kaspersky Lab reported that although spam decreased in 2012, it still represented approximately 72.1% of all Internet traffic. http://www.kaspersky.com/about/news/spam/2013/Spam_in_2012_Continued_Decline_Sees_Spam_Levels_Hit_5_year_Low

[††] For 2011 it was estimated at $388 billion in both material and time loss (Norton by Symantec, 2011).

[‡‡] See: "Find Out (ANYTHING) About (ANYONE)" http://www.xent.com/FoRK-archive/oct00/0050.html This site and other similar ones feature offers to let you "Find out SECRETS about your relatives, friends, enemies, and everyone else—even your spouse!"

And none of the prior instances addresses the ethical questions related to the cyberbehavior of governments (i.e., cyberwarfare,[*] privacy violations,[†] Internet blocking and censoring[‡]); or that of corporations (i.e., spying on employees,[§] intellectual property theft[¶]); or the behavior of "hacktivist" communities such as Wikileaks[**] or Anonymous,[††] and the Manning[‡‡] and Snowden[§§] incidents.

---

[*] When should nations actually go to war in cyberspace? This has become the subject of much debate as nation states create their cyber commands and work out the rules of engagement. Do we need a modern-day St. Augustine to develop a "Just Cyberwar" theory?

[†] The US Congress was so concerned with privacy protection after 9/11 that in the creation of the Department of Homeland Security they established a Privacy Office reporting to the Secretary. Furthermore, the 9/11 Commission recommended the creation of a Privacy and Civil Liberties Oversight Board eventually implemented through statute to advise the President.

[‡] The Paris-based *Reporters without Borders*, tracks this aspect of cyberspace life. In its 2012 report they put together a list of "Enemies of the Internet" that includes: Bahrain, Belarus, Burma, China, Cuba, Iran, North Korea, Saudi Arabia, Syria, Turkmenistan, Uzbekistan and VietNam.

[§] It is widely done and most often legally. There are serious ethical questions, though, around how, what, and when. For an ad from one vendor of spying software see: http://www.spectorcne.com/?utm_source=GOOGLE&utm_medium=PPC& refer=38252&cid=70170000000MLSu&keyword=Employee%20Monitoring& placement=&gclid=CNyZ1sqoo7kCFdKj4Aod6U4AvA

[¶] Corporations and governments often engage in this behavior. It is estimated that the United States alone loses approximately $300 billion per year. See: http://www.rawstory.com/rs/2013/05/22/international-theft-of-u-s-intellectual-property-cost-300-billion-per-year-report/

[**] On their website (wikileaks.org) they state that they "provide an innovative, secure and anonymous way for sources to leak information to our journalists." The ethics of their wide publishing of sensitive documents, both public and private, is controversial.

[††] *Anonymous* is a loose network of hacker/activists that often acts in support of Wikileaks and other causes. See their *YouTube* "Message to the American People" video https://www.youtube.com/watch?v=PIpfFXux-bg

[‡‡] PFC Bradley E. Manning was court-martialed and sentenced to 35 years imprisonment in July 2013 for passing classified material to Wikileaks starting in 2009. The leaked documents included war footage videos, a quarter of a million diplomatic cables, and half a million army reports. http://en.wikipedia.org/wiki/Bradley_Manning

[§§] Edward J. Snowden was a contractor for BoozAllenHamilton working for the National Signals Agency (NSA). In May 2013 he delivered a significant amount of classified material to the *Guardian* (previously known as the *Manchester Guardian*) revealing substantial details about the large-scale NSA electronic surveillance programs unleashing a significant amount of controversy over the ethical, legal, and constitutional aspects in terms of dealing with Americans' privacy. Snowden fled to Hong Kong from where he leaked the information and as of October 25, 2013 he was in temporary exile in Moscow.

17.3 Ten Commandments of Computer Ethics

Needless to say, as information technology started to expand and complement human cognition and enhance interconnectedness and communications, there developed a somewhat perplexing convergence of reality and virtuality that has exploded onto the scene with a brand-new set of ethical dilemmas around behavior in cyberspace. Hence, a need exists to focus on cyberethics as well as to provide some framework for people to behave responsibly online, especially when no one else is looking.[*]

There have been many attempts to develop codes of conduct for the field of computers dating back to the 1960s (Herold, 2006). The first professional code was adopted by the Association for Computing Machinery (ACM) in 1973 and shortly after that the Institute of Electrical and Electronic Engineers (IEEE), the British Computer Society (BCS), and the Australian Computer Society (ACS) all followed suit.

The Computer Ethics Institute (2013), which I cofounded in 1990 and still preside over, proposed its own code in 1992 in the form of the "Ten Commandments of Computer Ethics." Although a late entrant into the space, it directly addressed the social behavior of users where the previous codes focused primarily on providing guidance to IT professionals. Given that the timing of this framework coincided with the emergence of the Internet and the World Wide Web, they have wound up being one of the most widely distributed canons for cyberethics. In effect, a recent Google search (10/26/2013) for "Ten Commandments of Computer Ethics" yielded 103,000 hits (Computer Ethics Institute, 2013). They were commented on by Paul Harvey News (ABC News, 1992) and by National Public Radio's (1992) "All Things Considered." They have been translated into 24 different languages (Computer Ethics Institute, 2013), and have been addressed in news stories by the *Washington Post, Boston Globe, USA Today, Philadelphia Inquirer,* and other major newspapers. They have also

---

[*] Although the *Merriam-Webster Dictionary* defines ethics as "the discipline dealing with what is good and bad and with moral duty and obligation," the comment about how people behave online when no one is looking reminds me of a more useful and evocative concept of ethics as "obedience to the unenforceable" which was brought forth by Lord Moulton, a distinguished early nineteenth-century English jurist. In attempting to analyze human agency, he considered the area of action lying between law and pure personal preference to be "the domain of obedience to the unenforceable."

been featured in the *IT Ethics Handbook* (Northcutt, 2004), the *Whole Library Handbook* (Eberhart, 2005), the *Information Security Management Handbook* (Tipton and Krause, 2010), and many other reference manuals, textbooks, and publications.

Hundreds of K–12 schools, as well as universities, in the United States and abroad use it as an ethical framework to guide behavior when dealing with information technology, including the following:

a. Eau Gallie High School, Melbourne, FL.
   http://carolburns.edublogs.org/2009/01/15/ten-commandments-
   of-computer-ethics/
b. East Buchanan Community Schools, East Buchanan, IA
   http://www.east-buc.k12.ia.us/Technology/com/ethics.htm
c. Southwestern Oregon Community College, Coos Bay, OR
   http://www.socc.edu/search/index.shtml?cx=0008496668598
   10170851%3Ahjkvpgujdv8&cof=FORID%3A11&q=Ten+
   Commandments+of+COmputer+Ethics#164
d. University of Advancing Technology, Tempe, AZ
   http://www.uat.edu/academics/ethics_in_black_white_and_
   grey.aspx
e. Jabakan Pendidikan Negeri Kedah, Alor Star, Malaysia
   http://www.kedah.edu.my/sahc/a_portal/portal_tekvok/ict/
   nota_ict_n_soceity/Microsoft%20Word%20-%20les6.pdf
f. Saint Joseph's College, Rensselaer, IN
   http://www.saintjoe.edu/~timm/core10lks.html.

At least one, the College of Southern Idaho, threatens anyone who fails to abide by the Ten Commandments of Computer Ethics with "loss of computer privileges … or other disciplinary actions including dismissal from CSI."* They have subsequently been applied to e-mail (White, 1994) and adapted for geographical information systems (GIS; Blakemore and Longhorn, 2004).

17.4 Intuition, Intuition-Based Decision Making, and Experience

So how does all this relate to intuition-based decision making? As we all know, intuition is not magic. We may not yet be able to explain clearly how it works, but we do know there is no intuition in an

---

* http://www.csi.edu/stuinfo/labs/policy.html

empty brain. Individuals in a coma with a flat brain wave* are not capable of intuition, let alone any other cognitive activity. Unless there has been a period and process that lays the groundwork by building a substantial amount of expertise in a cognitive domain, it is difficult to make decisions based on intuition.

Some instances of intuition seem to work based on our sensory perceptions of signals picked up from other humans or animals. But this in itself is probably possible through the accumulated unconsciously captured repository of signals that allows us to trust ourselves in making a decision on who we like enough to befriend, hire, or marry.

There has been a lot of attention paid to the "10,000 hours" threshold required for mastering true expertise. Popularized by Malcolm Gladwell (2008) in his book *Outliers: The Story of Success*, he talks about the studies done on the amount of hands-on experience required for international chess masters, the Beatles, or Bill Gates to achieve success in their chosen field. Much of Gladwell's analysis was based on the work done by K. Anders Ericsson† and other researchers on expertise. That said, there is much controversy and there have certainly been important counterexamples of excellence, at least in sports, that would point to genetics rather than practice.‡ The debate of "nature versus nurture" will always be with us; however, no one disputes that practice is very important in the development of expertise.

Without going into a depth beyond the scope of this case study, I just want to establish that there were at least 10,000 hours thinking and working on issues of cyberethics under my belt by the time I wrote the Ten Commandments of Computer Ethics in 1992. Certainly, I had been dealing with issues of ethics and information technology, off and on, for over 25 years; and 10,000 hours on task can be logged comfortably in less than five years by

---

* We do need to keep in mind that certain drugs exist that substantially depress brain functions and can sometimes produce a flat wave in a brain that is not truly dead. http://www.mhhe.com/biosci/ap/saladin/nervous/reading13.mhtml
† Ericsson is a professor of psychology at Florida State University and one of the world's foremost authorities on the topic of expertise.
‡ The main counterargument was presented by David Epstein (2013) where he documented the case of two high-jumpers with a very different profile in terms of time on task, where the less experienced one is more successful. http://www.theatlanticwire.com/entertainment/2013/08/malcolm-gladwell-defends-disputed-10000-hours-rule/68624/

working eight-hour days, excluding weekends, and even allowing for a two-week vacation every year.

My first encounters with these issues were in reading the occasional accounts of computer crimes in the press during the mid-1960s or from colleagues' anecdotes after joining IBM in 1966. But it was my arrival in graduate school at MIT that marked my move into a different level of interest and involvement with cyberethics.

All new doctoral students in Course 6 (Electrical Engineering and Computer Science) are assigned an advisor. It was just my good fortune to be placed under the tutelage of a unique human being and computer science pioneer, Roberto Fano.* Aside from having developed some of the fundamental work on electric transmission lines and then on computer architectures, he became the director of Project MAC at MIT. Project MAC (Project on Mathematics and Computation) was the precursor to MIT's Computer Science Laboratory. It was created in 1963 with a Defense Advanced Research Projects Agency (DARPA) grant and Fano was its first director. It became very well known and respected for its pioneering work in operating systems, artificial intelligence, and the theory of computation. And Fano was one of the rare technologists concerned from early on with what he called in a seminal article (Fano, 1970) "the societal implications of computer science." Through our many interactions and conversations he started me thinking about the problem with more seriousness and rigor than in my previous intellectual dalliances.

I continued conjecturing and writing about these issues during the next few years at IBM, both during my stints working domestically as well as my four years in charge of government relations for the IBM South East Asia Region in Hong Kong. One interesting anecdote from these years was a lecture I gave in September 1983 in Dogo, Korea at an international workshop (Barquin, 1983). It was being translated from English to Korean by a simultaneous translator who almost choked when he heard me say "cyberethics." I have no idea whether I coined the term on that occasion—it seemed like a good way to label the topic being addressed and I had no idea whether it had ever been used before—but clearly the translator had never heard

---

* Roberto M. Fano. For his biography, see: http://www.itsoc.org/portal_memberdata/
RobertFano

the word and it took him some time and linguistic creativity to digest it and then translate it.

In the mid-1980s, IBM transferred me to Washington, DC where I was in charge of the company's public affairs programs, including the establishment of the IBM Public Affairs Institute. In dealing with what we called emerging issues, I was asked to work on cybercrimes, privacy, and other related problems where information technology seemed to be creating new ethical dilemmas or resurfacing some old ones in very different ways. As a result, I took on the responsibility of conducting outreach and creating an alliance or coalition to better understand and address some of these issues. This led to an agreement with the Washington Theological Consortium* and The Brookings Institution† to initiate conversations on the topic. The first event was a "convocation," entitled *New Ethics for the Computer Age?* and was cosponsored by Brookings, The Washington Theological Consortium, and IBM in 1986.

These activities were the prelude to the creation of the Computer Ethics Institute (CEI), which launched in 1990 with a loose affiliation to Brookings, given the dedication and involvement of their CIO, Jane Fishkin, who also became CEI's vice president. We held many sessions, workshops, and discussions starting in 1990, but the National Computer Ethics Conferences became CEI's feature event from 1992 through 1996. And this brings us precisely back to the Ten Commandments of Computer Ethics.

17.5 Deciding to Write the Ten Commandments of Computer Ethics

So, unknowingly, but nonetheless having 10,000 hours plus of expertise on the subject area, I was tapped to give the keynote lecture at the Institute's first National Computer Ethics Conference in May 1992. The question of a framework for cyberbehavior was very much on my mind when I announced the title of my speech: "In Pursuit of a 'Ten Commandments' of Computer Ethics" (Barquin, 1992).

---

* http://washtheocon.org/about/

† The Brookings Institution is a Washington, DC based public policy research organization often considered the oldest and most influential think tank in the world. It was founded in 1916 and conducts research and education in most aspects of domestic and foreign policy.

Preparing myself to be the keynote speaker for the very first National Computer Ethics Conference at The Brookings Institution was something I took seriously and worked on diligently. But the title of the speech was misleading in the sense that it was just a way of focusing attention on the need for a cyber code of conduct. In no way was there an intention on my part, early on, to write a canon for this field. But the closer we got to the date and time of the actual speech, and the more I read and reread the draft, the more I felt there was something missing. As I read my latest version the afternoon of May 7, I realized what was missing: the actual Ten Commandments of Computer Ethics.

Now I had to make a decision. Did I dare to tackle that task less than a couple of hours before my speech?

What is a decision? *Merriam-Webster's Dictionary* defines a decision as the "act or process of selecting a course of action." Hence decisions are invariably tied in some way to action. I had to decide whether I would write a "Ten Commandments of Computer Ethics" and deliver them with my speech later that day.

I had never written an ethical canon or a code of conduct before. If I were to attempt to do so, I would normally give myself ample time to do the research required for such a project, disseminate it to experts and peers, test the premises, and assess the results, and write and rewrite as needed. No way! Not enough time. What do I do?

Interestingly enough, there was little of the internal tension you might perceive from the paragraph above. I had an intuition—the power of knowing immediately and without conscious reasoning; something known or understood at once (*Merriam-Webster Students Dictionary*)—and then proceeded to write. In no more than 15 minutes I had written longhand, on a striped white paper pad, the Ten Commandments of Computer Ethics.

I showed them to a colleague at work who nodded his head in assent. Then I left for Brookings to deliver my speech. In the minutes before, I showed them to other members of the CEI board, one of whom caught a typo and another suggested changing a word or two. I gave the speech and CEI issued a press release a few days afterwards that was picked up by the Associated Press. The rest is history.

17.6 Conclusion

Once it hit me that I could not deliver a lecture that just teased the audience about the need for a code of conduct for cyberbehavior and not provide at least a first draft, I decided to write one. Never mind that I had only a short time between that moment and the appointed time for my lecture. My intuition assured me that I could do it, and I did. It could have been a disaster, dismissed by the public and laughed at by my peers. Yet, I had the base of experience and the wherewithal to make it happen. Thus, the Ten Commandments of Computer Ethics were born.

References

ABC News (1992). "Computer Ethics." Paul Harvey News, 6/11, noon.

Alvarez, L. (2013). Suicide of girl after bullying raises worries on web sites. New York Times, September 13. http://www.nytimes.com/2013/09/14/us/suicide-of-girl-after-bullying-raises-worries-on-web-sites.html?nl=todaysheadlines&emc=edit_th_20130914&_r=0.A

Barquin, R.C. (1983). MICOM – Affection to Society. *The Electronic Times*. Seoul, Korea, October 5, 13 (in Korean). Lecture delivered at *Microcomputers and Their Future Impact on Society, The Electronic Times First International Computer Workshop and Seminar*, Dogo, Korea, September 6–10.

Barquin, R.C. (1992). In pursuit of a "ten commandments" of computer ethics. Working paper. Washington, DC: Computer Ethics Institute. http://www.computerethicsinstitute.com/publications/whitepapers.html

Blakemore, M. and Longhorn, R. (2004). Ethics and GIS: The practitioner's dilemma. In *AGI 2004 Conference, Workshop on "GIS Ethics,"* London, October. 14http://www.spatial.maine.edu/~onsrud/GSDIArchive/gis_ethics.pdf

Boschert, S. (2013). Cyberbullying triples suicide risk in teens. *Pediatric News*, May 21. http://www.pediatricnews.com/specialty-focus/mental-health/single-article-page/cyberbullying-triples-suicide-risk-in-teens.html

Computer Ethics Institute (2013). http://www.computerethicsinstitute.com/

Eberhart, G.M. (Compiler). (2005). *The Whole Library Handbook*. London and Chicago: American Library Association.

Electronic Privacy Information Center (EPIC). "The Amy Boyer Case." June 15, 2006. http://www.epic.org/privacy/boyer/default.html

Epstein, D. (2013). *The Sports Gene*. New York: Penguin Group.

Fano, R.M. (1970). Computers in human society—For good or ill? *Technology Review*, March: 24–31.

Gladwell, M. (2008). *Outliers: The Story of Success*. New York: Little, Brown.

Herold, R. (2006). *Introduction to Computer Ethics*. New York: Auerbach. http://www.infosectoday.com/Articles/Intro_Computer_Ethics.htm

Levy, A. (2013). Trial by Twitter. *The New Yorker*, August 20. http://www.newyorker.com/reporting/2013/08/05/130805fa_fact_levy

National Public Radio (1992). "Computer Ethics Ten Commandments." 6/11, 5–6 p.m.

Northcutt, S. (2004). *IT Ethics Handbook*. Rockland, MA: Syngress,

Norton by Symantec. (2011). Cybercrime Report:2011. http://us.norton.com/content/en/us/home_homeoffice/html/cybercrimereport/

Tipton, H.F. and Krause, M. (2010). *Information Security Management Handbook*, sixth ed. Boca Raton, FL: Auerbach.

Volpe, M. (1992). Ten commandments of computer ethics issued by newly formed Computer Ethics Institute, press release. Computer Ethics Institute, June 12.

White, V.A. (1994). Ethical implications of privacy in electronic mail. In *Proceedings of Technical Conference on Telecommunications R&D in Massachusetts*. Lowell: University of Massachusetts, October 25. http://valinet.com/priv.html

18

Don't Take It Personal

An Intuitive Approach to a Simple but Delicate Matter

JOAN MARQUES

School of Business
Woodbury University

Contents

18.1 Introduction

Performing as the leader of a team always brings along challenges. But when you lead a team of highly educated people, you have an additional dimension of trials and tribulations on your hands. As the chair of a department of seasoned academicians, all with high degrees, stellar lists of achievements, and many years of teaching and research under their belts, I have learned that there is one key mind-set that can make a world of difference in the quality of my work relationships: not taking anything personally. I am very happy that an experienced departmental leader and friend gave me this advice when he heard that I was offered the chair position. He said, "Whatever happens, don't take it personal." I have to admit: it's not always easy, because sometimes it seems as if colleagues are deliberately out to undermine your authority, to badmouth you, to make you uncomfortable, and to point out the flaws in your performance. Indeed, some of these people may have those intentions, but it's never helpful for your peace of mind or for the quality of relationships to take it all personally. After all, if you go, there will be another leader about whom they will complain. People with high education levels seem to have a hard time following orders. They are intelligent, accomplished, and generally feel that no one should tell them what to do. I'm not sure if this is the case in all academic institutions, but I would be amazed if it were not.

A highly respected dean from the University of Southern California (USC) made the following statement in a presentation attended by leaders from various walks of life: "Leading highly educated people is much more challenging than leading employees in a business environment. There are different stakes involved, and the egos you're dealing with in academia are immense!" Reflecting on this statement, I have to admit that he was right. You need a pair of silk gloves to handle highly educated coworkers, and you better be prepared for the fact that their level of maturity in handling issues sometimes is suspect, as the following case proves.

18.2 Retention Campaign

A few months ago, I was approached by a team of institutional officers who were implementing a retention campaign and therefore were visiting all schools of the university to collaborate on contacting students with performance issues. The intention was that the advisors of these students—there was a list for each school—would connect with their advisees and find out whether there were any needs to be addressed. It was only halfway into the semester, but the officers did not want to wait until the semester was over and the damage was irreparable. At this point, students could still get some extra assistance to ensure that their performance would improve, so that they could still have good semester results rather than failing their classes again, getting disheartened, and dropping out. The philosophy behind this initiative was admirable, in my opinion. It could make a tremendous difference in the lives of young people with families, jobs, or personal problems. The students would (or at least, should) appreciate the extra miles the school was going to secure their educational success.

18.2.1 *Contacting Advisors*

Once I received the guidelines and agreed upon a deadline for reporting back to the institutional officers, I reviewed the case list that had been handed to me, and saw that behind the name of each underperforming student, the name of his or her advisor was included. There were 35 students' names and about seven advisors, including me. That boiled down to an average of 5 students per advisor. I compiled a uniform letter, which I planned to send to all advisors. The only section that would be different in each letter was the one with the names and the current status of the students they were advising. I sent the letters to the six other faculty advisors by e-mail with a strong request to (a) please contact their advisees, (b) find out how they were doing so far in the semester and whether they needed any assistance, and (c) provide me with their findings within a week. This would give me one day to compile all the retrieved information and report back to the university officers in a timely manner.

Responses were pleasantly surprising in most cases. Most of my colleagues replied within the next two days with updates that were useful for my report. One colleague needed additional nudging, because she was seemingly taking the easy way out by claiming that all her advisees needed extra help without providing any specifics regarding their current whereabouts. In a follow-up e-mail, I encouraged her to communicate with each individual student instead of merely sending her shortcut response. As a result, she sent a more detailed overview of her advisees' current status a few days later.

18.2.2 *Surprising Response*

What surprised me most about this project, however, was the reaction of one colleague, to be referred to hereafter as Clarice, whom I considered my best friend on the entire team. Clarice and I had a history together. Many years ago, we had both been bullied away from a department by the same administrator, but each of us had managed to pave a successful career path for ourselves nonetheless. As it turned out, this administrator was now one of the institutional officers in the retention campaign. Because so many years had passed, however, I no longer felt any grudge or discontent in dealing with this person.

As for Clarice and me, we had known each other well before this unpleasant bullying experience, but sharing that common history had brought us closer together in the past six years. This closeness was further encouraged by our common research and teaching interests. Over the years, we engaged in multiple scholarly projects together, gathered data, wrote articles, conducted presentations, and developed a relationship of mutual respect and appreciation. Clarice and I knew we could count on each other when it came to getting any job done. By being assigned the chair position of the department, I was placed in a supervisory position over my friend. Yet, this had not been a problem for either one of us so far. It seemed, however, that things were about to change.

Where I had expected that Clarice would be one of the easiest colleagues to cooperate in the retention campaign, she wrote the most humiliating response, not only directed to me, but to the entire team of institutional officers involved! Clarice was clearly upset and she vented that she had thus far been repeatedly harassed by the Student Monitoring Department (SMD) about contacting poor performing students during the past months, and that she had already done all she could. In unambiguous terms, Clarice first explained how she had attempted to communicate with these problem advisees in the past months, and then boldly asked if we now wanted her to stalk these students, call their parents to keep daily tabs, or move in with them to verify whether they were doing what they had promised to do.

18.2.3 *Considering Options*

My first response after receiving this angry note from my longtime colleague and friend was astonishment and dismay. I read the letter over and over again, wondering why this person, with whom I had such a great relationship of trust and openness, did not first come and talk to me to obtain clarification, or even to vent verbally about this task if she wanted to. Sending such a demeaning letter, not just to me but to all involved officers, was not only unprofessional, but absolutely uncalled for in my opinion. I contemplated this issue, and wondered what my next move would be. Should I write her up? No, that was not my style. She was still a good friend as far as I could tell. Should I talk to the involved officers about it? No, the situation was embarrassing enough as it currently stood. Should I write Clarice a harsh letter in return, and copy all involved officers on it, just as she did? No, that would probably just add fuel to the fire, and could make something that was still relatively small erupt in a bitter feud. Should I talk to the dean, who was my supervisor, and ask for his advice? No, because he would probably explain the formal line of action, and disregard personal factors. I had to listen to my intuition here. And that's exactly what I did.

On the day after I received Clarice's wrathful letter, there was a faculty gathering, and I saw my friend sitting across the table. I had been thinking about this case off and on, struggling with the various options I had in order to address this issue, but also keeping in mind that I should not let this issue consume my entire thinking, performance, or mood. Whatever led my colleague to lash out the way she did was *her* problem, not mine. I had not singled her out or maliciously targeted her, I had not accused her of being a bad advisor, and I had not put her on the spot in front of anyone. In fact, it was quite the contrary: she had been the one blowing this whole issue out of proportion. At least, that's how I looked at it.

18.2.4 *Allowing Intuition to Lead the Way*

After the gathering was over, I headed for my office, and it so happened, that Clarice headed in the same direction. Letting my intuition lead me, I casually asked her, "So, what was the reason for your letter yesterday?" She shrugged, and then said, "Well, I'm fed up with being harassed all the time by the Student Monitoring Department about these poor performing advisees!" I thought for a moment and asked if she had time to talk things through in my office. She accepted my invitation, and we went to my office. Although I always maintain an open door policy, I closed the door for this one, because I could sense her frustration. I couldn't quite place the look on her face. It looked like a mixture of fear, aggravation, fluster, and regret, but then again, who was I to interpret someone else's facial expressions? I internally called myself to order, and we sat down. "Okay, we're alone now. Please share your thoughts or feelings." "Well," Clarice started, "SMD's supervisor has been sending me e-mails all through the summer about these students, and I have diligently contacted them.

I have reported on my findings. They should be keeping better track of their records, before accusing me of not doing my job!"

A lightbulb switched on in my head, and I thought, "Ah! She feels as if she is being accused of underperforming! Was this her way of defending herself?" My heart went out to my friend as the fog of misunderstanding lifted.

> Clarice, we all received those letters from SMD over the summer, and we addressed their requests for action to different degrees. However, the fact that this team is trying to secure retention is a laudable one. It may aggravate us, especially if we would have all been as diligent as you are, but believe me, not many of us have been contacting our advisees to the same degree and with the same devotion as you apparently have! As you know, many full-time faculty members are absent during the summer and do not undertake any action of that nature then.

"Well," Clarice insisted, "Then SMD should keep track of the responses and not badger those of us who have already done their duty!"

"I can see your point, but this was not SMD 'badgering' you, Clarice. The letter to which you responded came from me, and it was just a uniform letter that I sent to all our advising faculty, with only the advisees' names differing."

And then Clarice said something unexpected, "Perhaps I am angry with you, then!" There was a moment of silence in the room, as I was trying to understand where that came from.

"Why is that?" I asked.

"Because of the tone of your letter!" Clarice exclaimed.

"The tone of my letter?" I blurted, "The letter to you had exactly the same tone as the one I sent to Merrill, Jane, Joyce, Dick, and Jerry! But they were not offended as far as I recall. They just provided me the requested information without any complication. Even the most difficult one of all, Joyce, did not find any reason to be offended about it. So, what was so offensive to you about my letter?"

"Well, we know each other so well! We're friends. Why did you have to send me a uniform letter? You could have written something like, 'Clarice, sorry for having to bug you with this, but these officers are driving me nuts with their retention issues, so let me know where you stand with these student cases.' That would have been much more acceptable to me!"

I thought about Clarice's comment for a minute. To me, this was like bolt from the blue. I didn't see that one coming. "Hmm. So, it was the fact that I wrote you a uniform letter, and you felt that, by doing so, I threw you on a pile with the rest?"

"Yes! And you placed a red exclamation mark to indicate urgency. What was the need for that?"

I really didn't know what to think anymore. "Don't take it personal. Don't take it personal." I kept repeating this in my mind, as I was searching for calm reasonable words to explain the situation to Clarice.

> Clarice, we're both management professors. You know as well as I that efficiency and effectiveness can spare us a lot of extra work. This was a work-related project. It may have sounded a bit impersonal, but the idea was to get things done within the given deadline. That's also why there was an urgency mark attached to the letters. Now, you and I are good friends, and I cherish that, but we also have a work relationship, and sometimes there is just not enough time to include a personal note to everyone. If I recap what I just learned from you in this conversation, I understand that your reason for writing this letter has to do with two major issues: (1) You feel harassed by SMD because they have written to you multiple times, and you had contacted the students before; and (2) You are upset because I wrote a generic letter to you with an urgency mark, which made you feel pigeonholed and belittled?

"Right!" said Clarice. "I was really upset about this whole thing, and perhaps I should have calmed down before writing this letter and making such a fool of myself." This was another surprise to me. So, at least she realized that she had been out of line. Maybe this heart-to-heart talk was leading somewhere after all.

"Well, perhaps I could have alerted you on this verbally, Clarice, but our other colleagues could then come and complain about not being approached the same way as you. One major issue is the fact that you sent your harsh reply to all the involved university officers, and I'm afraid that did not go over too well."

"I know," Clarice admitted, "The dean already came to me and firmly reprimanded me about it. I have been thinking about it since last night, and realize now that this was a premature letter, and that it would have sounded entirely different if only I had thought a bit longer before writing it."

I felt relieved.

> I am glad that you see that, Clarice. To be very honest, I have thought about responding to you right after I received your letter, but I realized that such communication would not benefit our work climate or our friendship. I think we both have some valuable takeaway opportunities here. In the future, I will at least include a note on top when I am sending a uniform letter to faculty, so that they don't feel specifically 'targeted.' However, I feel that you should understand that I cannot possibly write custom-tailored letters for every issue that emerges. In the future, you could consider giving your emotions a few thoughts, and possibly come and discuss matters with me before writing such a letter again and thereby include officers that have no clue where this comes from. Do we have an understanding?

Clarice had tears in her eyes as we got up and hugged each other. "I appreciate you," she whispered.

I said, "I appreciate you too, my dear friend. Let's not let these things come in the way of our great work-based collaboration and friendship. We cannot lose the trust or the dynamism. We need to keep talking before drawing conclusions."

18.2.5 Lessons Learned

After our heart-to-heart talk, my relationship with Clarice was restored, and we continue to engage in research and other professional projects together with great mutual respect. Yet, I have learned a few valuable lessons from this issue:

1. People have their own perceptions about things, very often influenced by pre-existing emotional baggage, which taints their views in directions that may not be readily understood by others. Clarice saw a reprimand in a letter that was just a general call to action in order to support a well-intended initiative. Where her perception came from is not at stake here, but it was there, and it made her respond to the uniform letter in an entirely different way than all others who received it.

2. Although it is wonderful to be friends with colleagues, there can be circumstances where the two relationships can complicate clarity in communication. In this case, where one of the friends was the supervisor of the other, it required a cautious call on intuition to keep both relationships afloat and healthy. If I had responded to Clarice's letter with a similar level of aggression, our relationship might have been disrupted to an irreparable degree, and our friendship would have definitely been affected lastingly.

3. Communicating assignments to highly educated academic workers requires as much consideration, clarity, and caution as it does in other work environments, but there is an additional challenge: the egos involved are sometimes larger, so the caution has to be even more intense.

4. A good old, face-to-face conversation can clear up many dark clouds. In situations where the air gets tense, it is best to engage in an open private conversation without other eyes or ears nearby. This allows parties to lower their guards and be more candid with one another.

5. Reflect on the issue at hand, consider it, think deeply about it, but don't let it consume you. After the initial sense of dismay, I considered several reasons why this could have happened, but also kept reminding myself that the world would still turn, regardless of how this issue would work out.

6. Don't take it personal. As stated in the introductory part of this case, that is not always easy, because there are always many ways in which we can feel personally targeted. I could have decided that my friend–colleague was trying to undermine or embarrass me before top officers, and taken a very rigorous approach to this matter. I could have decided to go the formal route, and win the battle, but lose a friend.

18.3 Conclusion

Allowing your intuition to lead the way requires confidence that the right outcome will be achieved. When dealing with people, we never have all the information at hand. Maintaining relationships, whether formal and informal, is like sailing on the ocean: sometimes there are unexpected hidden icebergs under the surface, and only our intuition will help us circumvent them. We are fortunate to live in an era where awareness is on the rise about emotional intelligence and the critical role our intuitive skills can play in the overall level of well-being in our work environments. The case presented above was resolved in a highly intuitive way, without hidden agendas, developmental charts, trend analyses, scenarios, or ratio investigations. The solution to the problem developed all by itself in an atmosphere of trust and good-will, and solidified and strengthened a relationship where a diehard systematic approach would have only led to further alienation.

19

Let's Have a Knowledge Conference!

LESLEY-ANN SHNEIER

World Bank Group

Contents

19.1 Introduction

The intuitive idea was to change an existing model of one knowledge talk per month, disconnected from any knowledge activities, and not giving anything back to the speakers, to a gathering of like-minded people who would share what they do, learn from one another, and network during the knowledge fair. The challenge was keeping it to a peer-to-peer learning workshop rather than a conference of talks by "gurus". Working with facilitators to design interactive sessions, AdobeConnect moderators to ensure active participation by an online audience, and combining a workshop with concurrent sessions with extended time at lunch for a knowledge fair led to a highly participative two-day knowledge-sharing event.

19.2 Genesis of an Idea

Talking to people at KM World in 2011, I realized that many people want to know what the World Bank Group (WBG) is doing these days to share knowledge. I also found myself longing to learn what others were doing. At the time, the WBG was holding monthly knowledge talks, bringing well-regarded guest speakers in to share what they were doing. The talks were wonderfully inspiring and thought-provoking. The discussions that followed were rich, although the WBG participants' comments tended to convey a sense of envy of the speakers' accomplishments.

To me, there seemed to be something of a disconnect between these two experiences.

On the one hand, WBG readily and easily found inspiring speakers, but we weren't sharing what we ourselves were doing. This may have been because we were no longer as well organized around sharing knowledge activities as we had been in the past. It may also have been because the culture of WBG is to believe that others are better than we are, and that we should learn from them. The model of these talks was one talk per month, not connected to any particular knowledge program or activities and there was no follow-up about what we heard or learned. Nor were we sharing anything about WBG with the speakers in return. This bothered me no end.

The part that really tugged on my brain was the desire of others to find out more about knowledge sharing in development in general. And then it hit me: why not bring people together at the WBG headquarters? We could listen to them, they could listen to one another, and to us. Instead of one-off talks from speakers to the WBG, we could all share and learn from one another, a gathering of like-minded people in a workshop environment. Not only would there be speakers in a workshop environment, but there would also be a knowledge fair in the atrium that would enable the organizations to showcase their knowledge activities and to engage in informal conversations.

19.2.1 From Idea to Action

Now, as an individual working part-time in one part of the organization, the challenge for me was to "sell" this idea to the central group charged with knowledge activities, the organizers of these monthly knowledge talks. I approached my boss, and outlined my idea of inviting people from other development organizations to gather in

Washington, DC. He thought it a great idea, and helped me convince the central group that they should host the workshop, and to let me organize it.

I wrote up my idea as a formal concept note so as to make it "official", and for them to pass up the management hierarchy for approval. They particularly liked the plan to invite other development organizations to participate at their own expense—no one would be paid to speak, no travel expenses would be paid—and the only cost to them would be food, audiovisual, and other space-related costs associated with the booths for the knowledge fair.

So far, so good! My intuitive idea had been accepted. I had the paperwork in hand for HR to charge my salary to the central group, so the hard part was over. Or so I thought. How wrong could I have been! At times, I felt like I was pushing a rock up a hill all by myself. My new manager in the central group still supported my idea, but somehow nothing much happened. Because I didn't work physically with that group, I didn't really understand the group dynamics or the office politics. Even after 27 years at the WBG, I still somewhat naively thought that, once the concept note and terms of reference had been approved, I would simply get on and deliver.

The first indication that things wouldn't go smoothly occurred around the question of who would sign the invitation to participate in the conference. In fact, I regretted even raising the question of who in the hierarchy should sign it. When push came to shove, I simply told them that we had not quite three months before the conference, and no one knew about it. I knew that if I extended an open invitation through KM4Dev (with about 2,500 members, a strong presence on a LinkedIn group, a website, and excellent wiki on all things relating to knowledge and knowledge management for development), I would generate much interest. Management agreed I could do this, in a so-called "informal" way. Within days, I had so many abstracts and ideas that it was clear the conference/workshop idea was a winner.

Now excitement started to build. It became clear to the management team that something was actually going to happen. A small team was assigned to help me brainstorm how to organize the conference. We designed a website on which people could register to participate, and on which all conference materials would later reside.* The challenge here was to enable external access and participation, so special web hosting arrangements had to be made and cleared with the WBG's office of information security.

19.2.2 Words Matter

When it came to choosing a title for the conference, I realized how important words were: I wanted to convey a sense of a "web" of organizations sharing knowledge, with an image like a spider web, or network analysis diagram. This got formalized as "mobilizing knowledge networks for development." So the abstracts that came in dealt with "networks" for development. Adding "mobilizing" led people to propose topics that dealt with putting networks of development people and organizations together to cover a particular type of topic. This wasn't exactly what I'd had in mind, but it made for a very interesting conference.

Another challenge was insisting that the speakers all be practitioners, and resist the WBG's proclivity of inviting gurus to speak. Eventually it dawned on me that the way around this dilemma lay in the words I used to describe the event: instead of a "conference", I called it a "peer-to-peer learning workshop". That was instantly recognizable and acceptable to all, although right up to the day of the conference, I was still resisting suggestions for experts and notable speakers that I should invite to speak.

19.2.3 Conference and Knowledge Fair

With the 30 abstracts in hand, we proceeded to iterate how to create a cohesive workshop. We decided on four tracks, collaboration, grassroots practitioners, KM practices, and platforms (i.e., knowledge hubs around particular themes), although several abstracts could have fit into more than one track. The four tracks and 30 topics became 16 concurrent sessions, held across two days. And, of course, we did invite some gurus for keynote presentations.

---

* All conference materials, PowerPoint presentations, AdobeConnect recordings, and brief session reports can be found here: http://web.worldbank.org/WBSITE/ EXTERNAL/PROJECTS/0,,contentMDK:23189356~pagePK:41367~piPK:515 33~theSitePK:40941,00.html

Once the agenda was settled, I sent out invitations to register to KM4Dev, KM.Gov, and other similar groups, as well as the development banks, NGOs, CSOs, foundations, APQC, and universities with KM programs. In the invitation and on the registration form, we stated quite specifically that no one would be reimbursed for travel, no one would be paid to participate, and that there was no fee to participate. Even so, several tried very hard to get funding. Responses came in thick and fast, and we had to close registration for onsite participation once we reached 300, the limit of our largest conference room. All in all, we had 300 onsite and 200 online participants. Clearly, the idea of the peer-to-peer workshop was generating tremendous buzz and there was a lot of interest in the topics.

What surprised me, though, was the less-than-enthusiastic response from within the WBG, both for speakers and for participants. In some cases, I had to plead with people to speak about their work, which I knew would fit in with the topics other organizations were presenting; without WBG speakers, we would not have been sharing what we were doing, my major premise for the event!

Then, suddenly, with just six weeks to go, management tried to stop the whole thing. It turns out that they just didn't "get it", didn't trust that this idea of a peer-to-peer workshop would work or would be worth it. The design was considered "loose". There were no respected gurus as speakers. Lunch time was too long. Was my intuitive idea dead in the water? Once more I had to write a justification note, explaining just what the purpose of the workshop was and why we should do it. Absolutely exasperated, I said we already had more than 300 participants registered (online and in person), and was not about to tell them that the WBG had cancelled the whole thing. If necessary, I would pay the food costs personally rather than admit defeat in public! Luckily, it didn't come to that, and we got back on track to deliver the whole event. So, my intuitive idea kept needing nurturing and defending in the face of a management team who preferred hard data and standard conference designs.

Crafting the knowledge fair was much easier than the agenda. The proposed booths somehow fell into themes more readily, so that similar topics from different organizations could be grouped together spatially. Protecting the time on the agenda for participants to spend visiting the booths was a lot harder. Every time management looked at the agenda and saw a two-hour lunch break, they wanted to stuff additional talks in that space. Nonetheless, the idea of participants carrying bag lunches (which we provided) around in the atrium while they networked informally, exploring the various booths and generally sharing knowledge prevailed.

In addition to the booths, we provided bar-height tables around which participants could chat and eat their lunch, as well as coffee service in the center of the fair. The buzz this generated was palpable, such that we had to beg people to come back to their workshop sessions. See Figure 19.1.

To help manage the conference, we pulled together a team of four facilitators, one for each track. We had two AdobeConnect experts who managed the plenary and keynote sessions and trained and

Figure 19.1 Knowledge fair.

supported a team of volunteers from within the WBG who managed the AdobeConnect for the breakout sessions. Another group of staff, known as Y2Y, or the youth group, volunteered to write up a report for each session. Getting people to fill these roles was very easy. The difficulty I had, which surprised me, was getting agreement that we needed track chairs. At the last minute, I was able to convince my manager that the track chair would "hold" the knowledge across his or her track.

One really lively meeting occurred with all the facilitators, AdobeConnect moderators, rapporteurs, and track chairs. We explored the various roles each would play, paying particular interest to ensure that our online audience would be active participants instead of passive listeners. My insistence that we include the online audience, which meant that our AdobeConnect group had to get advanced training, really paid off.

In addition, the facilitators worked with the participants in their track to make sure that they understood the design of the session, connected the various speakers and topics, and coached them on creating a "wicked question" for their topic. Each 90-minute concurrent session was designed as interactive short talks with presenters speaking for less than half of the session. The rest of the time was then devoted to small group discussions based on the wicked questions. The online participants were given a separate space for each wicked question and encouraged to have their own small group conversations. Finally, the facilitator brought the small groups back together and each group, including the online groups, then reported back to the whole group. This design was more successful in larger rooms where there was more physical space to break out than in smaller rooms where participants couldn't move around much.

19.3 Conclusion

It took six months from start to finish to bring the intuitive idea to life, to convene the people, and host the conference and knowledge fair, but it was so worthwhile. The feedback from participants, both in person and online, showed that they found the experiences and knowledge sharing invaluable, and that they had expanded their own networks. All the bios of speakers, PowerPoint presentations, and reports of sessions are still available on the website, which has now become a repository of knowledge-sharing activities by 30+ development organizations.

19.3.1 Addendum

Long before this event, I had had another intuitive idea. Way back in late 1997, I was charged with designing some knowledge management training for staff. I responded that people wouldn't attend training for something they knew nothing about, and suggested we do something to show staff what we meant. The idea was for an open house; however, as a really small team, we didn't have a "house" to open. As I walked through the relatively newly opened atrium in our main building, I realized here was space we could use. So, I suggested we have a "knowledge fair." As it turned out, no one knew what that was, because no one had ever done such a thing.

However, the event gained momentum and traction as soon as I announced that Jim Wolfensohn, then President of World Bank Group, would open the fair. Organization units began begging for spaces in the atrium. The real challenge came from the facilities management people who were concerned that their pristine atrium would be turned into a "Middle Eastern souk," which was exactly what I wanted!

When he opened the fair in late March 1998, a smiling Jim Wolfensohn looked around the makeshift booths and said we had brought his vision of a knowledge bank to life. He asked us to arrange a similar fair during the annual meetings of the WBG and the IMF later that year, which we did, this time with 50 booths. He later showed us a letter from someone who said that after spending two hours at the booths he had learned far more about development and the World Bank than he had learned in 20 years of attending the annual meetings.

Twelve years later, when I went to the same facilities management people to plan the knowledge fair for the peer-to-peer learning workshop, they had a huge book of plans and layouts and were eager to help me bring this fair to life. Knowledge fairs and similar events had become de rigueur in the atrium.

20

COPING IN A BIG DATA ENVIRONMENT

Analytics and Alignment with Organizational Change and Learning

DAVID HARPER

Applied Physics Laboratory
Johns Hopkins University

RAMESH MENON

IBM Corporation

Contents

20.1 Introduction

This chapter makes the argument that upon careful examination we will discover that Big Data may best be conceived as a return to the two core principles of organizational learning and organizational change. A related argument asserts that while organizations have begun to chase the Big Data dream, they have lost sight of some of the underlying principles that may provide context and structure to this pursuit. Before delving into the principles that we believe are germane to understanding the adoption of this new phenomenon, this chapter begins with a perspective on Big Data, followed by an overview of its core drivers. The chapter closes with a set of core principles and a framework that could serve as the basis for IT leaders to better grapple with Big Data strategies.

20.1.1 What Is Missing from the Big Data Discussion?

The gaps in the literature revolve around the notion that organizations seeking to enter the Big Data arena need to address a few fundamentals, namely the ability to understand the implications for organizational culture and the ability to learn and adapt to a new way of doing things. Current Big Data discussions hint at some of these themes but we argue for a deep look at a few of these fundamental organizational principles. We believe these provide a lens through which leaders could frame and plan for this new evolution.

20.1.2 Overview of Big Data

As science and technology evolve, the decision-making frameworks develop from simple qualitative and quantitative frameworks to multidimensional, context-sensitive, real-time analytical and predictive models that will enable new capabilities required for business and military leaders to make context-aware data-driven decisions. Information technology has evolved from back-office support systems to web-based systems enabling global commerce and social interactions and we see the trend moving toward more sophisticated cognitive computing systems such as IBM Watson. It is no surprise that information is a strategic asset both for business and the military in their respective missions.

Some of the essential characteristics of Big Data, as shown in Figure 20.1, are as follows:

- Increased volume, velocity, variety, and veracity of the type of data.

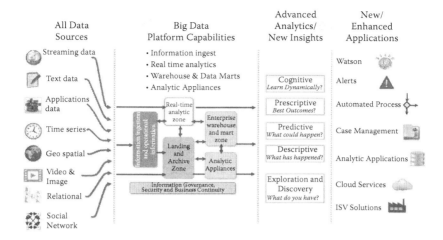

Figure 20.1   IBM Big Data integrates live streaming data (stream computing) with advanced machine learning. Cognitive computing solutions such as Watson can be used as enabling components in healthcare solutions.

- Ability to ingest data from multiple sources including sensors and free text such as social media, unstructured data, and metadata and other geospatial data collected from web logs, GPS, medical devices, and so on.
- The Big Data platform complements the existing data warehouse and mining capabilities by introducing advanced analytics and insights based on predictive and cognitive models to make context-aware decision making at any point in the past, present, or future.
- Modern information systems should be able to leverage these advanced Big Data capabilities as technologies, such as cloud computing, make it much easier to leverage these innovative technologies to position an organization in the future and differentiate it from competition.

We need to acknowledge that the world is changing. There is a significant shift of wealth from west to east; for example, by 2025, 45 of the top 100 cities will be in China according to McKinsey & Co., incurring economic pressures for the developed world to sustain growth. Innovation will help create new markets and technologies such as Big Data will be an invaluable asset for companies with the vision and ability to attract and retain top talent and help create an environment for them to be successful. This will differentiate good companies from great companies.

Growth of Big Data is being fueled by the confluence of social, mobile, cloud, and the Internet of things such as sensor networks. In this new era, traditional programmable systems will no longer be able to handle the volume, variety, velocity, and veracity of data, so things including cognitive computing, software-defined environments, and collaborative business models will become much more important. The ability to use these technologies to store, process, and analyze Big Data will be at a premium, as will the solutions that package all those capabilities together.

In recent years, we have seen the military use more UAVs (unmanned aerial vehicles) to fight the "war on terror". The UAVs are equipped with real-time sensors and powerful cognitive systems to help guide and drive the mission outcome. Big Data solutions can help detect new types of cyberattacks, employee engagement and motivation, and strategic input for driving innovation, transformation, and evolution.

Many of the Big Data components started with simple open source projects: for example, Hadoop is an Apache project written in the Java programming language. Hadoop evolved in 2007 based on the foundations of a Google-distributed file system based on university research supported by IBM and Google to solve large-scale Internet problems. Eventually, many other technology vendors came up with fully supported Hadoop-like file systems and high-performance storage subsystems, such as the general parallel file system (GPFS), that support Big Data, and a few have even packaged it as an appliance to make adoption easy and let customers focus on their core business and not worry about underlying technology complexity.

20.2 Big Data as Competitive Edge

In a recent study (Kiron, Ferguson, and Prentice, 2013), two-thirds of the respondents indicated that they were gaining a competitive edge from analytics. If organizations are looking to Big Data to gain competitive advantage, it would be noteworthy to once again return to the fundamental principles espoused by Porter (2008). Porter posited that organizations can retain their distinctive edge if they follow some seemingly commonsense tactics. These include starting with a goal, delivering a value proposition that separates them from their competitors, developing a distinctive value chain (e.g., Wal-Mart and Citibank), and having a willingness to forgo legacy infrastructures and instead focus on web-enabled technologies. The study by Kiron, Ferguson, and Prentice (2013) brings the argument full circle, indicating that 85% of the respondents agree that analytics creates a competitive advantage to a moderate or great extent. The study also found that there was strong agreement that analytics also helped to drive innovation.

Porter also reminds organizations that rather than competing on price they should focus on distinguishing the organization from competitors based on an understanding of their customers' needs. The literature (McAfee and Brynjolfsson, 2008) is replete with examples and case studies that point to the value of Big Data as a gateway to mine customer behavior. This is especially true in the retail industry, where IT-savvy organizations have come up with creative techniques to collect data about their customers and, more important, demonstrate the ability to tailor their offerings to match customer buying patterns (Kiron, Ferguson, and Prentice, 2013). It is also true in web-savvy organizations such as eBay, where product usage patterns are constantly examined and analytics are used to drive timely product enhancements (Kiron, Ferguson, and Prentice, 2013). So who benefits from these competitive data? According to Kiron, Ferguson, and Prentice (2013), a survey conducted in 2012 reported that 89% of marketing managers reported using analytics, specifically social data, to drive their decision-making process.

According to the Open Data Center Alliance (2012), Big Data use cases are not new but they can now benefit from a wide range of powerful technologies that enable access to multiple data types (e.g., structured and unstructured data). Specifically, these new technologies now empower organizations to pursue unstructured data that were previously ignored but now provide greater insight into their organizational assets. This report from the Open Data Alliance (2012) also points to the evolution of technologies such Hadoop and other open source tools as key enablers.

Davenport and Harris (2007) also confirm the value of analytics as a key enabler for organizations to blur the lines between their customer relationship management and their supply chain management processes. Davenport and Harris (2007) assert that organizations now compete by looking beyond merely simple statistical analysis and instead focus on "predictive modeling," integrating and aggregating internal and external data sources, optimizing their value chains by gaining greater insight into possible delivery challenges, and using "historical sales and pricing trends" (p. 84) to maximize their yields. More organizations are placing importance on performing trend analysis to drive marketing strategies. It is also undeniable that high-profile organizations such as American Airlines, Capital One, Citibank, and Marriott (Davenport, 2006; Davenport and Harris, 2007) have been early adopters of analytics and have used these techniques to drive some of their mission-critical business processes, such as electronic reservations.

Kiron, Ferguson, and Prentice (2013) indicate that 67% of organizations surveyed indicate that they are using analytics to gain a competitive edge. So how have these technology-savvy organizations achieved this competitive edge? The approach used by some firms can be best described as keeping it simple. For example, some of these organizations apply not only common tools and architectures but also common organizational structures (Davenport, 2006). In other words, they apply an enterprise approach, which incidentally also assumes an enterprise-level investment in IT dollars. According to Davenport, these organizations operate under the assumption that any business function can be improved with "sophisticated quantitative techniques."

Finally, it is evident that those firms which have successfully integrated analytics into their overall business strategy have done so with buy-in at the C-level. Organizations that make such commitments are considered leaders in the revolution (Kiron, Ferguson, and Prentice, 2013). Examples of this top-down commitment include Amazon, Procter & Gamble, and Harrah's, just to name a few. Organizations are also relying on the intelligence derived from Big Data not only to attract but also to retain their customers. These and other companies extol the virtues of Big Data and further make the case for this emergent IT trend. But the question remains, "Are we missing the mark when it comes to determining the framework(s) that truly drives an understanding of an organization's memory sources?" More important, how should organizations go about acquiring learning? The construct is not new but it appears to be missing from the Big Data discussion.

20.2.1 *What Is Organizational Learning?*

In this section, we discuss the perspectives on organizational learning followed by a more in-depth examination of one model that we believe is uniquely structured to be applied to Big Data implementation strategies.

The field of organizational theory has benefited from a wide variety of research and theories. However, the downside is that this has also led to a smorgasbord of definitions and linkages to the concept of organizational learning. The research on organizational learning does not agree on a single operational definition of organizational learning. The literature indicates that organizations acquire information from both the internal and external environment, interpret information from the environment, adapt, make decisions, modify assumptions and correct behavior, learn how to become more effective, and assess culture (Argyris; 1993; Argyris and Schon, 1978; March and Simon, 1958; Schwandt and Marquardt, 2000; Schein, 1996; Schon, 1975 Senge, 1990; Shrivastava, 1983). Garvin (1993, p. 80) defines the learning organization as an organization "skilled at creating, acquiring, and transferring knowledge, and at modifying its behavior to reflect new knowledge and insights," and also notes that a learning organization is skilled at four activities: "systematic problem solving, experimentation with new approaches, learning from past experience, and learning from the best practices of others" (p. 78). We assert this is exactly what Big Data organizations need to consider, specifically the notion of learning from best practices. Although we recognize that Big Data is still in its infancy, there exists a wide array of use cases that the early adopter organizations could analyze and upon which they could act. As experience accumulates, intuition based on this experiential learning can easily be applied.

Now let's turn our attention to one organizational learning model we believe encapsulates our earlier discussion. This organizational learning systems model (OLSM) is attributed to Schwandt and Marquardt (2000). We selected the OLSM to reframe this discussion and re-emphasize our argument for its applicability to the adoption of a Big Data strategy. The aim of the OLSM is to establish a framework that explains how organizations acquire information, learn, make decisions, and strategize in order to survive in a dynamic environment. The four subsystems of the model are summarized below:

1. The environmental interface subsystem permits information from external or internal environments to enter the organization (e.g., through benchmarking or scanning) and feeds this information to other subsystems within the model.
2. The action/reflection subsystem determines how the organization interprets new information, solves problems, makes decisions, formulates strategies, clarifies issues, takes action, and creates knowledge to attain its goals. The knowledge generated from this step (subsystem) is a result of the organization's ability to critically reflect on new information to adapt and survive. This subsystem is considered the nucleus of the model.
3. The dissemination and diffusion subsystem provides the structure for the organization. This subsystem determines how the organization organizes (or reorganizes), defines its management/leadership roles, defines formal policies and standard operating procedures, and communicates information.
4. The memory and meaning subsystem creates and stores the organization's processes (software processes), policies, and artifacts. These items are part of the organization's ongoing memory and permit the organization to use its intellectual knowledge to control and compete in its environment.

To summarize, a fundamental assumption of the OLSM is that no subsystem can stand alone. According to Schwandt (1997), an organization's strategies do not fail because of its size, age, leadership, existing knowledge structures, or its ability to scan the environment. Instead, he links strategic failure to a combination of all of these factors.

These four categories could benefit Big Data organizations because these learning models highlight the notion of creating knowledge. No doubt, on the surface these organizational learning models may appear to be somewhat complex to interpret, but we believe they are applicable to the current state of the Big Data market and could lead to long-term and sustainable implementation. It is also clear that when organizations apply the concepts derived from these organizational learning models, especially the ability to adapt and change, they too will reap the benefits we attribute to innovative firms.

20.2.2 It May Be All about Culture

So what does culture have to do with it? Well, it may be just one key piece of the Big Data puzzle. It's evident that those organizations (such as Amazon, Procter & Gamble, Harrah's), that have successfully deployed competitive Big Data strategies have done so by relying on the fundamentals of organizational culture. Examples highlight organizations such as Harrah's, which transformed from a rewards-based culture to a measurement-based culture. Studies (Kiron, Ferguson, and Prentice, 2013) support the argument that this cultural shift starts at the top, where analytics are a component of the corporate DNA and data are viewed as a core asset. However, in this chapter, we would be remiss if we did not include any discussion of organizational culture without drawing on the oft-forgotten frameworks that drive the concept. This may seem contrary, but if we revisit the early thinkers on organizational culture such as Schein (1985) and Hatch (1993, 1997), it would not be surprising to see an evolution of terms such as a "Big Data culture."

Therefore, organizations that are unable to transform their internal culture to view alternative points of view will be forever cast among the "analytically challenged." The ability to transform culture does not reside in the power of the server but more so in the executive suite's ability to transform the mindset of those who are entrusted to support, analyze, and innovate in ways that now seem contrary to current thinking. Moreover, organizations that can escape this mental lock-in (cultural block) will join the ranks of those seeking that competitive edge. The future is bright, but we can't forget the past.

20.2.3 Linking Organizational Subcultures to Change

A few pearls of wisdom for business intelligence leaders can also be found in Schein's (1996) discourse on organizational subcultures. He opined that "if we go back into the field and observe carefully what goes on when organizations attempt to improve their operations in response to new data from the economic, political and technological environment, we discover the critical role that culture and subcultures play" (p. 22). He also elaborated on the impact that organizational subcultures have on attempts to achieve organizational change. Schein (1996) proposed that the basic assumptions of a group determine how and when change will occur within an organization, and noted that organizations cannot operate silently within these subcultures. Instead, organizational leaders must recognize the worldviews held by each of their subcultures and communicate among them accordingly. In other words, change leaders cannot carry the same message to each subculture. Again the argument we make here is that although Big Data hype may be ruling the day, it would be difficult to ignore the core principles espoused by organizational theorists.

Our assertion is that organizational business intelligence leaders could learn much from some of these theorists. We are not calling for a stop to all engines, or as the title of this book implies "bursting the Big Data bubble;" We are not calling for a stop to all engines, or as the title of this book implies "bursting the Big Data bubble"; however, we are suggesting leaders pause and recognize some of the dynamics that may be at play when they attempt to implement Big Data solutions.

20.3 Organizational Subcultures and Implications for Change

Let's take a closer look at Schein's three organizational subcultures. Schein (1996) asserts that each carries a different set of assumptions based on their unique role within the organization. It is these disparate assumptions that make it difficult to implement change within organizations. Perhaps the greatest barrier to change is the layer of communication and translation that is required across these three communities.

Schein provided an excellent characterization of these communities when he introduced the concept of the cultures of management within an organization. In a Big Data context, Schein's (1996) three occupational cultures could be translated to the typical organization as follows: the executive subculture could be interpreted as the chief operating and chief information officers, the engineer subculture could be interpreted as the technical analysts who are charged with developing the complex algorithms, and the operator subculture could be interpreted as the owners of the business data.

20.3.1 What Is Each Subculture's Perspective?

How should change leaders communicate technology change in organizations? In order to communicate among these subcultures, it is important to modify the message at each cultural boundary (Schein, 1996). Schein's advice bodes well for the success of any change program because of the recognition that the change model affects all levels of the organization. To succeed, those charged with implementing Big Data strategies must communicate with all three cultures in the organization. The ability to understand the social and cultural boundaries and to craft messages according to each subculture's worldview could play a significant role in leading to a successful transition to a Big Data culture.

Let's recall that the executives are looking for a return on investment, and the business data owners are assessing how the change will affect their ability to respond to their customers. Likewise, the technical analysts (developing algorithms) are attempting to retain the "traditional" ways of working. In other words, these are software engineers who have been developing complex algorithms for several years and may not see a need to change their mindset. It is quite possible that they do not share the same set of assumptions about this new "hype" and hence the need for the organization to reinvent itself. Of course the executives will argue that such logic is flawed because they too have read the success stories of Big Data innovation. This success is driven by data scientists who are applying Big Data to create new insights and capabilities.

20.3.2 What about Change?

How do we help the analytically challenged organizations to adopt a new way of thinking? We have made the case for a competitive edge, customer attraction, and customer retention. However, we are still at the door of the Big Data revolution and this will require a change in all facets of the organization or, as recent studies have posited, "a new way of thinking." Recent examples indicate that even those organizations that have been around for a while, such as Match.com, managed to change the mind-set in the organization and are now viewed as "analytical innovators" (Kiron, Ferguson, and Prentice, 2013). This exemplar highlights the good news; we are in the early stages of the Big Data revolution. The question remains, how will the analytically challenged organizations adapt? What framework will they apply?

Earlier in this chapter, we highlighted the success stories of those organizations that took a top-down strategic and enterprise-driven approach to their Big Data initiatives. We now assert that it may not be possible for the Big-Data challenged firms to achieve similar strategies unless they return to the core principles of organizational change. We begin with Kurt Lewin's (1951) thinking. He posited that change occurs in three stages: unfreezing, movement, and refreezing. *Unfreezing* is the process of changing current behavior. *Movement* is the process of taking action to identify changes in the organization to modify current behavior, a core principle that is still relevant to today's organizations. We can also relate movement to the introduction of software-based technology change processes, such as Big Data, in an organization. And finally *refreezing* involves implementing the necessary structures to ensure that the change will take hold. Some writers refer to this step as institutionalization. The unfreezing step may involve the need to learn new paradigms in the organization. If we apply Lewin's model to the introduction of a technology-based software process, we can identify the unfreezing phase as identifying problems with the current mode of thinking within the organization. The movement phase would involve the use of the new practices, and refreezing would involve the introduction of policies and quality assurance procedures (McFeely, Paulk, et al., 1993) to ensure commitment to the change.

Schein (1993) extended Lewin's (1951) change model. According to Schein (1993), to make the unfreezing step successful, an organization must ensure the psychological safety of its employees during the change process. This can be achieved through executive-level commitment to the change. In terms of movement, Schein offered two approaches. First, the organization must identify a role model or mentor that members can identify with and who can help the members reframe their thinking. For some organizations, this may involve the acquisition of a data scientist to set the new direction. Second, the organization must scan the environment for information about the proposed actions or change initiatives. In other words, those organizations that are now embarking on a Big Data strategy should conduct an industry scan to learn from peers to identify competitive actions.

Finally, in terms of refreezing, Schein defined a two-step process. The first step involved defining new roles, collecting feedback, and continuing to adjust the new process until the recipients feel comfortable. The final step involved ensuring that all affected individuals fit into the new way of doing things. To accomplish this, organizations must engage the affected employees (technologist, business users, data owners) to help reframe their thinking. This is not a new idea; researchers such as Hatch (1993) have long argued that members of an organization who were not involved in the change process were more likely to reject it. In other words, it would not be possible to unfreeze if the change affects multiple parties but only one party has gone through the three-stage process. As described earlier, a Big Data strategy requires an enterprise commitment. It is not just an IT problem but an enterprise problem.

However, inasmuch as we are discussing a technology change, we must consider Moore's (1999) perspective on change adoption. He reminded us that change is a process of crossing the chasm between the five distinct groups (innovators, early adopters, early majority, late majority, and laggards) in an organization. According to Moore (1999), each group responds to and adopts organizational change based on a different set of assumptions. We realize that Big Data is still an evolving phenomenon, but a deeper understanding of these seemingly basic adoption principles may position leaders on a successful path. Although the market is replete with stories of how Big Data drives competitive advantage, the five stakeholder perspectives offered by Moore must be considered part of the human dynamic in any organization.

The change models discussed above offer several common themes. They refer to change as a process that first involves establishing the need for the change. In other words, why would a firm pursue a Big

Data strategy? If the driver is simply to be a follower, or because it is the next cool innovation, then that change may not take hold. However, if the strategy can be linked to a competitive driver then, as shown in earlier examples, it can offer the organization a distinct advantage over its competitors. The technology-based change literature would assert these actions could only be achieved through management commitment.

20.4 Conclusion

Upon careful examination of the extensive discourse on Big Data, both in the print media and the blogosphere, we discovered that there were a few elements missing from the conversation. We began this chapter with a brief perspective on Big Data and then highlighted the factors that have led innovative organizations to adopt and execute Big Data strategies to gain and sustain a competitive edge. However, we focused on a return to a few fundamentals we believe are the foundation of the pathway to a sustainable Big Data strategy, specifically, organizational change, organizational culture, and organizational learning. We were not aiming to deflate the hype associated with Big Data, but fear that the absence of these principles will make it difficult for organizations to adopt and sustain what has become the next innovation wave.

Therefore, we argued for a return to these core learning principles because we believe each offers a set of enduring concepts that could be of benefit to all Big Data stakeholders including CIOs, analytical innovators, business data owners, and even the analytically challenged. We would also assert that even organizations that are blazing the Big Data trail now should view this as a journey and take a cautious look at the discourse in the chapter. No organization is exempt from considering these fundamentals, specifically organizational learning and culture. Both principles could inform IT leaders on how to navigate the challenges associated with implementing this new technology phenomenon. The Big Data market will continue to mature. Likewise, we contend that as investment levels continue to rise, IT practitioners would be well served to align organizational learning strategies with their Big Data strategies.

In closing, it is hoped that this chapter has exposed the key stakeholders to a few practical frameworks. We believe these frameworks provide a lens through which leaders could model and plan for this new evolution. The Big Data journey has just begun and there is much we can learn from the organizational practitioners.

References

Argyris, C. (1993). *Knowledge for Action: A Guide to Overcoming Barriers to Organizational Change*. San Francisco: Jossey-Bass.

Argyris, C. and Schon, D.A. (1978). *Organizational Learning: A Theory of Action Perspective*. Reading MA: Addison-Wesley.

Asia Case Research Centre (2008). Citibank's e-business strategy for global corporate banking, HKU798. Boston, MA: Harvard Business School.

Davenport, T.H. and Harris, J.G. (2007). *Competing on Analytics with External Processes: Customer and Supplier Applications*. Boston: Harvard Business School Press, pp. 83–103.

Davenport, T.H. (2006). Competing on analytics? *Harvard Business Review*, January: 99–107.

Eaton, D., Deroos, D., Deutsch, T., Lapis, G., and Zikopoulos, P. (2012). *Understanding Big-Data – Analytics for Enterprise Class Hadoop*. New York: McGraw-Hill.

Garvin, D.A. (1993). Building a learning organization. *Harvard Business Review*, 71(4): 78–92.

Glaser, J. (2007). Too far ahead of the IT curve? *Harvard Business Review*, July-August: 29–39.

Hatch, M.J. (1993). The dynamics of organizational culture. *Academy of Management Review*, 18(4): 657–693.

Hatch, M.J. (1997). *Organization Theory*. Oxford, New York: Oxford University Press.

Kiron, D., Ferguson, R.B., and Prentice, P.K. (Spring 2013). From value to vision: Reimagining the possible with data analytics. *Sloan Management Review*.

Lewin, K. (1951). *Field Theory in Social Science*. New York: Harper & Row

March, J.G. and Simon, H. (1958). *Organizations*. New York: John Wiley.

McAfee, A. and Brynjolfsson, E. (2008). Investing in the IT that makes a competitive difference. *Harvard Business Review*, July-August: 99–107.

Moore, G.A. (1999). *Crossing the Chasm*, rev. ed. New York: HarperCollins.

Open Data Center Alliance. (2012). *Big Data Consumer Guide*. http://www.opendatacenteralliance.org/library/odca-documents/big-data-consumer-s-guide/open-data-center-alliance-big-data-consumer-s-guide

Paulk, M., Curtis, B., Chrissis, M., and Weber, C. (1993). The Capability Maturity Model SM for Software, Version 1.1. (CMU/SEI-93-TR-24). Pittsburgh: Software Engineering Institute, Carnegie Mellon University.

Porter, M. (2008). The five competitive forces that shape strategy. *Harvard Business Review*. January. http://hbr.org/2008/01/the-five-competitive-forces-that-shape-strategy/ar/1

Schein, E.H. (1985). *Organizational Culture and Leadership*. (2nd ed.). San Francisco: Jossey-Bass.

Schein, E.H. (1993, Winter). How can organizations learn faster? The challenge of entering the green room. *Sloan Management Review*, 85–92.

Schein, E.H. (1996). Three cultures of management: The key to organizational learning. *Sloan Management Review*, Fall: 9–20.

Schon, D.A. (1975). Deutero-learning in organizations – Learning for increased effectiveness. *Organizational Dynamics*, 4(1): 2–16.

Schwandt, D.R. (1997). Integrating strategy and organizational learning: A theory of action perspective. In Advances in *Strategic Management*, vol. 14. Greenwich, CT: JAI Press, pp. 337–359.

Schwandt, D.R. and Marquardt, M.J. (2000). *Organizational Learning: From World-Class Theories to Global Best Practices*. Boca Raton, FL: St. Lucie Press.

Senge, P.M. (1990). *The Fifth Discipline: The Art and Practice of the Learning Organization*. New York: Doubleday.

Shrivastava, P. (1983). A typology of organizational learning systems. *Journal of Management Studies*, 20(1): 22–28.

Weill, P. and Ross, J. (2009). *Defining your operating model: Making IT a strategic asset. In IT Savvy: What Top Executives Must Know to Go from Pain to Gain*. Boston: Harvard Business Press, ch. 2.

21

SOLVING AN EMPLOYEE TURNOVER ISSUE THROUGH OFFSHORE OUTSOURCING

ANDREW ISERSON

University of Maryland University College

Contents

21.1 Introduction

A civil engineering company containing a software house subsidiary had a significant challenge with turnover in the software development department. Staffing in the software house was based on contracts being executed. When a new project was acquired, new personnel were hired to deliver the project. Once the project ended, if a new project was not in place, the staff from that project was furloughed. Turnover in software development was sustained at over 100% a year. Senior management of software development was replaced and Human Resources did studies and implemented salary increases, but the turnover continued.

Executive management realized that this level of turnover was detrimental to the company's morale, products, and bottom line. The organization as a whole looked at this department as a liability to be given significant leeway in any corporate initiatives. Ability to have a standard architecture for the system was compromised as each new senior staff member entering found a better method of doing the work, thus any piece of software used many different design constraints, making it impossible to maintain. The delivered product was problematic, having to be patched repeatedly in order to provide a working system and avoid upsetting the customers.

Having been a seasoned manager in an information technology environment with a track record of notably low turnover for more than 10 years, I was hired by the company to manage the software development department. After being put into place, I found that many of the problems creating the turnover were easily solved. Standard techniques were employed treating employees fairly, communicating with employees on departmental and project issues, and allowing employees to become empowered. These changes took care of a significant amount of the turnover. But, even with these changes, there was still more employee turnover than I considered acceptable.

Employees who continued to leave the organization overwhelmingly indicated concern for losing their job as the reason that they had started job hunting. Everyone on the staff had experienced their coworkers being furloughed. Each time it happened, the rest of the staff became more ill at ease. Those staff members who believed they had a specific skill that was hard to replace and those who were on long-term projects were able to relax. All other staff members would again mobilize their personal search each time a furlough occurred. More than likely, one or several of the staff members would find a new position over the course of their hunt.

21.2 Challenge

A goal of operational management is to reduce voluntary turnover to insignificant levels. In that way, the staff is able to maintain a work environment free of constant change in personnel, responsibilities, and subject matter experts. The stability also ensures that institutional knowledge is maintained and usable by the organization for future projects.

Turnover within a software development organization creates many problems. These include: loss of credibility, institutional knowledge drained from the organization, constant introduction of new methodologies and technologies, cost of recruiting new staff, cost of training new staff, and ultimately negative feelings and concern of the remaining staff members.

As errors occurred on systems being delivered, the staff in other departments within the organization looked at turnover as a major factor. Whether this was true or not, perception is reality. The credibility of the software development department as a whole was always in question because the new hires were not yet familiar enough with the products being produced. Management of the department was taken to task over the continued turnover of valuable staff members, ultimately questioning their credibility.

The product being produced by the organization, as those produced by most software installations, is a complicated system. Even experienced software developers have a long spin-up cycle in order to understand the underlying requirements of the system and the existing mix of architectures that have been used over the years. Months or years have been needed by the senior members of the staff to understand the complexities and oddities of their assigned system. Each staff member has installed his or her own custom changes to correct or circumvent existing issues. As these staff members leave, this information is lost and subsequent staff members will begin the process anew while attempting to deliver new projects. Many times the changes are made using trial and error, which becomes evident to other internal departments and to the customers.

Requirements for new hires include knowledge of the existing technologies and architectures that are being used in the system along with new state-of-the-art technologies and architectures that are desired for future enhancements allowing the products to remain marketable. The new hires review the existing systems to determine places that the new technologies should be inserted. The addition of these new methods to the existing legacy methods adds significant complications to an already complex system. In addition, the new hires frequently do not fully understand the original requirements which created the reason that the system was structured in its current manner. Once the requirements are fully understood, additional changes are then added to the system. This new, more complicated system is the basis that future new hires will use as their starting point.

Bringing in new staff entails its own set of problems and issues. There is a significant cost, both hard and soft, of hiring new staff members that includes the hiring process and getting them to the point where they become productive. Costs of hiring new staff members may include: rewriting and getting agreement on position descriptions, advertising or using agencies for hiring, screening resumes, interviewing by multiple senior people, selecting the appropriate candidate, negotiating terms, and at times paying bonuses or moving expenses, paperwork, and background checks. These costs are not insignificant and with high turnover they can become quite burdensome.

Once the new staff member is onboard there are additional costs, usually being soft costs. The new staff members are not able to be productive immediately. In fact, the new staff members will often cause a net drain on the productivity of other staff members. The new hire will constantly ask questions to understand the requirements, existing architecture, and the development environment. Productivity drains can occur over the period of more than one project if the new requirements exist in different parts of the system.

Turnover causes anxiety for the remaining staff. As staff departs, their reasons for the departure are justified with the remaining staff members. At times when contracts end and employees are laid off, the remaining staff has their own parochial reasons for concern. Everyone would rather leave a job on his own terms as opposed to being laid off. Each time a contract ends and staff is laid off, the remaining staff updates their own resumes and renews their own job searches. When a peer finds a new position, the justification for leaving makes sense to those who remain. The remaining staff will again renew their job search causing a never-ending cycle.

As the manager of a systems development department, keeping turnover low is one of the fundamental issues to be addressed. By stemming turnover, many of the issues that have been described will no longer exist.

21.3 Situation

This organization's business is based solely on contracts received. Although a case has been made numerous times to invest in the product and keep a stable staff, the corporate culture is for all work to be based on contracts that have been received. The parent corporation performs their work in the same manner, based on contracts received. Senior contract staff in the parent company are in the position of selling additional work in order to maintain their jobs. This is possible because these senior staff members are frequently interacting with the customers. Senior development staff is, by design, kept in the background. In most cases, they have little or no interaction with the customer.

In this way, they are expected to produce more work, but this gives them little ability to sell additional products.

Staff being maintained only when billable work is available creates the need for additional staff with the start of new contracts. The contracts are priced, primarily fixed-price, based on the work to be completed by experienced staff. New hires are frequently hired before they are needed for the actual work in order to get them up to speed in time to start and, it is hoped, enabling the work to be completed on time. The actual hours and cost associated with the work being accomplished frequently require more hours than had been expected, causing overruns in the projects.

When projects are completed, normally with overruns caused by unresolved problems, senior management is of the opinion that those not billable should be furloughed. The project has cost the organization all of the project's profits and frequently more. Senior management is not in favor of putting this staff on overhead, costing the organization additional money until a new contract is received.

This layoff cycle fits with the culture of the organization. The parent organization believes that turnover brings new ideas into the organization. Projects executed by the organization, other than software development, are all customized and begin when the contract is received. In the software development organization the work is sold as a prewritten package (commercial off-the-shelf—COTS) with minor changes. What is actually happening is that the existing program base is used as base code and major amounts of new software must be developed to provide functionality that has been sold for the first time. Knowledge of the base code and architecture is required in order to deliver a product expediently. The layoff cycle creates a situation where software development, and thus the software product as a whole, is in a no-win situation.

The layoff cycle and all of its ramifications are wearing on the staff and create additional dissidence within the organization. This creates an environment for employee dissatisfaction, thus creating additional turnover.

21.4 Solution

The layoff cycle is the fundamental issue causing employee turnover resulting in project overruns and poor performance. Corporate culture condones the use of, and need for, these layoffs at the end of the contracts. Work has been done to try to change the corporate culture. Business plans, budgets, and risk reports have been produced, all to no avail. Attempts at increasing the cost estimates on new work based on using new hires to perform the work was unacceptable. With higher prices, the work will not be awarded and existing staff will have to be cut due to the lack of work.

The solution to this never-ending cycle is to find a method of no longer hiring each time a new contract is awarded and laying off when it is completed. With the number of different technologies that have and continue to be used in the systems, support for many technologies is required. The technologies include both legacy and state-of-the-art variants. While considering the various options, several other factors have to be kept in the forefront of the decision. The solution must be acceptable to senior management, the current employee base, and to the customers that purchase the product.

Offshore outsourcing, an industry buzzword at the time, was considered. Large offshore organizations have the ability to provide personnel with experience in a variety of technologies, both legacy and state of the art. Personnel can be made available for long or short periods as needed due to the number and variety of projects under their control originating from various different companies. At the end of each of the projects, the personnel can be reassigned to other projects for which the offshore company has contracts. The unit cost of the people working on the projects was significantly lower than the costs we were paying for staff. At the same time we could keep a core of senior people to design the solutions and oversee the projects. This seemed to be a perfect solution. Ultimately, the decision was made based on management judgment without specific quantitative models being used.

A lot of contradictory studies had been completed that go from being a major savings in operational cost all the way to a significant additional operational cost. Depending upon the source of the study the answer was always absolute, to either jump into or stay far away from offshore outsourcing.

In researching the industry and possible advantages, pitfalls, and opinions, a number of ideas came forward and were factored into the decision. Some espoused the idea that the work takes longer, costs more, and your intellectual property will be stolen if sent offshore.

Others brought forward that the costs are lower, the knowledge of the workers is higher, and the work will be completed faster.

With the differences in opinions in the industry, a management decision had to be made primarily through intuitive reasoning. No quantitative assessment was possible. Fundamentally opposing opinions were brought forward in industry research. In reviewing all of the issues and possible solutions, a decision was made and moved forward for approval.

The toughest issue was to sell the idea to the organization's management, current employees, and to the customers. Papers were written for senior management pointing out assumed quantitative and qualitative benefits of the idea. The benefits were assumed because there was no agreement in the industry of the benefits. No industry research had been completed that was universally accepted. Current issues that were created by the layoff cycle were pointed out with explanations of how this solution would solve the existing problems.

Presentations were made to the employees showing graphs depicting the current issues and how these would change with an outsourcing solution. The intention of management to stabilize the number of employees and thus eliminate layoffs was communicated. Many of the current employees understood and were happy. Other employees thought this was just another instance of management trying to sell an idea that would not be advantageous for their future employment.

Senior management expressed concern for the opinions of the customers about their work being performed offshore. Discussions were held and it was determined that no specific communications would be held informing them of this change. The subject would be reevaluated if a specific question or statement was made by the customer in reference to the work being accomplished offshore. This never happened.

The decision to solve the layoff cycle problem through the use of offshore outsourcing was put into place based on management's intuitive judgment. Then the reality set in. Putting this decision into place turned out to be neither the panacea that was predicted by some nor the disaster predicted by others. In fact, many of the issues encountered were not thought of or written about in the studies reviewed.

Cost turned out to be primarily a wash with the costs that were found when the work was accomplished internally. This was due to the fact that having developers offshore required that a more formalized system-development lifecycle be used. The developers working on the system did not have the ability to walk down the hall and ask questions. Questions and clarifications required a delay due to the differences in hours that were being worked.

Outsourcing firms have the expectation that accounts will continue to grow. The growth of the use of outsourcing was a function of the number of contracts that were received. There are a finite number of requests for this type of project, and this organization had already won a fair share of these projects. The number of projects to be executed was unlikely to grow at a rate allowing the relationship to grow at a level to meet the outsourcer's expectations. The result was an amiable split with this outsourcing organization and the need to move to a new organization. There are costs and inefficiencies that come with this type of unexpected move.

Communication was an issue, but not in any way that was anticipated. Setting up international telephone conferences was adversely affected by large fans that were required in the conference rooms of our offshore staff. The background sounds made the discussions harder to conduct.

Cultural differences created communication problems of their own. Priority issues that were expressed were interpreted differently than intended or expected. As the work progressed, this was better understood and the communications were changed on both sides in order to ensure that the expected communications transpired.

Configuration management issues caused unexpected system problems. The outsourcer purported to be certified at CMMI Level 5, using the ultimate in processes to perform the work. Issues were encountered reintroducing previously solved errors. These most likely were caused by inefficiencies in the process. Investigating these problems confirmed this opinion. The question asked of the vendor was how this could occur in a CMMI Level 5 environment. The explanation was that these specific projects did not use this level of process. The use of these processes was assumed, but never instituted.

The biggest surprise in retrospect turned out to be a blinding flash of the obvious. One of the main issues that was attempted to be corrected was the loss of institutional knowledge when contracts ended. The belief was that the institutional knowledge would be owned by the core staff that remained employed by the organization.

In reality, institutional knowledge was also housed with the outsourcer. The effect of this is that when we needed to release staff members on their side due to contracts ending, they were reassigned and might not be available for future projects. This caused many of the same problems as experienced previously and that this solution was expected to solve.

21.5 Management of the Solution

As is true with any decision, management must actively manage this solution. The issues presented above, along with a number of additional issues, had to be actively managed. Issues were made clear to the vendor and solutions were jointly determined and executed.

Cost was not a factor that was mentioned to senior management in the original request to proceed in this direction; therefore, cost was managed as any other budget item would be managed. In working through the cost issue it was determined that the cost estimate would be performed bottom-up. The outsourcing vendor would bid their costs as a subcontractor, much the way all contractors and subcontractors bid their costs. Costs for the core staff personnel time would also be estimated and projected costs determined. In this manner, a final cost was determined with a portion of the risk held by the outsourcing vendor.

Communications and cultural issues were handled by a local staff member of the outsourcing firm participating in the meetings, understanding what was being addressed, and following up to make sure that these concepts were understood.

To solve the configuration management issues, the outsourcer put additional effort into their processes and procedures. These efforts allowed this problem to be solved.

An overriding issue of the ultimate quality was solved by installing a more complete testing environment and procedures. All deliveries of code were extensively tested, ensuring that there were no surprises.

Decisions that are made, whether intuitively or using quantitative modeling are likely to fail without active management involvement. The success of this endeavor was a direct result of the oversight provided.

22

WHY I CONTINUED WHEN REASON AND LOGIC DICTATED OTHERWISE

MELANIE P. COHEN

IT Strategic Planning and Communications
US Department of Housing and Urban Development

Contents

22.1 Introduction

When you have had a long career in government, you sometimes can feel as if you have seen it all. You know when a new idea will take off and be successful and you know when it will be less than successful—not quite a failure, but not quite a success. You have seen the decision-making process in action. You have seen it work well and you have seen it fail miserably. But sometimes, you just know, whether it is a gut feeling, instinct, intuition, or just sheer determination because of your refusal to give up when you know something has value, that an idea is going to be successful. It is in those moments that you believe there is no amount of rational decision making that is going to get in your way. Because, sometimes, if you leave a decision up to rational decision making, it is doomed. So this is the story of how a staff meeting turned into a monthly webinar and has gained the attention of a federal government-wide audience.

22.2 Learning Organization

This story begins in January of 2009. My supervisor and I were talking about how to make staff meetings more productive. I believe that this is a conversation that must go on in every organization around the world, probably on any given day. Our dilemma was how do you make the most of your time together so that everyone in the room can feel as if he or she has learned something from the meeting? We would have a group of high-level managers gather at the same time each week, sit around an oblong conference table, and tell each other good news about their latest project. We would go around the table in the order in which we sat (I should mention that we generally sat in the same seats), and begin to talk about our latest success. People are not really actively listening and after you wait for your turn to speak, you're really not listening to the rest of your colleagues. The reason is you are not hearing anything new that you have not heard the week before or that you will hear the next week. After a few months of this same scenario, my supervisor asked me to think about how to make our time together in these meetings more productive. Little did he know that I had been thinking about this issue for quite some time. I was ready with a response.

First, let me say that I have never been a fan of the "traditional staff meeting." I was thinking about something different and new and wanted the people who attended these sessions to feel that they had spent a productive 60 minutes together. With the free rein to develop these meetings into something different, I began to think about how we could spend our time together and learn about something new. No more sitting around the conference table and giving good news about a project upon which only you were focused. My focus turned to learning. We were not just going to meet, but we were going to learn. And not just about something new in a technical field, but something new so that you could grow as an individual. I believed that the focus of the meeting needed to shift away from the everyday work at the desk and the immediate task and move to what I have always believed learning should be focused on: a change in knowledge, beliefs, attitude, and behaviors, with the emphasis on change. I soon realized I was not reformulating a meeting, but creating a change in culture. And to do that I would soon be working to develop a learning organization.

I follow the work of Peter Senge and he describes the learning organization as "continually expanding its capacity to create its future." The learning organization is essentially an ideal. It's a journey, not a destination, a goal toward which organizations grow and evolve. I decided that this was what I would try to create. The meetings would no longer be called "staff meetings," they would be retitled "learning sessions." With a simple name change, I had now taken the first step to creating a new culture. But what was this change going to be? What would it look like? And how would I know when it had happened? Perhaps in these sessions, we could have discussions on how to be a better leader or a better manager, how to better understand the people in our organization, or even how to shift and transform an organizational culture. I was excited by the possibility of change and the new opportunity, but I was wondering if such an idea would really be of interest to others. I discussed the idea with a few trusted colleagues to get some feedback and everyone thought that it was a good idea. Many felt that the traditional staff meeting was not a valuable way to spend time and were more than willing to try something new. I was emboldened by their confidence and I believed that I was on to something. I began to make a few calls to colleagues outside my agency who were experts in their fields just to ask if they would be interested in coming to our agency and speaking on their topic of expertise. There would be no monetary compensation, only my gratitude along with a cup of coffee. To my astonishment, all were willing to participate. In a way, it was like establishing a formal brown bag lunch, but without the lunch.

I must disclose that I am fortunate enough to have wonderful colleagues in industry, the public sector, and academia who are willing and able to share their knowledge with others. The way that I had envisioned the sessions would be to have outside experts come and discuss their area of expertise and I would introduce them and then help to facilitate a discussion. Our first "learning session" began in February 2009 with a discussion, "Turning Business Threats into Competitive Advantage." Each month, we would have a new session with such topics as "Implementing the Future: 3D Virtual Worlds in Government"; "Leadership Priorities: Business Leaders First, Technology Leaders Second"; "How Green Is Your Information Technology?"; "Introduction to Systems Thinking"; and "The Eight

Building Blocks of Customer Relationship Management." I led book discussions with books on business, leadership, and management topics designed to help people learn, grow, and develop. It sounds good so far, but let me tell you what began to happen.

As with many new initiatives, enthusiasm began to wane. There was always a core group of individuals who would attend each meeting, but then as time passed the reality of the day-to-day work began to creep in; there was always another meeting to attend, some other project that demanded attention, some other pressing priority, and then the worst thing happened, the senior executives stopped attending. Once the senior executives stopped attending, attendance began to drop off. It was at one point when we hosted a speaker on the topic of hybrid thinking (how to think through problems in new and different ways) and we only had about half a dozen attendees, that I began to question whether I really wanted to continue this effort. Not only was attendance waning, but my confidence was also. I have to admit that there were many times I questioned whether this effort was worth pursuing. It didn't seem as if people were interested. Needless to say, it became difficult to obtain experts to speak with us, especially if only a few employees would be in attendance.

22.3 Revisiting My Decision

I had no resources, I had no encouragement, and I was thinking that I had no interest. I asked myself a series of questions about why I should continue with this effort. With each question, I had few answers. The only answer that I could come up with was that it felt important. I know that if I had looked at it through the lens of rational decision making, I probably would have ended the effort. But instead, I went with my intuition. It felt a little muddled and confused, but I knew it was the right path to take. I had to continue. I just knew that it was important for the growth and development of the workforce, even if they didn't quite know it yet.

I shook my head and wondered, "Why was this happening?" I became introspective and took a close examination of my own thoughts and feelings about why this was happening. Was it something that I was doing wrong? Were the topics not of interest? Did I not really have a good sense of the organization and its needs? What could

I have done better? As I struggled to make a decision on whether to continue with the effort or abandon it, several thoughts entered my mind. I realized that this was a problem that was ambiguous. I came to the conclusion that the problem was not just poor attendance, but there was no precedent because we had never done anything like this before. So I struggled in my thought process. I came face to face with the dilemma of intuition versus rational analysis. I must say that I am a rational thinker. I prefer to rely mostly on logic and analysis when making business decisions. I like to analyze all the options consciously, formulate the main criteria for judging the expected outcomes of the options, and assign certain weights to those criteria to reflect their relative importance. Then, based on the expected outcomes and their weights, I rate the options by their perceived usefulness. Then finally, I choose the option that has the highest rating. But in this instance, I had no clear criteria. I had no data. I had nothing to analyze. So, then in my mind, rational decision making suddenly seemed impractical. When it came to the learning sessions, I was much more connected to my emotions. I knew that the option to continue felt right, even though there was no clear logic to prove it. I was determined to see the problem through despite the fact that logic was not on my side.

I spent a great deal of time thinking through the process of the learning session. I asked myself several questions. What was working right? What could improve? What topics can we talk about? I even thought about the time that these sessions were held. Should they be held in the morning instead of the afternoon? What can I do to make this effort more successful? I was now at the point where I could not and would not give up. I was determined to achieve success and nothing was going to get in my way. The difficult part was now knowing I had to trust my instinct that I had made the right decision to continue, despite the lack of facts which would justify continuing the effort. If my intuition was not enough, I refocused and began to think even more broadly about imperatives for the public sector. And then began to ask myself what the future of the public sector was. How was it changing? What small part can we play to help prepare the workforce? What could I personally do?

I have been thinking, researching, and writing about the public sector for some time. Admittedly, there are so many questions and few definitive answers. What does the future hold for the twenty-first–century public sector organization? Will organizations continue to be structured in a pyramid or perhaps be a circle? To what extent will the new public sector organization be virtual? How will virtual organizations be managed and led? How will a multi-generational, multiethnic public sector deliver the results that are needed for the American public? There is still so much work to be done to understand the impact of knowledge workers on the future public sector organization and ultimately their impact on society.

22.4 Changing the Learning Audience

There is a confluence of events that have created powerful drivers to transform the federal workforce and workplace. These drivers include shifting demographics; the workforce is changing in both complexity and responsibilities. These changes allow for new and diverse skills and talents to enter the workforce and the opportunity to restructure agencies to become more citizen centered and customer focused. Market force demands, as part of the austere times, that the government workforce be held more accountable for becoming leaner, flexible, and responsive for the delivery of services. New technology requirements require gaining access to and applying today's technology to recruitment, employee services, and citizen engagement.

As I thought about the future, suddenly it dawned on me that perhaps I was targeting the wrong audience. I was going to change the target audience. No longer would these sessions be limited to the upper levels of management. Not only would the audience change, but the topics for the sessions needed to change and focus on topics that are important to the workforce. The landscape of the public service workforce is changing. For the first time in modern history, workplace demographics now span four generations, which means that 22-year-old new hires can find themselves working side by side with colleagues who are older than they are by 45 years or perhaps even more. The existence of the multigenerational workforce poses unique challenges to today's public sector environment. A lack of understanding regarding generational differences contributes to conflict within working relationships, lowers productivity, and increases turnover. More seasoned staff can become frustrated by a seemingly aloof younger generation. Younger staff can become disenfranchised with entrenched hierarchical and bureaucratic structures. And those employees stuck in the middle can become frustrated with everyone. These shifts affect organizational culture because priorities, attitudes, and work styles differ with each generation.

It was at this point that I became invigorated and decided to expand the target audience and focus on topics that are important to a changing and dynamic workforce. I began to approach employees who had not been part of the previous effort and asked if they would be interested in attending discussions/presentations on a variety of leadership and management issues. The answer was not only a resounding, "Yes," but "When can we get started and can we invite others to participate." I then had a brief discussion with my supervisor to let him know that I would be changing direction by making these sessions more inclusive to our entire workforce. The direction that we had originally established had not been successful. We would now change focus. He had no objection and was pleased that I had given this so much thought and attention. The original effort as envisioned had not worked, but to me, it was a learning experience. The focus was too narrow. We were about to expand in ways that I would have never imagined.

I then opened these sessions up to anyone in our organization. I soon had people of all levels attending these sessions. And then the magic happened: someone asked if there was any reason that these sessions could not be open to others outside our department. In a short period of time, we had to move these sessions from a small conference room to a large training room. The word soon spread to our field locations. I then received a few calls from our field offices asking if they could participate in the learning sessions. What a change! A radical change had occurred. I moved from so desperately trying to push these sessions onto people, to now people asking me how they could participate. It was a 180-degree turn. But the good news was that this was only the beginning of the change. There would be much greater change to come.

22.5 Expanding the Scope

With the sudden increased demand, we had to figure out a way to get these learning opportunities out to the people who wanted to participate. I enlisted the help of our broadcasting branch, told them about what we were doing, and then asked about the possibility of doing an internal webcast. Is it possible? How would we do that? Is it really feasible? To me, the questions really always have been, "Why not? Why not think in a different way? Why not focus our efforts on the future of our workforce?" I always come to the same answer. "Let's do it and when can we get started."

We were soon doing internal webcasts. These webcasts would include a call-in phone number where people could ask questions of the speaker. We also would hold a live Twitter chat during the session and the audience was continuing to grow. To say that I was happy with the way that the effort was going is an understatement, but I was not happy enough. I wanted to reach more people. So, I took some additional action. In the beginning, when it was a small group of people gathered in a conference room, I had been trying to work with and meet the chief learning officers in the federal government. I thought that it was through this group that I could leverage the work that we were doing and bring it to a federal-wide audience. As long as we were doing these sessions, why couldn't we all benefit? And the change happened again.

It was in working with some of these chief learning officers that there was now this idea that we can all work together. Why not offer learning opportunities in the federal sector to those who want to learn? So, the new question was, how could we logically and cost effectively carry this effort out? We soon had the answer. Just as we were able to broadcast and do an internal webcast, we would now offer an external webinar. With the help of the chief learning officer community and the US Office of Personnel Management, I now had a very extensive e-mail distribution list. We had our first large-scale broadcast in April 2012 with a discussion and presentation on "Retention Efforts on Generation Y in the Public Sector." This was a great success. Not only were there a large number of people in the live audience representing different federal government agencies, but also a great number of people were viewing on the Internet. A staff meeting had become a webinar viewed around government.

I am delighted to say that we have been successful ever since. We have significantly changed the format over time. When we began, the sessions were more of a lecture with a short discussion.

Using TED talks as a model, these learning sessions have evolved to a talk show format that I continue to host each month. They are now much less formal, more intimate, and more engaging for our live audience to feel much more comfortable asking questions and contributing to the discussion. Always for consistency purposes, these sessions are held at the same time each month. We have hosted speakers on such topics as "The Art of Decision Making: Getting It Right Every Time," "Personality, Relationships, and Communication: Simple Yet Complex," "Personal Leadership Development," "If I'm Talking I Must Be Communicating: The Power of Framing," "Managing and Surviving Disruptions, Reorganizations, and Other Crises," and "Leading from Mid Organization—With Your Head, Heart, and Guts." These are just a few of the topics. Each month, our viewership continues to grow. We also archive past sessions that are available for viewing on YouTube.

22.6 Concluding Thoughts

One of the benefits of the initial struggle and somewhat muddled decision making was how I was able to grow and learn as an individual. The dictionary states that learning is "the activity or process of gaining knowledge or skill by studying, practicing, being taught, or experiencing something." So, learning is the process where knowledge is created through the transformation experience. I can say without hesitation that I learned and transformed during the process. I'll refer back to Peter Senge for just a minute and take a bit of liberty with his idea. According to Senge, learning requires a "shift of mind" that goes far beyond learning new tasks. It requires a change in our mental models and our frameworks for interpreting the external world. This shift involves the tension between the vision of the future and the current reality. I worked very hard to try to change the current reality. Through these learning sessions we have created a community of commitment to change. We are not simply a group of individuals who attend these sessions and who learn. These sessions have helped to establish the commitment to collaboration and awareness of self and others and of the whole. We have essentially helped to establish a commitment to create change within the culture of the organization.

So, what has been the result of the creation of the culture of commitment to learning? These learning sessions have become quite successful. We now have many hundreds of people who watch the live stream of the show each month. Not only have many of the guest speakers asked if it were possible to return for a second time, the guest speakers share the information with their colleagues (expanding and creating new networks) who are now approaching me to be guest speakers for future shows. In the past, I had to rely on the good graces of my colleagues to be speakers. I am now being approached by people in government, industry, and academia to ask if I would be interested in having them as speakers. With all that said, let me tell you what is the most important and most significant success of the learning sessions. I often receive notes or messages from people around government telling me that they found the session to be valuable, and of course those kinds of notes are gratifying in knowing that the sessions have been worthwhile. But, very often I receive a note from someone outside the Washington, DC area, generally an administrative-, entry-, or journeyman-level employee telling me how much they appreciate the opportunity to learn about topics that they may not have known ever existed, where they can sit at their desk and the learning experience comes directly to them. Most important, this new idea or piece of information has changed the way they think. This is what I have always believed learning to be: a change in knowledge, beliefs, attitude, and behaviors, and sometimes to change for the better you have to leave accepted models behind and rely on your intuition.

23

DECISION MAKING

Intuitive, Evidence, or Hybrid Approach?

MICHELLE MASON

American Society for Quality (ASQ)

Contents

23.1 Introduction

How do we make decisions? Is decision making abstract and based on illogicalities that have a subjective correlation? Are they based on factual evidence that lead to more informed and systematic results? Is there a hybrid approach of coalescing instinct and "gut" feelings with data and tools to inform judgment?

There is an assortment of scientific studies on how decisions are actually made, however, answers to these questions could take leaders in a variety of directions leading to variable results. What we know is that decisions are a part of our everyday lives, professional and personal. The decisions we make, large and small, affect others and could have enormously positive or devastatingly negative results.

According to Whitehead and Finkelstein (2009), leaders make decisions largely through unconscious processes that neuroscientists call pattern recognition and emotional tagging. These processes usually make for quick effective decisions, but they can be distorted by self-interest, emotional attachments, or misleading memories.

For example, Jürgen Schrempp, CEO of Daimler-Benz, led the merger of Chrysler and Daimler against internal opposition (Whitehead and Finkelstein, 2009). Nine years later, Daimler was forced virtually to give Chrysler away in a private equity deal. Steve Russell, chief executive of Boots, the UK drugstore chain, launched a healthcare strategy designed to differentiate the stores from competitors and grow through new healthcare services such as dentistry. It turned out, though, that Boots managers did not have the skills needed to succeed in healthcare services, and many of these markets offered little profit potential. The strategy contributed to Russell's early departure from the top job.

23.2 Are These Decisions Based on Abstractions or Fact?

Neuroscientists have studied decision making for years and believe that leaders make quick decisions by recognizing patterns in the situations they encounter, bolstered by emotional associations attached to those patterns. Most of the time, the process works well, but it can result in serious mistakes when judgments are biased (Whitehead and Finkelstein, 2009).

23.2.1 What Is Intuitive or Abstract Decision Making?

Intuition in the context of decision making is based on "gut" or hunches. According to Sinclair (2005) many think of intuition as a magical phenomenon, but hunches are formed out of our past experiences and knowledge. So although relying on gut feelings doesn't always lead to good decisions, it's not nearly as flighty a tactic as it may sound (Sinclair, 2005). Intuitive or abstract decision making also introduces myriad options for an organization to consider (see Figure 23.1). "Intuition is a highly complex and highly developed form of reasoning that is based on years of experience, learning and observation, facts, patterns, concepts, procedures and abstractions stored in one's head" (Matzler, Bailom, and Mooradian, 2007).

23.2.2 What Is Evidence- or Fact-Based Decision Making?

Evidence-based decision making is utilized in many businesses and organizations. Also known as data-driven decision making, where

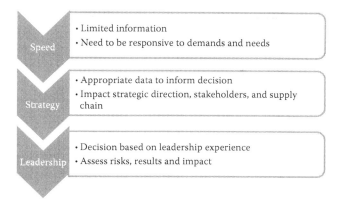

Speed
• Limited information
• Need to be responsive to demands and needs

Strategy
• Appropriate data to inform decision
• Impact strategic direction, stakeholders, and supply chain

Leadership
• Decision based on leadership experience
• Assess risks, results and impact

Figure 23.1 Decision-making drivers.

there is a commitment to analysis and feedback, using data to drive dialogue and engagement (ASAE, 2006). It is prominent in technical areas such as financial, healthcare, quality improvement, and the sciences, among others. As this concept is explored, it is important to recognize that decisions have a far-reaching impact on everyone. This causes some to base their judgments on facts rather than instinct and gut. Fact-based decision-making organizations analyze data to inform future directions. It is about data-driven decisions to support continuous improvement and learning, for example, entering new markets and new product development. Gathering, analyzing, and securing the proper information is utilized as the precursor to decisions (see Figure 23.2).

When is evidence-based decision making utilized? Leaders who are utilizing fact- or data-driven decision making are considering the following steps:

1. Define your information needs.
2. Identify the most important data to collect.
3. Design a strategy to analyze the data.
4. Develop a plan to turn the data into knowledge to direct your business strategies and future actions.
5. Evaluate the progress of your results.

This is modeled after the Deming cycle or Shewhart cycle called plan, do, check, act. The plan-do-check-act cycle (see Figure 23.3) is typically a four-step model for carrying out change for continuous improvement (ASQ).

Figure 23.2   Decision-making cycle.

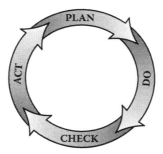

Figure 23.3   Plan-do-check-act cycle.

23.2.3 What Is a Hybrid Model for Decision Making?

A hybrid model of decision making provides the usage of both gut and instinct as well as data-driven decisions based on factual evidence (see Figure 23.4). It could start with a simple strategy of bringing both the abstract and technical leaders together to ask these questions. How significant is the decision? What are the business requirements? What are the risks? What are the rewards? Who are the stakeholders? How might we design a strategy to be both responsive and factual in our approach? Who should take the lead role? It starts with a dialogue based on your organizational culture or situation.

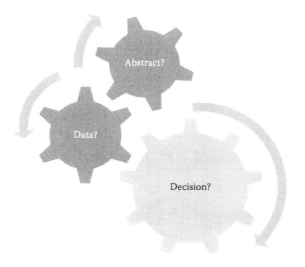

Figure 23.4 Working together: abstraction and data to make decisions.

23.3 How Do You Know When to Use One or the Other?

You are probably realizing that there is no formal science or an aggregated body of knowledge to respond to or address decisions based on instinct or fact. Many organizations defer to fact to mitigate risk. Instinct decision making might be utilized when under pressure to make a decision when no clear consensus is present. Many will look to the leader to make the "go" or "no-go" decision. The question to ask is, "Are you comfortable in that position without a support methodology to justify direction?"

"Regardless the process used; you must feel comfortable with how you reached that point. Peter Drucker calls it the *Mirror Test*. At the end of the day, a leader must have the ability to look in the mirror after the decision has been made and state that he or she has made the right choice" (Stanwick, 2014).

23.3.1 When to Use Intuition, Data, or Hybrid

Intuitive decision making is conceptual. It involves making abstract decisions on a hunch, inkling, or a feeling. In many cases, it is based on professional and personal experiences. In interviews with several Fortune 500 executives, they revealed that professional successes and failures inform the decision-making process when little quantitative or qualitative research is available. They typically use their leadership skills to assess risk and opportunity to move forward adequately. Despite the data available, gut and instinct might be more appropriate under stress. Many executives who primarily utilize this approach describe themselves as being visionary, creative, big-picture thinkers, and fearless.

According to ASQ, fact-based or evidence-based decision making helps you to understand how well an organization is performing; data on performance measures are necessary. Total quality management (TQM) requires that an organization continually collect and analyze data in order to improve decision-making accuracy, achieve consensus, and allow prediction based on past history. Evidence-based decision making requires research and analysis.

A hybrid approach combines these two approaches. One executive stated, "When I make assumptions based on limited data, it is experience based." Typically, these executives said they use a "situational management" leadership style. Many were adamant that the strategic direction of the organization should not be primarily guided based on gut. Start with what do we know? How do we know this? What do we need to know? Who else should be involved to fill in the gaps?

23.4 What Are the Tools and Resources Available?

Generic decision-making methodologies exist to support either direction, abstraction, or fact-based decisions. A helpful resource is the American Society for Quality, a global nonprofit membership organization whose mission is to increase the use and impact of quality in response to the diverse needs of the world.

References

American Society for Quality (ASQ): www.asq.org

ASAE & The Center for Association Leadership. (2006). *Seven Measures of Success: What Remarkable Associations Do that Others Don't*, 1st ed. Self.

Matzler, K., Bailom, F., and Mooradian, T. (2007). Intuitive Decision Making. Cambridge: *MIT Sloan Management Review* (Fall). 49, (1): pp. 13–16.

Sinclair, M. (2005). Intuition: Myth or a decision making tool? *Management Learning*, 36(3): 353–270.

Stanwick, Peter A. and Sarah D. (2014). *Understanding Business Ethics*, 2nd ed. Thousand Oaks, CA: SAGE, p. 96.

Whitehead, J. and Finkelstein, S. (2009). Why good leaders make bad decisions, *Harvard Business Review*, February, pp. 1–7. Reprint R0902D.

24

CONQUERING THE "WE DON'T KNOW WHAT WE DON'T KNOW" DILEMMA BY CONNECTING PEOPLE TO EXPERTS

LINDA HUMMEL

Act Knowledge LLC

Contents

24.1 Introduction

Picture this: a business unit (BU) of a large, global manufacturing conglomerate realizes that internal research being conducted around the world is unknown to many who could use it; voice of the customer (VOC) is collected but not shared widely; and critical knowledge resides in the heads of their experts, with no way to capture and disseminate it easily. In short, they didn't know what they didn't know. Let us call this company HI Corporation. As a knowledge–based organization, whose key competitive advantage is its intellectual capital and the expertise of its employees, they were not managing their knowledge to their advantage. This led to duplication of efforts, repeating mistakes, and excessive time searching for information. The result was lower quality, productivity, and efficiency. This chapter describes the case of how key intellectual capital was unlocked and made available globally through several intuition-based decisions.

24.2 Global Manufacturer's Expertise Locator System

The evidence was clear: the large BU of HI needed to initiate a knowledge management (KM) program to leverage its corpus of intelligence and spur innovation. Sponsored by the chief marketing officer (CMO) and the vice president of sales and marketing, a prime motivation for KM was to "invent once—use multiple times." Due to my past work experience in Accenture's world-class KM organization, as well as designing and implementing KM programs at NCR-Teradata (a leader in the data warehouse industry), and NCR Professional Services, I was brought on board to establish HI's program.

In any new KM program, a best practice is to assess the organization's culture around sharing and hoarding of knowledge, receptiveness to collaboration, comfort level with social media tools, organizational churn (i.e., layoffs and other changes affecting morale), and upper management support for KM. I also make it a priority to identify key knowledge processes and content, primary content repositories, content management practices, and key subject matter experts (SMEs).

The HI BU culture was decent in knowledge sharing and collaboration as well as upper management support. The organizational churn was relatively low, and so was social media tool usage. I considered these characteristics while creating a multiyear KM strategy, identifying specific KM approaches. They also factored into my intuitive decisions.

A fundamental business pain point was the excessive amount of time needed to find key knowledge. Information was stored in multiple repositories with minimal guidance as to what type of information to store in which repository. Each one had its own search engine and user interface. If an employee did not know where the information he or she was seeking was stored, he or she would have to search repositories one by one until finding it. After due diligence, Google Enterprise Search Appliance was selected as the federated (i.e., across multiple repositories) search engine and was the first part of the KM infrastructure to be deployed.

Early in the startup of the program, I created a KM roadmap to chart our course for the next four years. Each year had a KM theme and built upon the previous ones: knowledge capital (explicit) = > human capital (tacit) = > social capital = > enterprise capital. See Figure 24.1 for an example of a roadmap like this. With the Google Search Appliance greatly improving findability of explicit information across the enterprise, I knew it was time to move up the KM value chain and better manage tacit knowledge. Tacit knowledge is the wisdom, experience, and expertise in the heads of employees that is difficult to codify and put into explicit form in a document. Due to its intangible nature, the challenge was to transfer it efficiently at the time of need. My intuition was telling me that despite this current challenge, tacit knowledge was even more valuable to a company than explicit information, and had the potential to create even greater competitive advantage. This was new territory for most KM programs in 2009.

I define intuition as a process where we sense or know something is true without analytical reasoning. It bridges the gap between the conscious and nonconscious parts of our mind. In practice, it pulls from our ideas, thoughts, and education, as well things we have seen, done, and experienced with all of our senses. Intuition makes new connections seemingly without any conscious effort.

My subconscious mind was incubating the idea of transferring tacit wisdom and experience from one person to another. About that time there were some new KM approaches to tacit knowledge management: communities of practice (CoPs), after-action reviews (AARs), and knowledge elicitation practices to name just a few. Consider this common business scenario: during the course of performing his job as a knowledge worker, Lee has a question requiring

Figure 24.1 Example KM roadmap.

specific experience or expertise. For example, can a highly toxic chemical be shipped to a customer via FedEx? Lee needs to know the answer immediately. At HI and many other large companies, the typical action would be to go to one's internal network and pick one or more people who might either know the answer or know someone else who might know the answer. Note that the strength and diversity of a person's internal professional network is highly dependent on years of service, the cross-functional nature of the role, geographic location, language, and so on. The typical channel to connect to internal contacts was by telephone and frequently they were not available so the knowledge worker would leave a voice message. The issue would remain open until Lee (in this example) got a response or answer back, or another name to pursue. As you can see, this process could take many days, was inefficient for the multiple people involved, and did not produce a timely resolution.

This is where my intuition as the KM expert started to come into play. What if the strengths, areas of expertise, and professional interests of all 75,000 employees were "known" to a system? What if their profiles and contact information were displayed (as well as the current time in their local time zone) to make connecting fast and easy? Think of the competitive advantage generated if, through a simple search, I could find and connect to the best people to address my questions within seconds. My subconscious immediately knew this could be a vital KM tool for my BU. The challenge now was to convince others it would be worth the investment, especially if their intuition did not align with this.

24.3 Is Locating Experts the Silver Bullet?

The HI BU KM program implemented the role of knowledge practitioners (KP), KM champions in each BU product line (i.e., sub-BU profit and loss centers) who were domain experts for their product line and were responsible for deploying KM in their organization. We compiled an SME list that was located on the knowledge portal and searchable via the enterprise Google Search Appliance. The KPs centrally maintained the SME list for their organization. This was a step in the right direction; it could connect people who needed knowledge with those who had it. However, the

SME list was tedious to maintain. If a KP moved to a new position or left the company, and there was a gap in replacing that KP, multiple changes in SMEs could and did occur over the interim. Likewise, SMEs came and went, ensuring the expert list upkeep was a continual effort. Most important, in a very large company, it was nearly impossible for a knowledge practitioner to know all the SMEs in his or her domain, thereby making the expert list inherently incomplete.

A few of the more mature KM programs in the industry had experimented with a richer employee directory called expert locators. Expert locators were centralized, as in the above example, built using spreadsheets, wikis, word documents, and the like, or decentralized, based on employee profile data. The issues with the centralized model were noted above; there were drawbacks to the decentralized model as well. Most relied on employees populating their own profiles and keeping them up to date when acquiring new skills/areas of expertise or job assignments.

HI Corporation had a large internal IT organization and a home-grown centralized content management system, as well as a newer, internally built social media platform (SMP) that was deployed primarily by "word of mouth." The SMP had a profile for each employee that he or she could edit. It also provided the ability to create groups. The groups functionality allowed CoPs/teams to store documents, have discussions, keep a calendar, and so on.

My intuition connected the dots of my experience with communities of practice, discussion forums, and expert lists, and the potential of the SMP to deliver more value by managing tacit knowledge in the heads of our experts and all employees. The challenge was how to make it happen. In hindsight, it seems logical to create an expertise locator system (ELS), but at the time, it was not a commonplace KM tool. The typical employee/user was not aware of the concept and did not request such functionality. Even the supportive leaders at my HI BU were skeptical; they had not heard any internal requests for such a function. They were aware of the numerous KP comments about our centralized version being high maintenance and lagging behind the current state of expertise in the company at any moment in time. Lastly, KM budgets are typically anemic, and the lack of pull from my users was a major obstacle.

Yet I intuitively knew that a large global organization, which was growing at a fast clip through mergers and acquisitions, in a highly competitive industry requiring quick action and product innovation, needed a better, faster, smarter way to manage tacit knowledge and connect people to expertise. How did I know? The mission of the KM program was to connect people to the knowledge and people they needed to do their jobs. The pieces were coming together in my subconscious mind and making some noise in my conscious mind. I listened to my intuition and kept championing and selling the ELS concept internally to HI senior leaders and KPs. I examined budget details to find some "startup" funding, proposed a phased approach that could be discontinued at any time, and took on most of the effort myself to make it a real project.

Before racing off in one direction, my intuition also told me that I could avoid mistakes of other programs and build on their successes. The two best ways I have found to do this are first, to tap in to the amazing network of KM professionals in the CoP called SIKM Leaders (SIKM stands for systems integrators knowledge management) led by Stan Garfield, and second, to run a search in the APQC (American Productivity & Quality Center) knowledge base. APQC is a member-based nonprofit and one of the world's leading proponents of business benchmarking, best practices, and knowledge management research.

I posed the following question to the SIKM Leaders Yahoo group list serve:

> We are in the process of determining whether to make an investment in an Expert Locator system. I know several of the great minds here have implemented these types of applications—can you share the lessons you learned? For example, if you had to do it all over today, what technology would you choose? What are the top 3–5 most important customer requirements/features? What worked/didn't work?

Their response was amazing. This was not surprising, because as a profession that promotes knowledge sharing, KM practitioners are very generous with sharing what works and does not work in their KM programs.

The responses provided qualitative lessons learned, suggestions, and recommendations; the anecdotal knowledge sharing was invaluable to me and reinforced my intuitive decision to move forward with the ELS. The responses were about half for and half against decentralized ELS. Although some responders had positive results from a decentralized ELS, several had struggled with getting employees to populate and maintain their own employee profiles. I was no stranger to influencing people to a shared—and new—goal; cultural issues have always been the major challenge for KM programs. One of the cornerstones of a well-designed KM program is to understand an organization's cultural willingness to change. Knowing this in advance gave me ideas on the design and best way to communicate the ELS.

24.4 Challenges

Deciding to move forward based on intuition and some external research was only the beginning of the project challenges. Other challenges cropped up along the way, some anticipated, some not. For example, I expected needing to sell the future benefits of the system to my manager continually. I kept her informed with regular updates, and to her credit, she gave me the freedom to create the program with minimal restrictions (no doubt she was following her intuition on this as well).

As with any IT-related KM project, the HI ELS development had a phased approach, with standard "gated" reviews. Using the SIKM responses, information from APQC's knowledge base, and my intuitive ideas, I drafted the requirements document. Then, I sat down with my IT program lead who provided several good feature ideas based on the internal social media platform's capabilities (as well as some technical limitations), which served to round out the requirements document.

The project went to development. The ELS was designed as a front end to the internal social media platforms Because the SMP was a centralized tool for all BUs of HI it was being developed and maintained by the central IT function at corporate headquarters. After submitting the functional specification, they came back with an initial version. The corporate IT organization demonstrated it for the KM team: by typing an expert's name in the search box, it brought back their SMP-based profile (prepopulated by the back-end Human Resources system with name, organization, job title, location, and phone number, as well as a link to his or her direct manager's profile).

24.4.1 Lessons Learned

This was wonderful! I now had white pages on steroids. Moreover, a major lesson had been learned: while I had been calling it an expert locator (inasmuch as at that time there was no standard nomenclature for such a system), the interpretation by IT was to find an expert by name. That was the moment it became clear that three more letters were essential. I needed to call it an exper*ise* locator to avoid such confusion. As I reinforced with the IT team, the business problem was that a user does not know who the expert is, and so is unable to enter a name in the search box. It was a step forward to have a person's full profile available. However, users needed to be able to search using topical keywords (such as knowledge management or competitive intelligence or the name of the process chemical the user needed to ship) and find the most relevant experts across the company and their profiles. The ELS used profile fields such as work responsibilities, a self-identifiable job title, and professional interests in its search algorithm to determine relevancy. The user could then use years of experience and geographic location (for time zone if timing was critical) to determine whom to contact.

An unanticipated challenge was the concern by both management and SMEs that "advertising" the experts' abilities would lead to an influx of questions and usurp their valuable time. However, an interesting lesson learned was that the experts discovered the "what's in it for me" rather quickly. The experts gained insight into issues in their area of strength around the larger organization by joining in the new connection and nurturing the relationship with the knowledge seeker. They appreciated finding out about projects, customers, and issues in their area of expertise that they otherwise might not have heard about until much later. They welcomed the opportunity to share their hard-earned lessons learned so that colleagues could avoid repeating mistakes and be more efficient. In addition, often they intuitively understood that by contributing to the success of the larger organization (not just their part of it), their bonuses could be larger as well.

24.4.2 Culture Effect

An anticipated challenge came in the form of changing the culture. From a KM perspective, I could envision the ELS connecting people to people; enabling knowledge sharing, transfer, and retention; and appealing to the (mostly) younger people who used social networks outside of work. Yet most people using the social networks (MySpace, Facebook, Twitter, LinkedIn, etc.) were "lurkers" (i.e., people who merely observe), not creators or contributors. Couple this with some comments I received from my SIKM inquiry that even with a profile-based, robust ELS, corporate users could be hesitant to reach out to a total stranger. Once again, I realized the importance and challenges associated with the culture aspect of KM. Culture change is the area most in need of attention in a KM program and the area where high-quality KM programs expend most of their effort.

Drawing from my experience in KM and that of others who responded to my SIKM query, as well as some general info on social network use, I came to the juncture of another intuitive decision. I knew that even with solid technology and a decentralized, profile-based ELS, culture would play a role in both populating profiles (input) and ELS usage (output). Each was vitally important to the success of the ELS. The plan for the former was to communicate well, leveraging staff meetings, knowledge practitioners, communication channels, and word of mouth. An application was created by IT that reported for each manager at HI what percentage of his or her organization had populated their profiles (or not) and when they were last updated. The KM team encouraged managers to run the application and create their baseline before we communicated the importance of populating profiles. Managers could periodically use the tool to measure their progress toward 100% completion, and communicate as necessary based on progress.

The more challenging issue was how to help users become comfortable reaching out to experts they did not know. This is where intuition came into play. LinkedIn had introduced the concept of social distance, that is, showing if a network connection was a first-, second-, or third-level contact. A LinkedIn user could ask a first-level contact to introduce him to another LinkedIn member, or see who and what he had in common with another person by connectedness and profiles. I knew from personal experience how useful both features were to growing my professional network. I envisioned the ELS doing the same thing for HI employees. Not only could it connect someone needing information with the person/expert who had that info in the short term, but also it provided the knowledge seeker with a person to call upon in future situations for questions that arose in the expert's area of expertise. They might even find a common area of interest and connect on a more frequent basis.

Before that could happen, I had to solve the problem of usage. As before, this was uncharted territory. Relying on instinct, I pushed IT for a network view such as that LinkedIn provided, that is, a way to show a user all the connections in her network in a visual format. Unfortunately, this was not possible with our in-house technology. Nevertheless, we were able to include a form of social distance, incorporating "in-common" information. For example, if the expert and I had a group in common (e.g., the HI cross-BU knowledge management CoP, or the Refinery Knowledge Sharing Network) or we both reported in through the same organization, the ELS would display this under the expert's profile. This gave the user a sense of connectedness to the expert, and potentially a way to "break the ice" when reaching out with a question.

Here is one example of the time the ELS saved and the efficiency it produced. Just before it was deployed, a KP was looking for an expert in a new market in South Africa to respond to a request for proposal. The KP called a contact, who called another contact, who, after a three-day delay due to missed connections, time-zone differences, and being unavailable, provided the name of an expert. Using the HI ELS, this very same expert was the top expert search result, displaying in less than two seconds, along with her contact, profile, and in-common information. The two people involved in the earlier, non-ELS search would not have been interrupted, thus avoiding that productivity loss, and the response back to the customer would have occurred days earlier. In addition to expert names, the search results provided the names and links to related groups (i.e., CoPs) to tap into for a whole network of possible experts, as well as links to relevant blog discussions to search when the user had additional questions.

24.5 Conclusion

With minimal existing data, my strong inclination to pay attention to intuition made the decision process on this project easier. Intuition also played a large role in adjusting to cultural barriers. It did not eliminate all risks, but it did eliminate much of the hesitancy to move forward. The HI ELS was very successful, garnering more and more usage over time and positive feedback from users. The combination of a decentralized, user-maintained, profile back end; a rich search results page which included not only highly relevant expert matches but also links to groups, blogs, and microblogs around a topic; and a social distance feature to overcome barriers to participation, led to a powerful KM approach.

25

INTUITION

How Experience and Values Helped Create a Successful Career

RICK SMITH

(formerly with) Georgia Department of Transportation

Contents

25.1 Introduction

When asked to write this chapter, I did what I learned a long time ago. I did a gut check. Having never written a chapter-length document detailing anything, let alone on how I make decisions, it was necessary to do some introspection and also run the idea by family and friends. I am the perfect candidate to write a chapter on intuition-based decision making given that making decisions on the fly is something I know about. Most of the important decisions I have made over the years both in my personal life and in my professional life have been based on experience and gut instinct.

Even with a full workload at work and the pressure of writing a dissertation, the invitation was enticing because it is an opportunity to share a different perspective and approach to decision making with an audience who may be looking for affirmation that intuition decision making is as effective as data-based decision making.

Putting to use what I learned over time for making decisions of this kind, I talked it over with family and friends. They all encouraged me to accept the offer. When it came down to making the final decision, however, it was still mine to make. Using a common decision-making technique, I weighed the pros and cons by listing them, then made the decision based on the longest list. Obviously, the pros outweighed the cons. I did a final gut check just to make sure. Feeling no anxiety about my decision, I accepted the invitation.

What does it mean to make decisions using your intuition? That was the question posed to 60 business leaders by Burke and Miller (1999) in their investigation into intuitive decision making. The participants defined five types: (1) experienced-based, (2) decisions based on feeling and emotions, (3) cognitive-based decisions, (4) subconscious decisions, and (5) values- or ethics-based decisions. In my career, I have used each type given a particular situation. Development of my intuition-based decision making is the result of my career path and my position in the organization.

25.2 In the Beginning

Data-based approaches to decision making were a concept of the future for the department when I decided to provide supervisor/manager skills training to the customers of a technical assistance program. This was especially true in the employee development office in which I worked. At the time, my unit offered the same classes each year based on previous offerings. We also received requests from office administrators when they had identified a training need. Now several years later, focus on data is gaining more emphasis. Even so, the need for decision making intuitively will persist.

In my position in the employee development office, I was assigned to manage the Local Technical Assistance Program (LTAP). The LTAP, which has been in existence for over 30 years, provides training and technical assistance to city and county public agencies. The position had been vacant for a time when I took the job of LTAP director. I came into the position not as a career-training professional, but as an engineer who had graduated from college a few years earlier. Not having sufficient experience to draw from to make decisions regarding what training the program should deliver was a weakness and an opportunity.

My lack of experience, no formal training in adult education, and unfamiliarity with LTAP taught me early that I should not trust my own judgment when making decisions in my role as LTAP director. I also learned early in my new position to check with other managers, coworkers, and, yes, family and friends when making program and personnel decisions.

It was during this period that I began to develop practical intuition. Dr. Paul Wong, the noted psychologist and researcher, identified seven types of intuition. Three of the seven have application in business. They are interpersonal intuition, such as character judgment; practical intuition for problem solving; and expertise intuition, which relates to having expert knowledge and information about a specific topic (Newton, n.d.). At this point in my career, I had none of the identified types.

As I worked and gained experience managing the LTAP, I made what I think are the usual mistakes that come from scheduling and conducting training. There were times when my workload was so heavy I would forget to complete a critical task such as scheduling a location for an upcoming class before advertising its availability. In a rush to locate a facility, I would overlook the obvious red flags such as using too small a room or not asking how many would attend. My decision making in these situations was not where it needed to be. Over time, however, I learned from my mistakes. I began to look for the red flags I had overlooked before. Learning from my earlier mistakes improved my decisions when selecting locations and the timing of my training announcements.

For most of LTAP's existence, the focus was on delivering technical training to the workforce of public agencies responsible for the construction and maintenance of their roads and bridges. It was this historical focus on technical training and the total lack of soft-skills training offered through the program that made me aware of an opportunity for the program to have a greater impact on the operations of our customers. I felt that all the technical training would not ensure success if managers and supervisors did not have the skills they needed to motivate their employees and to handle the personnel issues effectively that inevitably arise when the majority of the workforce is at or below the poverty level.

Many areas of the state the program serves are rural and lack industries that support a high level of government services. On more than one occasion while traveling on an outreach effort, I would find myself visiting with a mayor or council member whose office was located in a small building that housed the sheriff's office, the courthouse, and administrative offices. The point being these small governments had few resources available to train their supervisory staff properly.

Looking at professional associations in the state that represent local governments, I noticed they provided professional development opportunities to elected officials and administration-level employees on topics necessary to manage and serve the residents of that local government, including management and supervisory skills training. The primary provider in this case is a branch of a leading university in the state. The purpose of the branch, in fact, is to assist elected and appointed government officials and administrators in improving their knowledge and skills through continuing educational opportunities.

A similar relationship existed between state agencies and another state agency formerly known as the State Personnel Administration (SPA). SPA, at the time, was responsible for administering several human resource functions common to all state agencies. One of the functions included the professional development of the state's managers and supervisors. The department routinely provided supervisory and managerial skills training to state employees who worked at the various state agencies. Annually scheduled courses were available to all agency employees. Agencies could also schedule closed classes on an as-needed basis.

There existed at one time a three-tiered management certificate program offered by SPA. However, some agencies, including the agency which employs me, did not recognize the value of the content that was delivered. Managers with whom I worked believed the concepts and principles taught were not those the department supported. Managers in other agencies must have believed the same was true of their department. SPA dropped its management development program years before due to lack of demand and the fact that the material taught was often in conflict with the management culture of the individual agencies. However, SPA continued to offer individual classes. My department continued to purchase their soft-skills classes on a class-by-class basis, spending approximately $70,000 to $80,000 per year.

I saw an opportunity to provide a valuable service to LTAP's customers using my department's ongoing relationship with SPA.

LTAP offered the same technical training classes year after year to our customers, which led to a drop in participation. Participation began to drop off noticeably. Offering soft-skills training seemed to be an obvious solution. Instinctively, I knew a program designed to deliver supervisory training to public works supervisors would increase the level of participation to where it had been.

Working together with SPA, we developed and delivered a structured curriculum designed to provide managers and front-line supervisors with the management skills necessary to manage their employees. The curriculum was widely accepted. Participants finished the program within two years, inasmuch as the classes were offered statewide on a rotating basis. All participants received a certificate of completion. By simply organizing existing training into a curriculum, we were able to increase class enrollment and to provide needed management training to our customers.

The program drew the attention of my department's training director. Management soon realized the benefit of offering a structured curriculum to supervisors and managers. Soon after, management introduced the program into the department. However, department leadership took the program one step further. It mandated supervisors and managers in the maintenance division to complete the program. Some years later, the professional organization that represents public works employees developed their own version of the program, eliminating the need for LTAP to continue offering it.

I did not realize at the time, but I had begun to make decisions based on intuition because of the experience of collaborating with others to develop and implement a program.

25.3 Targeting the Next Group

The department employs maintenance workers whose job it is to perform activities necessary to maintain the transportation infrastructure. The department was under increasing pressure to maintain the state's infrastructure at an acceptable level. Department leadership made a strategic decision to spend more dollars on maintenance and less on building more bridges and roadways. A large percentage of the workforce was maintenance workers; many of them were satisfied with remaining at their current position on their short career ladder.

Maintenance workers must advance up three levels of their career ladder before moving into a supervisory position. The dispersion of equipment operators up and down the career ladder created a diverse set of skills and experience. The department tried to account for the disparity in skills by distributing the workers equally among the crews. A typical work crew employed one or two equipment operator ones, one or two equipment operator twos, and one or two equipment operator threes.

The challenge to management was employees were not moving up their career ladder quickly. Many of the employees were content to remain in a position where they were comfortable with the duties and pay of that position. It was decided they needed an incentive to move to the next step. The department had already put financial incentives in place. The only requirement to gain additional compensation through promotion was time in the position. The department needed qualified workers who could perform at the advanced level required to support the new strategic objective of maintaining the existing bridges and roads. The goal was to have all equipment operators achieve the equipment operator three position through skills development training. The objective was to pull employees up the career ladder through training.

Utilizing incentive theory, employees are pulled up their career ladder by incentivizing training rather than simply making the training available and expecting employees to work through a series of modules to become eligible for promotion. In the beginning stages of developing a human performance solution, training professionals conduct a needs assessment collecting data from managers and the target audience. One benefit to a needs assessment at the beginning is the results will confirm that the problem needing to be addressed could be solved by training. Employers spend thousands of dollars developing training, thinking the identified performance issue can be corrected with training. In this case, we did not conduct a needs assessment.

The team (of which I was a member) felt, based on our collective experience, that a training program would be the best solution. Therefore, we began the development process without the benefit of information typically available after conducting a needs assessment. In addition, when we had completed development of the program, we did not conduct a summative evaluation. A summative evaluation (sometimes referred to as external) is a method of judging the worth of a program at the end of the program activities (summation). The focus is on the outcome.

The program partially achieved its stated goal of pulling equipment operators up their career ladder. The goal was not completely achieved because many long-term employees were not motivated to move up. The influence of an employee's tenure should have been intuitive to the team members, but we did not consider it.

This program was the second major development project of my career. Going into it, I did not have the experiences that would have provided input into decisions made over the course of the project. However, the lessons learned added to my earlier experiences. I would soon have the opportunity to apply my combined experiences to decision making on the next project.

25.4 Solution Worth Modeling

The program created for the maintenance workers was deemed a model that fit the problem. The multitiered model was applied to other work groups. Before long, a program was created for other key work groups that had well-established career paths. As with the first program, the programs that were to follow had a multitiered design with monetary incentives to pull the employees up the career ladder.

In the original program, management created training to develop the skills needed at the next step of employees' particular career ladder. They were required to take all trainings for each level before being eligible for promotion. This new model added additional incentives such as a bonus for completing the training at each level and eligibility for promotion. The program design was adapted from the "push–pull" concept used by the marketing and employee development industries. A push strategy brings the training to the learner in the form of classroom or instructor-led training. The pull strategy makes available to the learner training that is informal or just in time. The learner has access to chunks of learning such as training videos and e-learning courses for use or reuse at any time.

The adaptation included a blended learning of self-study, classes, and monetary reward for completing each level of training.

25.5 Rollout of Employee Learning Management System

The Training and Development Office identified a need to develop an application that would automate many of the administrative duties of managing, scheduling, and delivering training. The application ultimately selected had many features that enhanced employee experience with training such as viewing in real-time their training record, enrolling in courses, and capturing information on training activities that occur on the job or when travel is involved. Training administration benefited from the selected application because it eliminated the need for manual input of hundreds of training records a year, generating reports of training including course offerings and how many employees attended in a given region of the state.

The application was an off-the-shelf product that the state had purchased but no agency was utilizing until my department began to use it. There was minimal tailoring allowed, as other agencies may want to use it in the future. Because all agencies potentially would be using it, we could not change it the way we had conceived the application in the beginning. Even so, it required a great deal of effort on the part of the implementation team to populate the application. Even with the time spent on this phase, the team did not consider an implementation plan.

As team leader, I made the decision to have a soft rollout. There were no data to support this decision. The team had no prior experience in the rollout of an application of this kind. Initially, we trained the learners to enroll in activities. This was quite a change. Prior to the rollout, we notified managers and supervisors of a scheduled class. They would select the employee(s) to attend a class, and then submit a list to the course manager. With the new application, employees were able to search the application for scheduled classes and enroll in one. The system sends an e-mail to the employee's supervisor notifying him or her of the employee's enrollment request. Other than a few technical glitches related to logging in to the application and the manager–employee reporting structure, the rollout was successful.

According to Rogers' diffusion of innovation curve, attempting to convince a group quickly to adopt a new idea (in this case a computer application) is useless. I was not aware of the curve prior to implementation of our training application. With the change requirements, it was intuitively obvious that the best approach was to roll it out gradually. The more the employees used it, the more they would be accepting of the application. As it turned out, there was little pushback from the users. Over time, we were able to utilize the initial user experience to enhance the training we had created beforehand.

25.6 Knowledge Management (KM): A Critical Need Addressed

It was six or seven years ago when my predecessor, while conducting workforce planning, realized there would be an exodus of employees within five years. One of the goals of the workforce planning initiative was to inform employees that what they do supports the department's strategic objectives. Leadership wanted to make visible to each employee a line of sight. It was during the analysis phase that the determination was made that several employees in key positions could be retiring soon. Projected retirements for 2013 were as high as 43 in key management and leadership positions. It is more than likely the manager reported his findings to leadership. However, no action was taken to develop and implement strategies focused on capturing and retaining the institutional knowledge the department would soon be losing. In 2010, I assumed the leadership role responsible for all aspects of employee development. In this role, I was encouraged to innovate to identify solutions to the department's human capital challenges in the area of employee performance. At the same time, through my studies of the learning transfer research, I saw an opportunity to address the long anticipated exodus. Admittedly, I was behind the curve already as employees had begun to retire and the department was losing some critical knowledge.

At this point in my career, I had learned to combine intuition with data analysis in decision making, employing intuition in concert with deductive processes. For this project, the combined approach was critical because I only had access to minimal data that were not updated often enough. To compound the lack of real-time data, employees eligible to retire were submitting their retirement papers and leaving on short notice. Therefore, other means were necessary to identify and talk with employees who would be leaving soon to document their tacit knowledge before they walked out the door.

In my position, the opportunity existed to work on an internal research team with the responsibility of recommending research projects. At this point in my career, I was confident in my understanding of the department and, as I mentioned, I had been granted a lot of discretion as it relates to originating solutions for employee development. A plan began to form to slow the loss of tacit knowledge and eventually decrease the loss to an acceptable level—a knowledge management plan, if you will.

The plan involved a combination of leveraging internal research activities with the research I was conducting on KM and the techniques commonly used in the transportation industry. As a member of the research committee, I suggested KM-centered topics for research. Ultimately, the research committee selected the KM-centered topics as worthy of investigation.

Knowledge management is not something new to the transportation industry: several state transportation agencies from around the country had already developed programs. Instincts and the years of experience I gained informed me I should reach out to the other states to learn from them what worked and what did not work. In addition, I learned there was a movement at the national level to begin work to solve the problem many states were having with the loss of institutional knowledge. I located the group that was doing this work and became involved, as I had done many times before over my career, realizing the opportunities that would open up to me.

By intuition, I knew I would meet other professionals who could assist me in carrying out my idea to develop and implement a KM program. I did meet other professionals, a few of whom were considered experts in the field of KM. That little voice inside was telling me in order to have this idea to have a KM program accepted by top leadership, they would need to be sold by bringing other voices. At the same time that we were losing experienced and knowledgeable employees there had been a hiring freeze in place. One of the consequences for the freeze and the loss of employees was that employees who were already carrying a heavy workload were now expected to do even more with fewer employees. I knew from experience to suggest that department employees take on additional work that was not core function work would be difficult to sell with my voice alone. Therefore, for that reason I decided to invite an expert in to pave the way for the development of a KM program.

The expert was welcomed in a manner fitting for a guest speaker and subject matter expert. I could tell, however, not everyone was convinced of the need to initiate such an undertaking. Leadership needed more convincing.

Some months later, I decided I needed help. A lesson I learned years ago through experience is you need help with carrying out multiple tasks including educating people in an organizational form, a committee, or in this case a task force. Once a task force was established, the number of knowledge-capturing activities increased, and we delved into video and began work on a website to be used by employees to exchange knowledge. The plan was unfolding nicely. It was as if I had written my plan and distributed it to everyone. In reality, I had shared it with few people.

Even though the plan was coming together nicely, my gut told me more was needed in terms of convincing leadership of the need to have a KM program at this time. The decision to get involved in activities at the national level was beginning to pay off as I began to get calls and recommendations to serve on national-level committees from colleagues with whom I had just developed relationships. When presented with these opportunities, I knew I had to act on them. I did not seek input from others as I have learned to do. Instincts told me leadership would look favorably on the recognition the department would receive. In addition, expectations were that all employees including leadership would be better informed and as a result move to furthering the initial plan of establishing a sustainable KM program.

According to Wikipedia, "In organizational theory, *knowledge transfer* is the practical problem of transferring knowledge from one part of the organization to another. Like knowledge management, knowledge transfer seeks to organize, create, capture or distribute knowledge and ensure its availability for future users" (http://en.wikipedia.org/wiki/Knowledge_transfer). Whereas learning transfer, according to Wikipedia, is the transfer of learning, usually described as the process and the effective extent to which past experiences (also referred to as the *transfer source*) affect learning and performance in a new situation (the *transfer target*; http://en.wikipedia.org/wiki/Transfer_of_learning). There is enough commonality between the two concepts to allow me to apply what I was learning in my study of learning transfer to the knowledge management initiative I convinced department leadership to support. When I undertook this initiative, I was told by some in leadership this was long overdue.

The KM effort and the others I described in this chapter were examples where intuition played a key part in the conceptualization and eventual implementation of critical training efforts needed to move the department even further.

References

Burke, L.A. and Miller, M.K. (1999). Taking the mystery out of intuitive decision making. *The Academy of Management Executive,* 13(4), 91–99. Knowledge transfer. (n.d.). In Wikipedia. Retrieved April 7, 2014, from http://en.wikipedia.org/wiki/Knowledge_transfer

Newton, C. (n.d.). The Use of Intuition in a Business Decision. Transfer of learning. (n.d.). In Wikipedia. Retrieved April 7, 2014, from http://en.wikipedia.org/wiki/Transfer_of_learning

26

APPLICATION OF INTUITION-BASED MANAGEMENT IN AN ADMINISTRATIVE PROJECT

An Airport Industry Case (Frankfurt Airport)

DIETER H. FRÜAUFF

Frankfurt Airport

MARION KAHRENS

1&1 Telecommunication AG

Contents

26.1 Introduction

The airport industry in Germany represents one of the traditional industries. It has reached maturity in various ways, starting in the mid-1990s with the market entry for the privatization of the airport industry (Forsyth, Niemeier, and Wolf, 2011). This was followed by the deep impacts generated by security and policy decisions after 9/11 (Kirschenbaum, 2013), and concluding with the ongoing focus on cost and pricing, so now the pressure to benchmark airport performance is paramount (Francis, Humphreys, and Frey, 2002; Cheng, Tsai, and Lai, 2009; Adler, Liebert, and Yazehemsky, 2013; Voltes-Dorta and Lei, 2013). Depending on the specific geographical region and the status of privatization, there have been an overlapping of themes in the past 10–15 years. These structural changes influenced the airports in different ways. From the perspective of the airport-services industry, the general rationale existed for consolidation and mergers, including improving technical efficiency, reducing transaction costs to customers, eliminating market imperfections, overcoming regulatory restrictions, and getting access to resources (Forsyth et al., 2011).

26.2 Airport Industry Background

In general, the airport industry is strongly linked to two groups of stakeholders: the airlines and airline alliances, and the general public such as governments, authorities, and the community. This explains the interbranch assignment of airports to the public and economic sector. The rationale mentioned above influences the different segments and airport models, which can be distinguished by the business content as follows (Forsyth et al., 2011):

- Aviation: Including the charges and fees for landing, parking, and takeoff
- Nonaviation: Not directly related to air transportation, for example, commercials, or leasing terminal facilities

• Ground handling: Comprising a diverse set of services such as catering, cleaning, fueling, and pushing off of aircraft from terminal piers

Depending on the government policies and the geographical region, airport pricing follows either the single-till approach (includes nonaviation) or the dual-till approach (separated examination of aviation and nonaviation revenues). Historically, the infrastructure of transportation such as railways and nowadays aviation has had deep impacts on regional and business development (Appold and Kasarda, 2011). The different regulatory framework, linked with the technology structure, created an ambitious environment for operations and administration regarding efficiency and cost reduction programs.

The development of airport cities in the United States such as Michigan's Detroit Region Aerotropolis, in Europe (e.g., Amsterdam Schiphol, London Heathrow, and Frankfurt airports), in Asia (e.g., Singapore, Kuala Lumpur, Hong Kong, Tokyo, Shanghai, Bangkok, and Seoul), and in recent years particularly in the Middle East, such as Dubai, Abu Dhabi, and Kuwait shows the third driver for the change in the airport's business environment. Airports try to increase their business mainly from two business sides (aeronautical and nonaeronautical revenues). Typical improvement options for airports consist of the top nonaeronautical revenue (such as retail in airport cities) followed by regulatory management, CAPEX optimization (such as terminals and airport cities), improved operations (on land and airside), and marketing and pricing (Goulmy, Stern, and Eggenkamp, 2012).

26.3 Frankfurt Airport Case

Following the board of directors' decision, three independent billing departments (consisting of different aeronautical revenue streams) were merged into one major billing department. The objective of this centralization was to achieve an administrative cost reduction. Due to the existing long-term employment process, knowledge is mainly stored as intangible and hidden knowledge within employees' minds. The explicit knowledge stored as job and task descriptions is just rudimentarily given. In addition, due to the operational interdependencies and requirements, billing processes are embedded in a continued path of process complexity. For the responsible takeover management team, the following two major problems occurred: There were risks in loss of knowledge due to employees leaving and the risks of dysfunctional incidents because of missing process descriptions and lack of transparency within the different processes.

26.3.1 Intuition-Based Management

Based on this environment, the takeover team needed to decide quickly on the general approach and project structure. Within the team, it was clear from the beginning that typical project procedures best fit together with discussions, and benchmark analysis would not work in this case. The spotlight moved quickly to the most experienced manager for the decision making. The intuition-based decision was to use the SECI (Nonaka's socialization-externalization-combination-internalization) model as a structural vehicle to join the recentralization process of knowledge transfer, sharing, and creation during usual business activities.

26.4 Managerial Decision Making and Decision Styles

26.4.1 Nature of Intuition

Cognitive styles describe how people gather, interpret, and use information for their individual situations. In general, two different types of thinking can be distinguished: one can be described as analytic, deductive, rigorous, formal, and critical; and the other refers to synthetic, inductive, informal, diffuse, and creative (Nickerson, Perkins, and Smith, 1985). The types of thinking are determined by the modes of consciousness. The analytic or rational style implies viewing parts of a situation in sequences, whereas the holistic or intuitive style includes the whole situation at once. The use of intuition means unconscious pattern recognition (Millett, 2011). These authors focus on the description and the line of demarcation between intuition and rational thought; however, Dane and Pratt (2007) explored and defined intuition as affectively charged judgments that arise through rapid, non-conscious, and holistic associations. The main assumptions behind this definition are that decision accuracy is often inversely related to decision speed and intuition is a means to manage this tradeoff: that intuition is the integral part to complete successfully tasks of high complexity and time pressures and that the need for intuition may especially affect organizations in changing environments (Dane and Pratt, 2007).

26.4.2 Intuition in Organizational Management

Since the 1930s, the two types of thinking have been discussed in the context of management and the conclusions are that organizational effectiveness needs both types of information processing depending on the individual situation, for example, for decision-making (Hayes, Allison, and Armstrong, 2004). Traditional approaches in management theory focus on analysis and planning to support systematic decision-making processes. This follows the rational type of thinking (Hayes et al., 2004). But executive work often involves immediate decisions rather than reflection and planning. In some circumstances, decision making has to rely on relational and simultaneous rather than systematic information processing. In the late 1980s, the discipline of cognitive science devoted attention to the nature of expert problem solving and decision making to gain insights into the behavior of experts (Simon, 1987). There is a continuum of decision-making styles involving a combination of the two types of thinking and related skills. The growing understanding of organizational intuitive processes and the specific knowledge that is required to perform particular judgments might deliver new approaches for improving expert judgment (Simon, 1987). The major characteristics explore intuition in relation to managerial decision making and bring together the processes and outcomes: intuiting involves holistic associations, is fast, and results in affectively charged judgments (Dane and Pratt, 2007).

26.4.3 Expertise-Based Intuition

Expertise in general is a level of specialized skills and knowledge in a given domain or area. Experts achieve this level of performance through their specialized knowledge and the application of reasoning strategies acquired in periods of experience and practice (Salas, Rosen, and Granados, 2010). Expertise-based intuition is different from intuition in general, which describes rapid and affectively charged judgments. Expertise enriches intuition with situational sense making, mental knowledge-based simulations, and problem assessments. Expertise-based intuition can be defined as the rapid generation of single decision options through domain-specific knowledge and pattern recognition.

26.5 Model Application

26.5.1 Relationship between Tacit and Explicit Knowledge

Although the characteristics and descriptions of explicit knowledge are clear, the term "tacit knowledge" carries different shades of meaning. It has been considered as inseparable from human activity and embedded knowledge (Orlikowski, 2002). Furthermore, stages of knowledge management include collecting, storing, making, and using the information (Märtensson, 2000). The main characteristics for tacit knowledge have been described as inexpressible (in a codified form), subjective, personal, and context-specific. In contrast, explicit knowledge is seen as codifiable, objective, impersonal, context-dependent, and easy to share (Hislop, 2009). From a business perspective, the question arises how an effective approach to identify, explore, and extract knowledge could be implemented.

The cyclic model SECI illustrates four stages of socialization, externalization, combination, and internalization (SECI) and delivers an integrated approach to implement a process to create, disseminate, and capture the knowledge of business processes among individuals and working groups (Nonaka, 1994; Nonaka and Takeuchi, 1995; Nonaka, Toyama, and Konno, 2000). Within this model, exchange between the two spheres of knowledge (tacit and explicit) in different steps and stages is assumed (Oguz and Sengün, 2011). Whereas the tacit sphere reflects the more personal and hidden knowledge, the explicit sphere can be summarized as codifying and decrypting conversion in written and visible storage.

26.5.2 Process Meetings Conducted According to SECI

The centralization of the three departments had been managed in a project that covered the development of a process inventory to fulfill the completeness requirements (accounting standards). The intuition decision making (see Table 26.1) was to conduct the project activities by applying the SECI model.

Table 26.1 Key Objectives of the Intuition Process

INTUITION DECISION-MAKING–BASED PROCESS	MEETING ENROLLMENT BILLING DEPARTMENT AREAS	PEOPLE INVOLVEMENT
Study of knowledge management impact on business processes (centralization, cost reduction, and change effect)	Airport charges: 15 Ground handling: 12 Other services: 25	Airport charges: 8–10 people Ground handling: 3–5 people Other services: 6–8 people

Employees who were involved (billing experts and business process supervisors) had from 3–35 years' experience with the company. The meetings for the process definitions in accordance with the billing content were conducted in parallel. The business process supervisors and project-supporting external students prepared the documentation. The billing experts as process owners were responsible for the review of the process descriptions based on their tacit knowledge.

26.6 Application of Intuitive Decisions

26.6.1 Program Challenges and Complexity

The major challenge consisted of unknown business details from the three different departments. In addition, the job descriptions and manuals were incomplete and created by different standards (aviation such as charges and fees versus ground handling including different sets of services). The quantity of subprocesses and process steps was unknown. The process integration level such as manual, automatic, and test process steps was not clear as well. The time needed for tasks was based on the decentralization level from the previous organizational structure.

26.6.2 Expertise-Based Decision Making

The expertise-based decision-making process in this project was as illustrated in Figure 26.1. This process is embedded in the organizational influence (such as internal and external stakeholders) and the timeline, including the predominant intuition stage and predominant control and data analysis stage. The process in practice consists of three different intuition levels.

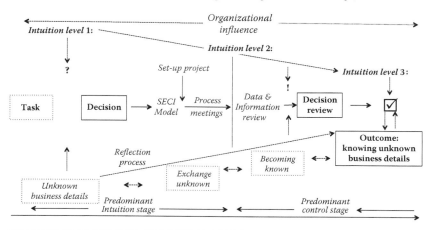

Figure 26.1   Expertise-based decision making. (Developed by present researcher.)

Table 26.2   Process Analysis Key Figures

NUMBERS OF PROCESSES	AIRPORT TRAFFIC CHARGES (AC)	GROUND-HANDLING SPECIAL SERVICES (GH)	OTHER SERVICES (OS)	TOTAL
Main processes	6	6	19	31
Subprocesses	33	10	91	134
Total	39	16	110	165
Average sub/main	5.5	1.7	4.8	4.3

26.6.2.1 Intuition Level 1   The Intuition Level 1 consists of the given task and the unknown business details. The unknown business details are on the highest level at this stage. The expertise-based intuition stems from the ability of generalization, including past experiences and having an open mind for new solutions. In this case, the adoption of the SECI model was the unknown component to manage the unknown and hidden business details faster and more efficiently. The structure and the project phases followed the requirements of the three different units of analysis (airport charges, ground handling, and other services; see Table 26.2). Part of this stage was the creation of a series of process meetings. This phase of the project was in general highly dominated by intuition-based management. This includes the core decision for using the SECI model and the decisions during the process meetings and the exchange procedures. In general, the flow of decision making followed experiences of what happened in the past, what is adaptable at present, where are there similarities and differences, and how does it work among processes, systems, and employees.

26.6.2.2 Intuition Level 2 The Intuition Level 2 consists of the conversion of collected data and information. Based on this clash of data and information, the next level of expertise-based decision making occurs in accordance with the following questions:

1. When are detailed process descriptions achieved sufficiently?
2. How many further meetings and review steps are needed?
3. At what level is comparableness for the departments given?

During this level, the characteristics of the intuition-based decision making changed from the helicopter view into closer assessments and adjustments. The intuition-based decisions were more fact influenced and distinguished by different units of analysis (three former departments). The impact is shown in the different forming of process descriptions and quantity of process meetings (see Table 26.2). The main characteristic of this level is the finding of the previous unknown, which transfers the subdecision processes to an automatic stage and a gut feel (Sadler-Smith and Shefy, 2004; Salas et al., 2010).

26.6.2.3 Intuition Level 3 At this level, the gap between intuition level on one side and the unknown business content on the other side is nearly closed. The degree of intuition-based decision making is low. Focus is on the sense making in decision making to complete the project. This includes the closing of the process meeting across the different departments and the approval of the process forms.

26.7 Outcomes and Organizational Change

26.7.1 *Transparency in Process Inventory*

The process meetings create data and information. Subsequently the previous unknown business details become known process details. The three units of analysis (airport traffic charges, ground-handling special services, and other services) consist of different processes. The first outcome contains different degrees in the data–information–knowledge assignment. The differences are shown in Figure 26.2.

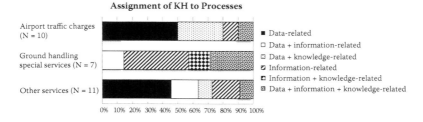

Figure 26.2   Assignment of knowledge hierarchy (KH) to billing processes. (Developed by present researcher.)

The assignment illustrates the different structures of the processes and links to the unknown but expected complexity. This was the first acknowledgment for the intuition-based decision making on intuition level one. The adapted SECI model as a tool had worked sufficiently. It showed where differences such as data relations between airport traffic charges and ground-handling special services exist. From the management perspective, this was important for further decision making based on increased facts and measurement with underlying assumptions such as complexity.

26.7.2 Performance Insights in Processes

The outcome of the process inventory revealed transparency of the business details. A distinctive structure among the three process areas was expected and was one of the key questions at the intuition level one to be answered. The spread in quantity such as the total of 16 processes in ground-handling special services and 110 processes in other services surfaced. The major review during intuition level two focused on the investigation of the process measures such as manual, automatic, and test steps, as shown in Figure 26.3. This classification should deliver the key drivers for future business process reengineering and dissemination of knowledge management.

The allocation shows a majority of manual steps in all billing process areas. This outcome emphasizes the need to reengineer the processes. This development demonstrates the linkage and exchange opportunities between intuition-based decision making (based on experience of process and business skills) and the application of process models such as SECI. The outcomes of process ratios and steps created are the basis for the future decisions.

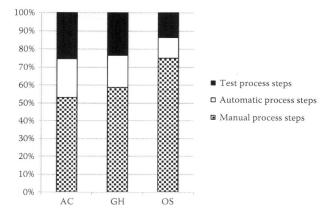

Figure 26.3   Allocation manual, automatic, and test process steps. (Developed by present researcher.)

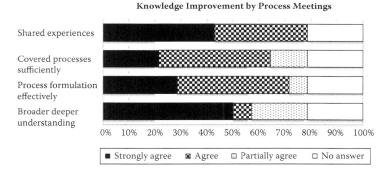

Figure 26.4   Knowledge improvement by process meetings. (Developed by present researcher.)

26.7.3 Process Meetings and Knowledge Sharing and Transfer

After the completion of the process inventory, the participants were asked to evaluate the outcomes of the process meetings. They had to evaluate the shared experiences, process sufficiency, the effectiveness, and the knowledge sharing and transfer effects regarding improved understanding (ranging from strongly agree to strongly disagree), as shown in Figure 26.4.

There is an overall agreement visible. The option "no answer" has been chosen by representatives who did not attend the process meetings. The outcome demonstrates that the process meetings created predominant agreement in the range of 60% to 80%. This includes the sharing of experiences, broader understanding, and the process activities.

26.8 Conclusion

In this case, the intuition-based decision making could be applied and observed as follows:

1. Intuition Level 1, which consisted of the major decision made regarding the assumption that the SECI model is applicable (Salas et al., 2010).
2. Intuition Level 2, the stage in which the first results of the process meetings, such as process inventory ratios (quantity of processes), could be considered. Based on that, the decision from level one was reviewed and further specifications such as investigation of particular business processes and areas was made.
3. Intuition Level 3 consisted of the complete set of the outcomes based on the SECI process meetings and the delivered process inventory. In addition, the previous unknowns in business details are now the grounding basis for future intuition-based decision-making referring to the processes.

References

Adler, N., Liebert, V., and Yazehemsky, E. (2013). Benchmarking airports from managerial perspective. *Omega*, 41(2): 442–458.

Appold, S.J. and Kasarda, J.D. (2011). Seeding growth at airports and airport cities: Insights from the two-sided market literature. *Research in Transportation Business & Management*, 1(1): 91–100.

Cheng, M.-Y., Tsai, H.-C., and Lai, Y.-Y. (2009). Construction management process reengineering performance measurements. *Automation in Construction*, 18(2): 183–193.

Dane, E. and Pratt, M.G. (2007). Exploring intuition and its role in managerial decision making. *Academy of Management Review*, 32(1): 33–54.

Forsyth, P., Niemeier, H.-M., and Wolf, H. (2011). Airport alliances and mergers—Structural change in the airport industry? *Journal of Air Transport Management*, 17(1): 49–56.

Francis, G., Humphreys, I., and Frey, J. (2002). The benchmarking of airport performance. *Journal of Air Transport Management*, 8: 239–247.

Goulmy, M., Stern, S., and Eggenkamp, G. (2012). Moving from good to great: Using smart benchmarking to improve airport performance. *Journal of Airport Management*, 7(2): 119–128.

Hayes, J., Allison, C.W., and Armstrong, S.J. (2004). Intuition, women managers, and gendered stereotypes. *Personnel Review*, 33(4): 403–417.

Hislop, D. (2009). *Knowledge Management in Organizations – A Critical Introduction,* 2nd edn. Oxford: Oxford University Press.

Kirschenbaum, A. (2013). The cost of airport security: The passenger dilemma. *Journal of Air Transport Management* 30: 39–45.

Märtensson, M. (2000). A critical review of knowledge management as a management tool. *Journal of Knowledge Management*, 4(3): 204–216.

Millett, S.M. (2011). Managers as visionaries: A skill that can be learned. *Strategy and Leadership*, 39(5): 56–58.

Nickerson, R.S., Perkins, D.N., and Smith, E.E. (1985). *The Teaching of Thinking*. Hillsdale, NJ: L. Erlbaum Associates.

Nonaka, I. (1994). A dynamic theory of organizational knowledge creation. *Organization Science*, 5(1): 14–37.

Nonaka, I. and Takeuchi, H. (1995). *The Knowledge-Creating Company*. New York: Oxford University Press.

Nonaka, I., Toyama, R., and Konno, N. (2000). SECI, Ba and leadership: A unified model of dynamic knowledge creation. *Long Range Planning*, 33: 5–34.

Oguz, F. and Sengün, A.E. (2011). Mystery of the known: Revisiting tacit knowledge in organizational literature. *Journal of Knowledge Management*, 15(3): 445–461.

Orlikowski, W.J. (2002). Knowing in practice: Enacting a collective capability in distributed organizing. *Organization Science*, 13(3): 249–273.

Sadler-Smith, E. and Shefy, E. (2004). The intuitive executive: Understanding and applying 'gut feel' in decision-making. *Academy of Management Executive*, 18(4): 76–91.

Salas, E., Rosen, M.A., and Diaz Granados, D. (2010). Expertise-based intuition and decision making in organizations. *Journal of Management*, 36(4): 941–973.

Simon, H.A. (1987). Making management decisions: The role of intuition and emotion. *Academy of Management Executive*, 1(1): 57–64.

Voltes-Dorta, A. and Lei, Z. (2013). The impact of airline differentiation on marginal cost pricing at UK airports. *Transportation Research Part A: Policy & Practice*, 55: 73–88.

Index

Note: Page numbers ending in "f" refer to figures. Page numbers ending in "t" refer to tables.